William Sharp—"Fiona Macleod"

William Sharp—Fiona Macleod

William Sharp, 1896
From an etching by William Strang

William Sharp—"Fiona Macleod"

1855-1905

Flavia Alaya

Harvard University Press

Cambridge, Massachusetts

1970

To my parents

ACKNOWLEDGMENTS

My first thanks must go to Professor Jerome Buckley of Harvard University, who first supported my proposal to do a critical biography of William Sharp, and to Professors Carl Woodring and John Rosenberg of Columbia University, who patiently read and criticized the manuscript in its early stages, extending to me both their wide knowledge and their gratifying encouragement.

Further and special thanks are due Noel F. Sharp, whose recollections and insight into his uncle's career were infinitely more valuable than he himself would ever give them credit for being.

Many others assisted me at every stage of research. Mr. James Ritchie of the National Library of Scotland advised me of the Library's Sharp and Geddes collections and opened them to my use. His gracious help, and that of other members of the Library's staff, made a pleasure of my work in Edinburgh. In addition, Elizabeth G. Jack of the Glasgow University Library searched the university records for information on Sharp's student years; the reference librarians at Butler Library, Columbia University, helped me to locate and obtain rare editions of Sharp's works; and New York University helped finance my trip to Scotland to complete my research.

Others who will protest their inclusion in this reckoning nevertheless deserve my gratitude. Chief among them is Professor Amy Charles of the University of North Carolina who, when she might have been doing her own research, generously gave time to help me with mine; thanks also to Mrs. Nancy Clemente, of Harvard University Press, who patiently and wisely guided author and manuscript through publication.

And last thanks to those ever-increasing members of my household, who learned to know even better than I the trials of living with a dual personality, and who bore them with a grace that could only come of loving.

F. A.

CONTENTS

Illustrations

William Sharp—"Fiona Macleod"

A place adumbrated itself in his thoughts, wherein
those sacred personalities, which are at once the reflex
and the pattern of our nobler phases of life, housed
themselves; and this region in his intellectual scheme
all subsequent experience did but tend still further
to realise and define. Some ideal, hieratic persons
he would always need to occupy it and keep a warmth
there. And he could hardly understand those who
felt no such need at all, finding themselves quite
happy without such heavenly companionship, and sacred double of their life, beside them.

—Walter Pater, *The Child in the House*

I stand beside the gold-flamed pine-boles and look
with hungry eyes against the light of a sun that never
rose nor set.

—Fiona Macleod, "Hy Brasil," *The Silence of Amor*

INTRODUCTION

Time, Place, Perspective

William Sharp was born in Scotland in 1855 and died in Sicily in 1905. Between those two points lie fifty years and perhaps a thousand miles, a brief span of earth and of life. Yet brevity is relative. To the men and women of Sharp's time the distance between Scotland and Sicily, though it was a mere hint of the lengths Sharp traveled in his lifetime, was a significant one. To have been born in the Celtic north and to have embraced the Latin south, and to have found affinities with both such diverse racial and climatic characters, were facts impressive in themselves—then. Time has tended to make them less impressive. A shrinking world has weakened those geographical polarities to which Sharp responded so keenly and made many forget their significance.

What has happened to those fifty years is stranger still. A man who dies at fifty dies young. But the half-century that divides the high Victorian era into which Sharp was born from the dawn of the modern era upon which he last closed his eyes is long and tumultuous enough by historical standards for many lifetimes, and the changes in attitude it contains sometimes polar enough to defy reconciliation.

Alert and sensitive to the distances we now diminish, Sharp was equally alert and sensitive to the experience of those years we now find so complex. The great scope of his brief but varied career, a reflection of the scope of his times, gave him opportunity for a continual and conscious discovery of its opposites, tensions, and polarities. He bridged both geographical and psychological distances—bridged them, or painfully expressed their division in his art.

The oldest child in the teeming family of a provincial Scottish merchant, Sharp suffered early and deeply the disparity of values between his parents' generation and his own that has since become the common sign of modern change. He felt an abiding sense of singularity: rejecting his family and his native Scotland, he turned toward an industrial and mercantile Europe, heaving in clumsy and thoughtless urban growth, and knew with ever-increasing poignancy

1

the loneliness it mercilessly exacted as the price of art. Yet it was not a world altogether uncongenial. Through years in which he slowly gained uneasy fame as a popular writer and sought respect as a serious one, he was the object of the protective and absolute devotion of his wife Elizabeth, and the intimate of many artistic and literary circles in London, Paris, New York, Rome, and Edinburgh. But though he was notorious for his charm and good looks, though he was outgoing, willingly befriended, and apparently well fit for the life of the publishing careerist, Sharp remained always somewhat distant and elusive. Like the classic hero of a Thomas Mann novel, desperately protecting the vital center of his creative powers from the invasions of a bourgeois world, he represented in his life, and recreated through the secrecy of his female pseudonym Fiona Macleod, the very type—and since then the stereotype—of the modern artist. Under that pseudonym as well he expressed the sexual opposition he harbored within himself, again reflecting internally one of the most significant social tensions of his time.

The many-sidedness of Sharp's era was in every way the mark of his career. He was a world traveler—one might even say a world wanderer, consummately stricken with the travel fever of his generation. As realist, aesthete, symbolist, and local colorist, he played the full range of roles offered by contemporary literary art. Both exploiter and victim of the most extraordinary publishing explosion in history during the London eighties and nineties, he spilled his creative energy into every kind of enterprise: art and literary criticism, travel writing, journalism, biography, poetry, drama, short stories, and novels.

A great deal about the life of that complex time might be learned from the study of William Sharp now, at the distance of yet another half-century and more of change. It revivifies the history, perhaps even clarifies the disordered spectacle of such an era, to find so much of it embodied in the life chronicle of a single man. Yet a truthful biography must be more than the history of an era writ small. Every man is singular: at least in that respect Sharp was right about himself. Unlike the broad, abstract portrait just sketched, a biography must convey a *bios*, a life, and has to display a process of growth, accretion, and change. It needs to understand causes; it needs to understand motives; it needs to understand how a man understood himself.

With William Sharp, unfortunately, a great deal of this understanding must be conjectural. Past efforts repeatedly hint of the same difficulty: there is something about William Sharp that nearly defies biography. Although time has thrown the experiences of social change in Sharp's lifetime into jarring new perspectives, revealing much that was not known before, it has left the mysteries of Sharp's internal life practically untouched, and thus, if anything, more mysterious than ever. There is nothing in the stuff of Sharp's history alone guaranteed to make hard, realistic sense out of his illusion of a unique literary mission, nothing concrete to explain completely his eccentricity in choosing to write under the name of a woman, nothing positive with which to penetrate the mystery of his cryptic utterances about himself and everything he produced as Fiona Macleod. By now it may have become impossible to know with certainty what were the deeper experiences that formed him and led to the feminine bias of his major work, experiences that every literary biographer, in this day of psychoanalytic judgments, is under sentence to investigate—his relations with his family, with his wife, and with the woman who was the effective cause of his taking the name and literary personality of Fiona Macleod. Relatives of intimates may survive, but the intimates themselves are gone.

Perhaps, too, no one may ever know fully the extent to which Sharp was conscious of his own motives. His work is there and it remains the same work, regardless of whether it was produced by an illusionist convinced that a female spirit dwelt in him, a hypocrite exploiting public sensibility, or an artist quite above hypocrisy, consciously forging a literary tool. Whereas the pure critic, if he exists, may resist the lure of the intentional fallacy, the biographer-critic, who wishes to trace the relationship of man to work, cannot entirely substitute literary analysis for analysis of motive.

But the challenges on this side are more than equaled by the temptations on the other, temptations that have not often been resisted. The same Sharp "mysteries" that no document has yet fully unlocked have proven too fascinating to await the application of an analytic technology. Sharp is a novelist's fantasy realized. He has readily lent himself to interpretation as a self-romanticizing madman, frenzied wanderer, religious cultist, and literary opportunist, half-missionary, half-charlatan; he has been obviously suspect as a transvestite, using his unusual sympathy with women as grounds for one of the most curious literary hoaxes of the nineteenth century. The effect of this perspective upon his reputation as an artist is clear. Even in this era of supposedly enlightened sympathy for the abnormal, such imaginative evaluations of Sharp have stalled any genuine appreciation. Now, having for more than sixty years suffered every exaggeration of the most eccentric aspects of his personality and the most dubious aspects of his work, he is a literary figure in utter disrepute.

The process by which this disintegration occurred is interesting in itself. In 1911 Richard Le Gallienne, though not attempting a literary appraisal as such, described Sharp in terms that inescapably reflected on the value of his literary production, attributing to him "a certain histrionism," and drawing attention, through a series of innuendoes, to the sensational nature of the female inspiration that motivated the Fiona Macleod writings.[1] Again in 1913, on the crest of the first full wave of anti-romantic sentiment that has characterized until recently much of twentieth-century criticism, Paul Elmer More dismissed Sharp as an inheritor of what was weakest and most meretricious in Wordsworthian and Shelleyan romanticism.[2] But his animadversions were not merely literary; they were permeated with invidious judgment of the man. "No doubt," he said of some early Sharp poetry illustrative of his persistent bent for rhapsodizing, "no doubt the youthful bard thought he was uttering some startling spiritual truth and, as is the way with youthful bards and their accomplices, cursed the world for its obstinate deafness. As a matter of fact, that sort of pantheistic revery was exasperatingly easy then, and now; Wordsworth and Shelley and a little contempt for reason are the formula responsible for a stream of that kind that trickles clammily through the nineteenth century." The mystery exploited by Fiona Macleod is, he continued, the kind "which has pleased so many other romantic writers, and which has its roots in the rather naive desire to pose as the prophetic instrument of some vast renovation of ideas, when really the prophet's mind, instead of labouring with ideas, is floating on a shoreless sea of reverie, and tossing with indistinguishable emotions."[3] Others of More's opprobrious phrases would be familiar to anyone who knew the modern anti-romantic tradition, whether or not he also knew the work of Fiona Macleod: "the fluttering of tired nerves," "meaningless rhetoric," "pure poetic convention."[4]

But the flood tide of the anti-romanticism represented by More, and by his fellow, Irving Babbitt, was still to come in the scholarship of his and the next generation. Writing in *Modern Language Notes* in 1918, Georgiana Goddard King thought she was exploding the value of Fiona Macleod's work by throwing doubt upon its authenticity as pure Gaelic lore. She concluded that Sharp's work under the pseudonym, passed off as genuinely Celtic, was "sheer pastiche."[5] Some years after King, but not far behind her in spirit, came Dorothy Hoare, whose comments on Fiona Macleod appeared in a 1937 study of the use of saga literature by Morris and Yeats. Fiona Macleod, she says, rode into popularity on the coattails of the Irish movement. Her writing is "sentimental," her symbolism "dim," "almost meaningless."[6] Later still, in a survey of minor writers of the later nineteenth century, Samuel Chew disposed of Willliam Sharp in a single sentence that summarized the views of previous critics: "His fame was due to the verse and prose published under the pseudonym 'Fiona Macleod' which are in the most exaggerated manner of the 'Celtic Twilight' school."[7]

Even men who had known Sharp, and who, as members of his generation had shared in its predilections and prejudices, suffered a reversal of feeling toward the era, and the men, they had survived. Ernest Rhys is a particularly remarkable example. Like Le Gallienne, he had been Sharp's friend and associate and—more—supporter of his causes. Such a cause was Fiona Macleod herself (apparently Rhys was not one of the sacred few admitted to knowledge of Sharp's secret authorship). Rhys sang her praise in 1900, calling her an "incalculable writer," considering her work "vital and individual," "harmonious and natural," and designating the task she set herself "an errand of miracle."[8] By 1931 he had thoroughly reconsidered his estimate. Sharp, he said in *Everyman Remembers*, "was one of those younger men much influenced by Addington Symonds, Pater, and Swinburne, not always for their own good." His works, Rhys claimed, "do not stand the hard test, and in the end fall into that limbo in which are hidden so many lost books of verse, so many romances that once delighted sentimental readers, and so many novels which had a month's run before they dropped into the pit." As for Fiona Macleod, all sympathy was scuttled once the secret was out. She became "the master stroke of magic" of a "veritable literary chame-

leon," and her Gaelic paraphernalia was reduced to "romantic camouflage."[9]

In a similar spirit, Arthur Waugh, in an article in the *Spectator* in
1936, thought it not improper to speak of a man whose colleague he
had once been as a "dilettante," a "skillful euphuist." Fiona Macleod
was for Waugh, in effect, no more than a lucky literary coup, to be
understood in the terms used by Edmund Gosse to explain why he
had never been fooled for a moment: "I have always understood that
certain of the less saleable productions of William Sharp were being
foisted on editors under the forged name of the Celtic siren. I think
I have said so more than once."[10]

The one consistency these writers share is an evaluation of Sharp
based almost exclusively on his work as Fiona Macleod. "The Celtic
siren" has, in fact, stood as the single immovable obstacle to any just
interpretation of Sharp's literary career. Even those few writing in
his praise have simply turned the same coin to the other side, finding
admirable and inspiring precisely the same Fiona Macleod work that
the tough-minded saw as sentimental and romantic camouflage.
Thomas Rudmose-Brown's encomiastic tribute of 1906 was nothing
more than a tribute to Fiona Macleod and her dream visions.[11]
Sharp's wife herself could not resist the same bias, when, in her
Memoir (1910), while presenting an estimate of her husband's production more sympathetically divided between his two "personalities,"
she nevertheless felt it necessary to divide that estimate, and to treat
Fiona Macleod as the culmination of Sharp's literary power.[12] And
Sophia Fiechter, who published her intelligent essay in 1936, with
all the supposed advantages of distance and impartiality, nonetheless
concluded that Fiona Macleod was Sharp at his best—the best he
could be, considering the tragically self-defeating division of his talents
into what she agreed were two opposing streams.[13]

The clear fallacy in all these views is the use of the biographic
fact of Sharp's secretive pseudonym as almost the entire basis for
literary judgment; the presumed split between the achievements of
Sharp and the achievements of Fiona Macleod has been accepted as
dogma. It is curious but true that, had Sharp left the real identity
of the author of Fiona Macleod's work a secret after his death, he
could not have succeeded more thoroughly in having that work
judged as an entirely distinct body. The price exacted for that death-

bed revelation was high, as Sharp must have known it would be. His wife and friends were forced by it to endure both the sorry private jokes about his female proclivities and the ready public accusations of charlatanism. There is only one purpose for which he could have wanted them to pay such a price: to be judged by posterity as the author of all his work.

It was not an extravagant demand. There is good reason to believe that he recognized, as no thorough student of his work can fail to recognize, the intimacy in point of genesis between the imagination that produced the work known as Sharp's and that known as Fiona Macleod's. This intimacy is everywhere evident, but was consciously fostered after 1897 or 1898. A survey of Fiona Macleod's production from that point until Sharp's death shows two revealing things: that nothing like her first rush of stories and poems between 1894 and 1896 was ever conceived again; that by 1898 Fiona Macleod's capacity for imaginative production had been almost totally exhausted, and there was no work thereafter that adhered to the classic Macleod type—the bardic, visionary, or mystical treatment of life in the Celtic highlands or islands. Instead, the later production contained only one work that might be termed "visionary," and it was a traditional, almost Elizabethan allegory, "The Divine Adventure." Two Celtic plays, published in 1900, were no doubt conceived some time before, during an intensive period of dramatic writing. Everything else of significance is nonfiction—first-person relations of Celtic life and manners, "spiritual history," philosophizing on the Gaelic heritage, criticism, commentary on the connections of literature and race, "studies," particularly of folklore and symbolism.

None of this bears the stamp of an imagination unique, distinct from Sharp's as such. What in the end he seems to have protected behind the pseudonym was privacy, and not a special kind of inspiration. Differing only slightly in vocabulary and tone, the criticism was equally good under either name, and grounded in similar literary values. Probably Sharp's best imaginative work from his last period was his novel *Silence Farm*, published in 1899 as his own and not as Fiona Macleod's.

There is, then, no reason to speak of Sharp's production as two distinct bodies of work. To do so has been all too easy for those in a position to pass judgment upon him, and in this respect Sharp has

7

suffered at the hands of his friends no less than his enemies. But the enemies had the additional advantage already alluded to, a popular and critical taste that has shared a largely unsympathetic view of the "decadence" and artificiality of the literary developments of the later Victorian period, especially the nineties. Such generalizations are longlived; even attempts at objective assessment have run afoul of them and continue to do so. Reputable literary histories often still represent the artistic spirit of the last years of the nineteenth century as some combination of amusement, indifference, and cynicism, a muddy blur of "yellow" and "mauve." As undergraduate study aids, such broad characterizations may have their place. When they become automatic, as they have a way of doing, they merely help to make all the artistic intentions of the writers of this period suspect. Obviously Sharp would be the first to suffer from an attitude that looks upon his special form of imaginative fabrication as part of a pattern of deliberate fakery.

When More grudgingly redeemed his subject's allegedly hard-headed "Sharp" side from the generally contemptible froth of Fiona Macleod,[14] he was even then making a totally characteristic gesture, unjust not only to Sharp but to the mercurial and various spirit of the age that Sharp so brilliantly epitomized. The man was like the era—of such variety that to judge it by any single line of development is to misrepresent it. In this sense, at least, Elizabeth Sharp's biography is tentatively fair, though disappointing: it does not recreate a whole man who organically unifies his own disparities.

But time, in the long run, saves rather than destroys. The era of genuine reevaluation and reinterpretation is upon us, and like the thinkers of the period to which Sharp belongs, we may perhaps now begin to grasp what we are not yet completely able to resolve, and to know what we may not yet completely understand.

On this score, a biography of Sharp has its own intrinsic apologetic. When a single man is as responsive as Sharp was to so many different streams of literary and philosophic thought and makes a compound of so many movements of mind, English and foreign, he provides a kind of existential logic for their unity. If nothing else unites the influences of Wordsworth, Shelley, Emerson, Whitman, Tennyson, Arnold, Ruskin, Swinburne, Morris, Hardy, Meredith, Yeats, Zola, Maeterlinck, D'Annunzio, and Verga, Sharp unites them. If his loose connections with Pater, Swinburne, and Symonds justify his being classified as an "esthete," there is yet nothing amused, indifferent, or cynical, either about his personal ethics and his solemn passion for the relevance and social value of his art, or his strong sympathies with the activist proponents of the feminism and radicalism of his day.

It may be that we still have a warped view, or no real view at all, of the psychological and philosophical motives behind those movements classically identified as decadent. To consider some examples, research may well prove that the sexual freedom advanced by many of the so-called decadents was almost always accompanied by a social or even a physiological rationale, and that it was contrained by an extremely demanding sense of the intimate psychological obligations created by human relationships, obligations which the writers thought were unrecognized or falsified in the canons of conventional morality. The refined artistic sensibility of men and women of Sharp's era, often criticized by social realists of their own time and after as too precious and out of touch with reality, was perhaps a transfer of a sense for precision and an awareness of nuance from the world of morals to the world of the imagination. The eclecticism of the era, in which its detractors see violations of the integrity of the artistic medium, may well represent an early version of the modern McLuhanite's total experience. We may indeed borrow some insight from radical artistic theory in our own day, which declares that no single art form is sacrosanct.

Other critiques of the decadence, particularly that ill-defined aspect called the "twilight" because of its dependence on crepuscular vagueness and mystery, are hard on the allegedly "escapist" need for fantasy and myth. But deeply underlying the infatuation with myth and folklore among Sharp's contemporaries was a real quest for knowledge, for a new understanding of the life and mentality of primitive cultures and of children. Besides, as Oscar Wilde's playfully shocking "Decay of Lying" brings home, the art that realists found escapist only thinly disguised outraged censure of the values of an over-urbanized and over-mechanized civilization.

From the partisans of English rectitude comes still another thrust, an attack on the passion among later Victorians for things French and foreign, viewed as both eccentric and lewd. Yet, sympathetically considered, that same passion appears as a healthy reaction to the petulant anti-Gallic middle-class sentiment of their time. It was united in Sharp and other members of his generation, moreover, with a genuine philosophic commitment to the solidarity and union of mankind. To the charge of lubricity there is never really any answer, since the grounds of attack are constantly shifting. What was considered morally repulsive might have been then, as it is now, clinically sexual (and justifiable as social realism) or erotically fantastic (and justifiable as psychological truth). Some of Sharp's depictions of childbirth and labor—his poem "Motherhood" and his one-act drama "The Birth of a Soul," for example—and his use of images or themes of nudity (*Sospiri di Roma*, "The Passion of Père Hilarion") left him occasionally open to such charges. Fiona Macleod was generally more delicate and discreet, if not downright proper.

Attacks on Sharp's morals ordinarily came after his death and from another quarter entirely. They were based on the revolutionary shift in taste that decreed the "artifice," "pastiche," and "vagueness" of his Celtic work a forfeit of artistic integrity. Fair judgment, however, must be grounded in the knowledge that Sharp's Macleod tales, his prose poems, and his "studies" were exercises in literary impressionism, a widespread late nineteenth-century experiment in conveying experience colored by memory and association. Such impressionism is no more artificial than any other artistic means of ordering the maelstrom of experiential data.

The same relativism can go farther. What our hardened generation calls "sentimentality," whether it appear in Sharp or in other more significant writers of his period, was an attempt to express a profound and sincere compassion and reverence for the poor and the weak, the detritus of a cruelly advancing industrial civilization. This is how Henry James read Pierre Loti at the time, how Sharp himself read Loti, Maeterlinck, Hardy, and Yeats—not as writers indulging the impulse to tears, but as gentle and loving men. It is how, if we were to acknowledge it, modern readers continue to respond to Proust and Joyce.

The fact is that every judgment we have made in sweeping condemnation of this era, whether it condemns a formally careless, an amoral literature, or apparently amoral or immoral men, is a judgment condemning the possibly naive but nonetheless often transcendent ideals of moral and social regeneration with which the later Victorians invested their art and their artists. Even Sharp's kind of transvestism—

a transvestism not of the flesh but of the imagination—was implicitly sanctioned by contemporary anthropological studies of prophetic and visionary types, and by the "new spirit" of humane, compassionate sexuality expressed in the writings of such men as Edward Carpenter and Havelock Ellis.

The trouble, of course, in dealing with Sharp and his era is that the present-day reader is confronting revisionary romanticism from the vantage point of even further revision. We are suspicious of the lines of development the same movement underwent before us. Sharp and his contemporaries were themselves inclined to call their romanticism "neo-romanticism," like everything else of significance in the nineties, "new." For a time it represented, in Sharp's mind at least, a movement of reaction, a protest, defined in obedience to the Swinburne-Baudelaire formulae, against "Grundyism"—the prudish and prosaic. But implicit in this definition, and explicit later on, was the knowledge that a protest based merely on the rejection of sexual inhibition and moral convention was unsatisfactory and imprecise. What Sharp proved to be reacting to was something larger, more pervasive, something to which his work, in whatever genre, whatever style, under whatever name, opposed itself, by asserting the sanctity of nature, human or otherwise, and calling for the conservation of privacy, intuition, and personal values.

What most clamored for the sacrifices of these values in his time was a forcefully self-conscious national society, a configuration of moral and social prescriptions, surrounding him, surrounding everyone, and demanding conformity and service to a national purpose. As so often happens in the history of ideas, it is paradoxically possible to lay the blame for the creation of this powerful concept of nation on romanticism itself. One of the several revolutions for which romanticism had been responsible was the discovery that man was reflected in and indeed coextensive with his environment. Political circumstances in England may not necessarily have been themselves romantically motivated, but as they more and more gave a name and an identity to that environment, and a banner of empire to its purpose, the power that enables a great nation to turn everything in it to its use worked almost inexorably to mold the individual man, no matter how otherwise renegade, in the national image, and join him to the mystical body called Great Britain. Men are not forever capable of sustaining the anxious

11

inspection of their own private values thrust upon them by the romantic upheaval. It was possible for the Victorian to cling to the "image" of his breed and upbringing, to a cluster of values, moral, social, and spiritual, provided by a secure if narrow conception of his national tradition. As Jane Austen put it in *Emma,* "It was a sweet view—sweet to the eye and the mind. English verdure, English comfort, English culture, seen under a sun bright, without being oppressive." However ironic in intention was Austen's version of it, the "sweet view" was to become the quiet, unquestioned persuasion of several subsequent generations of Victorians. H. G. Wells, attempting in his *Experiment in Autobiography* to characterize what he considered his fairly standard schoolboy mind of the late seventies, supplied hard confirmation.

> It was made a matter of general congratulation about me that I was English . . . a blond and blue-eyed Nordic, quite the best make of human being known . . . We English, by sheer native superiority, practically without trying, had possessed ourselves of an Empire on which the sun never set, and through the errors and infirmities of other races were being forced slowly but steadily—and quite modestly—towards world dominion.

The educational process by which these truths had been inculcated was clear, as were its ultimate psychological effects:

> I was taught no history but English History, which after some centuries of royal criminality, civil wars and wars in France, achieved the Reformation and blossomed out into the Empire; and I learnt hardly any geography but British geography. It was only from casual reading that I gathered that quite a number of things had happened and quite a number of interesting things existed outside the world of English affairs. But I looked at pictures of the Taj Mahal, the Colosseum and the Pyramids in very much the same spirit as I listened to stories about the Wonders of Animal Intelligence (beavers, bees, birds' nests, breeding habits of the salmon, etc.). They did not shake my profound satisfaction with the self, the township, the county, the nation, the Empire and the outlook that was mine.[15]

Sharp may not have been a great man, but he was a recalcitrant one. He could not yield to this persuasion, and in reacting against it he guaranteed himself a wholeness that defied even his own inconsistencies. In this light, and this light only, can be understood his frenzied movements—from Scotland, to Australia, to the South Seas, to London, France, Italy, Germany, America, Africa, Greece, and back to Scotland again—and only thus can be understood his frenzied reduplication of pseudonyms and identities. He was in flight—in flight from the orthodoxies and convictions that a century of political expansion had given to the individual Englishman to secure his identity with the national fate and turn the romantic's sense of dislocation, and his quest for identity, to excellent political use.

A rebellion against such disciplining of the personality is the implicit credo of the romantic faith. Nothing characterizes the romantic temperament if not its mobility, its "negative capability," the exercise of its renegade nature through projection into all the phenomena of the external world—and beyond, if need be, into infinity—in a continual process of experiment. And even while temporarily lending itself to practical ends, that volatile element was still alive in the Victorians, surviving in what may be called the sense of place. The romantics had, of course, discovered "place," that quality of personality possessed by certain configurations of permanent objects in space. Wordsworth had submitted to its influence. So had Byron, though differently. Scott had dramatized it and made it work in the very action of his novels. But the Victorians, who had been somewhat liberated from the anxiety which had been its original motive among the romantics, revelled in it at home or on their travels, and turned it into an active diversion. The world literally became their drawing room, each place a gimcrack on the shelf, unique in its kind—"colorful," "beautiful," "sublime," "picturesque."

Possessed of the romantic's temperamental mobility to an extraordinary degree, Sharp was especially well suited to act as a heightened reflector of the Victorian taste for place. But the taste itself was widespread. The fascination of Victorian popular literature with the foreign had grown by the end of the century to an obsession, and almost every serious writer was in some way touched by it. Anthony Trollope owed an essential part of his popularity to his travel writing. John Ruskin, for some time an arbiter of Victorian middle-class taste, both reflected and fostered the same tendency; our own era, nursed on travel literature, can easily miss the significance of his concern, so exquisitely expressed in his autobiography, with the *places* rather than the people that had the most profound effect upon his life. Another taste-setting Victorian,

Robert Browning, used nationality and race as essential resources for the delineation of character. Particular landscapes and cityscapes too had an intrinsic ancillary function in his dramatic monologues. George Eliot tried Browning's Italian vein in prose with Romola, and her greater novels represent the sense of place in one of its best forms among the Victorians. Hers is no mere regionalism, but a deep sense for the efficacy of community in shaping people's lives. Hardy, too, evokes a familiar English setting with a full awareness of its power, with him a fateful, symbolic power that the term pastoral, as applied to it, utterly fails to convey. "Place" did not have to be countryside or province either, as Dickens's London eminently well attests. Matthew Arnold exhibited another aspect of this tendency, the isolation and characterization of racial qualities, but even he was not averse to writing into his Essays in Criticism peculiarly evocative descriptions of places—Oxford, Pompeii, Assisi, the coast of Wales. In all of these writers, and in more, places became analogues for moral states and even metaphors for entire movements of civilization.

The growing sense of place had other ramifications, too, to which Sharp and other Victorians were susceptible. On the continent, where boundaries were more flexible than the coastline of the British Isles, the romantic impulse to provide places with character had functioned also in the opposite direction—to provide peoples with their proper geographical limits. The Europeans had begun early, and their literature on the influence of climate and region on art and character was already copious by the end of the first quarter of the nineteenth century. It was Mme. de Staël who had led the English to discover, with such delight and awe, their own national character, and it was through her, certainly, that cultural determinism was assisted on its way to England and influenced the thinking of the English on issues of nationalism. That famous Victorian byproduct, the fascination with Italy (eventually to play so important a part in Sharp's career), was a result of this influence combined with the sense of place already described: it was a country where characteristic and compelling places had proliferated in semi-tropical abundance; and it was also a symbol of the national character discovering its homeland, its physical definition. The combination, however contradictory in practice, had an irresistible imaginative appeal.

This Zeitgeist worked a profound effect upon Sharp. That he was a Scotsman, bred in a peculiarly Scottish landscape, familiar with the highlands and the isles, was important, but not at first for the obvious reason that it would someday make him a Celtic writer. It was first important because it made him *not* English at a time when, to most of the English, to be English was to be everything. It was important because it delayed, temporarily at least, any confrontation with, and perhaps conformity to, the English national character in all its Victorian intensity. He was bred on the romantic fascination with nature— nature for itself, untitled and universal—and the romantic breadth of natural sympathy; he had traveled almost around the world before he was twenty-five. These experiences became his resources, and these made him a cosmopolitan before he was anything else. His psychological baggage was essentially a problem of identity that initially had no conscious connection with his nationality. But his ticket to a literary career was issued by a Victorian public pleading for someone to delight their sense of place, and in delighting theirs, he exaggerated his own. Places, nations, nationalities, were not mere physical pauses in his restless wanderings: each became a separate analogue for his various perceptions of his own personal identity. Each was systematically recreated in his work, and, by an organic principle of accretion and growth, adapted to his entire outlook. Fiona Macleod, the self-sufficient Celtic recluse who was the antithesis of her roaming creator, was no final resolution. She was merely one of a system of pauses and experiments, the whole of which represented an instinctive anti nationalism, a convinced cosmopolitanism. This is why, though Fiona Macleod was so closely associated in the popular theories of literary history with a nationalist movement, Sharp spoke through her to reject emphatically any association with that movement's strictly nationalist aspect.

Sharp's union of cosmopolitanism with his problem of personal identity was no private eccentricity. Both were there, all around him— the cosmopolitanism a persistent and growing bias away from high-Victorian nationalism; the problem of identity, even sexual identity, a growing malaise in the artistic mind. The connection between them is evident in the mask consciousness and symbolic nationalism of Yeats, in Stevenson's Jekyll-Hyde doppelgänger, in the taut strain between the poles of the civilized and the primitive in the work of Conrad, and in the American-European dialectic of Henry James. Like Sharp, they were "foreigners" all. Only slightly later, the same link between psychological and physical alienation became functional in James Joyce

15

and T. S. Eliot, and, owing to the influence of the most important political event of this century, the First World War, even in such native-born Englishmen as E. M. Forster and D. H. Lawrence.

The nature of Sharp's cosmopolitanism, then, and its evolution out of his problem of identity, can illuminate a period of transition in English literature that has long proven problematical and difficult to define. That is the underlying premise of what I hope will be a useful study of William Sharp, for it would be egregious to suggest that, despite the fine quality of some small portion of his work, he can be restored to anything resembling the reputation he had as Fiona Macleod in his own time. No one would now even wildly surmise, as some of his contemporaries did, that Fiona Macleod and William Butler Yeats were the same person. It would take a very fervent apologist to claim him a writer of vital importance and pardon his obvious shortcomings—the thinness, the occasional false heightening of mood, the flagging creative energy exhibited in so many of his narrative and lyrical efforts, and the failure of confident execution revealed repeatedly by slackness in vocabulary and style. Added to these is the mystery Sharp allowed to surround the genesis of his Fiona Macleod work. Increasingly tough-minded generations accustomed to scrutinizing the origin of every hyphen a poet puts to paper will with time find this mystery, with its suspicion of epicenism, only more unreasonable and irritating. What merely adds a certain luster to a great talent will blight and obscure a lesser one.

Yet there remains much that can and should be redeemed. There is a flagrant injustice in the superficial rendering of Sharp's work and life that has cast him as the epitome of what men like Paul Elmer More and Irving Babbitt regarded as a disintegrating romantic ethos, the sum of all they found reprehensible in "emotional naturalism." In the half-century since Babbitt threw out his keenest challenge to the romantic vision in *Rousseau and Romanticism*, and More contributed his contemptuous sketch of William Sharp to *The Drift of Romanticism*, no fully adequate reply has been given either to the general or the particular charge that the romanticism of the nineteenth century began in potential degeneracy and ended in degeneracy realized. The reputation Sharp enjoyed in his lifetime might have declined in any case after his death, yet it never would have been so effectively obliterated had he not so easily provided a scapegoat upon whom anti-romantic critics might discharge much of their animus toward what they viewed as a literature without genuine moral life, a vision of flux without permanence, an ethic of sympathies without values and sensibility without restraint, a failure to arrive at any controlling "superrational perception" by which to order and interpret a response to nature.[16]

There is no better argument for reassessment of William Sharp than the fact that he provides so illustrative a case for the important historical reaction that such views represent. And there may be no better praise of him than to say that an authentic delineation of his life and work would be, in a real sense, a reply to that challenge, and perhaps the best way in which that reply might be delivered. As the contemporary of many striking but abused and puzzling men, Sharp provides, as lesser writers so often do, a focal point for contemporary influences and contemporary tendencies. And finally he suggests in his own strange unity-in-diversity what can now be seen only dimly—that there is a valuable, even admirable unity in the diversity of the greater men who surround him.

1

THE CHANGELING

First Years

Sharp's early family life has not been exhaustively documented. Elizabeth Sharp's *Memoir* (1910)[1] and his own brief autobiographical sketch for *Mainly About People* in 1900,[2] remain the only authoritative sources, and neither his wife nor he saw fit to do more than provide a scant few of the facts of his childhood, as though providently aware of what a future generation might want to do with them.

He was born in Paisley, Scotland, on September 12, 1855 ("on a day," Elizabeth reminds us, "when the bells were ringing for the fall of Sebastopol"), the first child of Katherine Brook and David Galbraeth Sharp, both of substantial middle-class stock. Seven more children followed him, two sons and five daughters. Sharp's wife recalls that "he believed himself to have been born under a lucky star."[3]

One impression emerges irresistibly from both Elizabeth's casual chronicle and his own. The details they include all point to William as a child of unusual and distinctive traits, whose early life was marked by strange impressions in which his family did not share, and by events in which they participated only shadowily. The details they omit leave a near vacuum where one would ordinarily expect to find a real and living family, with the inevitable human problems arising from the combination of two human parents with eight very human children. The omission seems remarkable. Being an eldest son surrounded by such a family is not something a child can be expected to ignore, or a man expected to forget. Yet forget he apparently did. All we learn of his sisters and brothers is from Mrs. Sharp's *Memoir*. She and William were first cousins; they met when he was eight. "My impression of 'Willie' is vivid . . . eager, active in his endless invention of games and occupations, and a veritable despot over his sisters in their play."[4] He entertained them and his London cousins with stories, and teased and frightened them with his fantasies of nature. But of only one of his sisters do we hear any more thereafter—and then a good deal thereafter

18

—his sister Mary, who became his secretary, entrusted with the important task of handling the correspondence of Fiona Macleod. His parents, too, receive slight treatment. David Sharp was "a partner in an old-established mercantile house,"[5] says Elizabeth. William describes him as "a man of considerable means."[6] Both agree that he had "a great love of the country, and especially of the West Highlands."[7] It was on account of this love that the elder Sharp took a house in the country every summer, and it was through him that William was "initiated into the arts of swimming, rowing, and line fishing."[8] Elizabeth adds that David Sharp was a "genial, observant man, humorous and a finished mimic,"[9] implying perhaps that a flair for impersonation passed from father to son. William's mother receives passing mention. While William tells nothing of her himself, Elizabeth describes her as having been brought up by her father "to read seriously and to take an interest in his favorite study of Geology. It was she," continues the *Memoir*, "who watched over her son's work at college, and made facilities for him to follow his special pursuits at home."[10]

There would almost appear to have been a conspiracy between Sharp and his wife not to discuss his family at any length, beyond these simple, nearly impersonal, childhood recollections. Whether the close dependence on Mary during the Fiona Macleod period was the result of an intimacy that had survived childhood, or of a renewed association arising from convenience on his side and common sisterly loyalty on hers, is impossible to determine. There is simply no evidence either way, and Mary, as Elizabeth speaks of her, is no more than a disembodied handwriting. Sharp's parents, of course, were important during his adolescence, when he was in the process of promoting, and they of thwarting, his natural inclinations toward an intellectual career. But even in their restraining roles, Elizabeth treats them rather evasively, her husband barely at all. She, for her part, seems to suggest that the obviously deep difference of temperament that divided William from his parents was something upon which it was unnecessary to dilate. She tells us, for example, that because of frail health William "was considered too delicate to be subjected to severe mental pressures; and he met with no encouragement from either parent in his wish to throw himself into the study of science or literature as a career." But there was, by implication, more Philistinism than philanthropy in their motives. "Such a course seemed to them to offer no prospects for his future."[11]

19

His parents' motives were indeed an odd compound of severity and indulgence. Although they appear to have exerted pressure on him in the choice of a career, they also permitted him almost complete freedom in physical activity. He himself reports that the summers of his adolescence were filled with "boating, sailing, hill-climbing, wandering. From fifteen to eighteen," he writes, "I think I sailed up every loch, fjord, and inlet in the Western Highlands and Isles."[12] It is possible, of course, to interpret this permissiveness as his parents' device for exhausting William's resistance to their control of his "future prospects." It did not. During the summer of 1874, when he was eighteen, he "took," as he says, "to the heather," joining a troupe of gypsies, and wandering all over the countryside with them for three months.[13] It is even possible that he intended this excursion somehow to be a permanent escape. Elizabeth speaks of the "truant" (the gentle epithet will be noted) having to be "recaptured," which he was only "after considerable trouble."[14]

Brought to heel after this escapade, however, Sharp seems to have temporized with surrender. "At my parents' urgent request," he says, "I not only resumed my classes at the University, but entered a lawyer's office in Glasgow . . . to learn something of the law."[15] How real was his acquiescence is perhaps indicated by an added parenthesis—"on very easy conditions, hardly suitable to a professional career." Whether the easy conditions were a shrewd arrangement devised by William himself, or merely another example of his parents' ambivalence, is not made clear. At any rate, this is the last mention of the familial consequences of William's behavior. His father's sudden death very soon thereafter, in August 1876, removed paternal opposition to his hopes, and undoubtedly with that opposition much of the stuff of filial defiance. "Our home circumstances were altered," says Sharp quite simply, meaning, one would guess, in the financial sense. That the results of the loss were more profound may only be inferred. "About this time, too, partly from excessive overwork at college, my health gave way."[16] He was precipitously sent to Australia to recuperate, but also to test his prospects elsewhere. He never completed his education at the University of Glasgow.

Sharp, for his part, does not offer any defense of his parents, but neither does he imply that there was anything especially inimical in their attitude toward him. His tone throughout his biographical sketch is whimsical and detached, as though nothing in these youthful duels with his father and mother had ever really touched him emotionally. Only his wife seems to have borne even the smallest grudge towards the wardens of William's first years. Following his "recapture" after the gypsy episode, her narrative has it (couched as usual in the passive voice) that he "was put into a lawyer's office, ostensibly to teach him business habits, but also the better to chain him to work, to the accepted conventions of life, and to remove him out of the way of the dangerous temptations offered by the freer College life with its long vacations."[17] Had she forgotten the easy conditions of which her husband spoke? Perhaps. But it is rather probable that this fact was as irrelevant to her account of her husband's development as emotion or resentment were to his, and for the very same reason.

Their reason was, quite simply, that in the formation of the *real* William Sharp his family had hardly shared at all. "The three influences that taught him most in childhood were the wind, the woods, and the sea,"[18] says Elizabeth with simple emphasis. Practically from his infancy, William took "delight in open-air life."[19] He was inclined, like many imaginative children, to have fantasies of "presences" in nature, and in this view he was encouraged, not by his parents, but by a "Highland nurse," who filled his imagination with Gaelic folklore,[20] and later by an old fisherman, Seumas Macleod, who seems to have been to him the embodiment of a kindly and fatherly nature god, and whose surname Sharp eventually selected for his pseudonym.[21] His real playmates were not his sisters and brothers and cousins, but the "invisible" ones in the natural world around him. He thought, Elizabeth recalls, "that a belt of firs had a personality as individual as that of any human being, a sanctity not to be disturbed by sport or play." For awe of paternal authority he substituted awe of the universe. "There was some great power (he could not define the feeling to himself) behind the beauty he saw . . . that awoke in him a desire to belong to it." And he wrote later of trying to invoke that power: "I desired terror."[22] In effect he was a spirit, not a child. What could a family have been to such a spirit but an encumbrance?

His family was, in fact, an encumbrance he tried with obstinate, almost pathetic frequency to shake off. The gypsy excursion was only the last and most serious of a long series of attempted escapes. He says that it must have been his "wandering" Scandinavian blood that first sent him off at the age of three, only to be found in the garden, "a huddled little white heap at the foot of a great poplar."[23] At the age of nine he ran away from boarding school three times.[24]

The mention of the "wandering" Scandinavian blood is significant, too, as part of the habit both Sharp and his wife had of defining his genealogy in racial rather than personal terms. Elizabeth's account is particularly affected by the glamor of race. Infinitely more important than any of his mother's maternal offices, for instance, was her Scandinavian descent, from which Sharp had allegedly derived his splendid blond looks as well as his desire to roam.[25] And his father's Celtic blood was apparently not diminished by the mercantilism of the man into whom it had flowed. It was characteristic of Elizabeth to find a friend's description of William so memorable: "He was a Viking in build, a Scandinavian in cast of mind, a Celt in heart and spirit."[26]

Nearly everything in their accounts, in short, is designed to give William a unique and special benediction, to portray his family as a mere accident in the life of what should have been a free spirit. Were Sharp's refractory responses to discipline evidence of a churlish and spoiled disposition? Not in the least. Elizabeth is positive: William "at all times hated the restrictions and limitations of conventional life."[27] Sharp himself is only less shrill, equally positive: "By natural instinct," he says with delight in his youthful individualism, "I was 'agin the Government.' I remember the rapture with which I evaded a master's pursuing grip."[28] Did he ever regret the anxiety his disappearance "into the heather" had caused his parents? That adventure was, he conceded with mild sarcasm, " 'a sad waste of time and opportunity' (of course), but an enduring happiness for the rest of my life."[29] These are no mere devices to avoid the expression of rancor. They are part of a deliberate effort to recreate out of the materials of Sharp's early experience a child who has been given a special dispensation to do as he likes —a child whose very weaknesses are marks of special blessing that only the profane can misinterpret. It is an attempt to suggest for him an existence that is almost biologically independent of his family.

It must be said in Sharp's defense that the treatment he himself gives to his childhood is not, like his wife's, deliberately romantic in tone. But his restraint is not indicative of perspective, for his account, written in 1900, is that of a man who was already divided in his public image. The rhapsodic self represented by Fiona Macleod he kept as a thing apart, and none of the early visionary experiences is included in the article in *Mainly About People*, no doubt lest some Fleet Street detective make the connection Sharp was so determined to avoid. The restraint was all the easier because as Fiona Macleod he had already detailed the romantic episodes of his childhood, in a piece of veiled and fictionalized autobiography that had formed the prologue to a collection of twice-told Celtic tales for children, *The Laughter of Peterkin* (1895). There Peterkin is without doubt Sharp himself, liberated from perspective and restraint by the camouflage of pseudonymous authorship. He is a glamorous and special personality, his imagination filled with "Laughter, Wonder, and Delight," the beautiful fantasies with which he surrounds the natural world only vaguely understood by the uninitiated adults around him.[30] Peterkin has that same capacity Elizabeth had attributed to the young William for peopling the world with supernatural creatures. He does not disguise his feeling that he is more a member of the race whence they come than of the human race in which he actually lives.

Elizabeth, not surprisingly, readily avails herself of this material, and of another "autobiographical" essay by Fiona Macleod, "The Gaelic Heart." From the latter she takes the story, so often quoted by commentators sympathetic to Sharp as evidence of his peculiar visionary powers, that he was once visited by a mysterious "lady of the woods," who gathered "blueness," like foam, out of the flowers.[31] The manner of Elizabeth's retelling asks the reader for more than a willing suspension of disbelief regarding these intimations of immortality. Though she tries to maintain a hold on reality with a well-placed aside about "other imaginative and psychic children," it is clear that for her too his membership in another kind of race might have been actual. "He seemed to feel himself different from the other children of his age," she writes, "and would fly off alone to the hillside." He was precociously aware of his "special" character: "He realized that his playmates understood nothing of the confused memories of previous lives that haunted him. To his surprise he found they saw none of the denizens of the other worlds . . . so familiar to him . . . He found . . . that he had an inner life, a curious power of vision unshared by anyone about him; so that what he related was frequently discredited . . . He needed from time to time to get away alone."[32]

By what strange alchemy had Sharp's memory and his wife's observation been so transformed? He was, obviously, an imaginative child, clearly forced, as Elizabeth is well aware, to subdue his imaginative display and seal it off into a private, inner life. His frequent attempts at escape were the commonplace expressions of a child's will to assert his fantasy, and not to sacrifice it to the disciplines of adult life. But this assertion did not diminish as he grew older. To leave home and join the gypsies was to cultivate the rift between him and his bourgeois Glasgow world. To become their "sun-brother" was only to flatter his conviction of uniqueness, an essential part of the "enduring happiness" he derived from the experience. The escapes of his youth were translated in later life into a pattern of evasion and flight. Like many artistic personalities, divided between public and private selves, he suffered the fantasy of imposture, and, consciously or otherwise, considered himself the son of other parents than his natural ones; but unlike most other artistic personalities, he nurtured his fantasy as he matured with notions derived from folklore and spiritualism, and gradually, relentlessly, drove an ever deeper and deeper wedge between his real origins and his imagined ones. The return to Glasgow University, presented as a concession to his parents' will, was hardly that in effect. There he studied "literature, philosophy, poetry, mysticism, occultism, magic, mythology, folklore,"[33] none of which was precisely designed to arouse paternal pride and favor. Indeed his wife says that "the immediate result" of this reading "was to turn him from the form of Presbyterian faith in which he had been brought up." What she does not say is that such was undoubtedly its subconscious design, for its even more important result was to give him "a sense of brotherhood with the acknowledged psychics and seers of other lands and other days."[34]

The exigencies of life, and indeed the attractions of normality, made real and complete flight impossible. But Sharp could take flight into imposture itself. It took time for him to give that imposture a permanent shape, but slowly he developed a secure and angerless faith in himself as an artistic prophet and deliverer to justify his resentment against his family. He became a changeling, with special gifts of communion with another world, content in the happy knowledge that only he knew the secret truth.

Remarkably, Sharp's fantasy was not something in which he ever fully submerged himself. It was conditioned by reality, and expressed as the opposing, secret side of a dual existence. The "deliverer" was not the real, but the "other" self, to whom the "real" William Sharp, bound to the ties of this life, was a spectator. His life in London during the late seventies and eighties for a time held this duality in abeyance, and then began to have the reverse effect of exacerbating it. With the writing of "The Gipsy Christ" early in the nineties, the notion of the other, redeemer self reemerged with full force.[35] By then, too, he was already well on the way to giving new form to his private dispensation in the figure of Fiona Macleod. In her work the Christ concept persists, appropriately transformed into a female Christ, a woman who would come in her turn to deliver the race.[36] The same fantasy was otherwise expressed in the figure of the changeling, actual or believed, of which Oona in *The Mountain Lovers* (1895) is one example; and sometimes in the Fiona Macleod work a child or young poet undergoes a kind of ritual initiation into the "mysteries" at the hands of Christ or the apostles, or of some other divine creature momentarily assuming an earthly shape. The child himself is understood to be "special," independent of any normal worldly ties.[37] But the changeling type could also be cast as the son or daughter of lost, unknown, or mysterious parentage, as is the case with Alan, in Fiona Macleod's *Green Fire* (1896). Sometimes it was further sublimated into a figure of some spontaneous or parentless birth, a free spirit, born or reborn into an utterly independent existence, like Cathal of "The Annir-Choille" (1895), who takes his passage into "the green life."[38] Although the changeling is mainly a conception of Fiona Macleod's, it can be found also in transitional work like the impressionistic dramas published as Sharp's in *Vistas* (1894): in one of these, "The Passion of Père Hilarion," a young priest casts off his past along with his robes, and swims across the river to join the pagan spirits in timeless irresponsibility and joy.

In William Sharp's usually realistic fiction, most of it dating from the eighties, the same theme found its expression in circumstances similar to those used by Fiona Macleod in *Green Fire*. Lora Cameron's mysterious parentage in *The Sport of Chance* (1887), and Sanpriel's in *The Children of To-morrow* (1890), are illustrations, but so also is Margaret Gray's in *Silence Farm*, published in 1899. These works serve, because of their greater realism, as further confirmations of the kind of alienation Sharp seems to have suffered from his family. The families in these novels, none of them, curiously, tested by moral conflict, are invariably broken—the Camerons by villainy and catastrophe, the Acostas in *The Children of To-morrow* by a fatal curse.

The significant exception to this melodramatic rule, and that an exception only in part, is *Silence Farm*. There the family is indeed unhappy—excruciatingly so—but only in this novel is family unhappiness explained in primarily psychological terms. It is perhaps not surprising that the Ruthven family consists only of father and son—at least until the end, when the girl whom the father has kept as his domestic is revealed as his unacknowledged illegitimate daughter. From the outset, the conflict between the generations is a deep, tense war of incompatible minds that finally erupts into a violent physical struggle. For a time father and son appear to be at war over the girl herself, whom the young Ruthven, in ignorance of the blood tie, wishes to marry, and whom the elder does not have the courage to admit is his own daughter. But the essential source of their trouble is an utter division in temperament and outlook. The son is a modern, a skeptic in religion, and a confused freethinker, if not freewheeler, in morals. The father, deeply tormented by his own guilt, has developed, as his only means of living with himself and his weakness, an implacably authoritarian and self-righteous Presbyterianism. The son at last sets distance between them, and goes off to America alone in permanent self-exile.

The parallels between the Ruthvens and the elder and younger Sharp are difficult to resist, except for one important fact: the younger Ruthven, as Sharp presents him, is cruelly self-willed, and an almost entirely unsympathetic character. It is the daughter instead who is intended to attract and engage our respect, and she does not run. She stays, endures, and, after her father's death, sustains all the dignity left to the Ruthven name. Yet the apparent discrepancy here with Sharp's own experience is no discrepancy at all. By the time of the completion of this novel, Sharp had already "become" Fiona Macleod, a woman, and not a woman merely, but a Scot, restored to all the native ties to which Sharp had, in effect, made himself an alien. It was "she," of course, that private, imaginative self of William Sharp, who was indeed the "illegitimate" child of Sharp's father, betrayed, despised, and humiliated, but eventually transcending her suffering. The story thence becomes a fable, delineating the entire course of Sharp's psychological life.

Another question this novel inevitably raises is one which it is impossible to omit from any discussion of the psychological roots of Sharp's work in the experiences of his childhood. Was there anything in that experience by itself that might have urged him to identify the "illegitimate" part of his nature as female? Whatever the origins of this notion, it appears to have taken hold of him quite early. He was still in his twenties when he wrote to a close friend, "Don't despise me when I say that in some things I am more a woman than a man."[39] One probable source of this feeling is fairly obvious. His father's stern authoritarianism was a quality of manhood which the rebellious and sensitive young William must early have found distasteful. But there was, on the feminine side, something perhaps even more compelling. A psychoanalyst has observed that we who have become accustomed to invisible and antiseptic childbirth may often forget that it was the rule until very recently for women to have their children at home, and the emotional impact this had on older children must have been immense.[40] To say this was true in the case of William Sharp, the eldest of eight, is to be guilty of no exaggeration. Childbirth is one of the most obsessive preoccupations of his work, from beginning to end. The frail and sensitive boy, whose father encouraged him in every manly physical exercise and no doubt looked upon a literary career as smacking of the effete, may easily have repressed these impulses of sympathy for the suffering of women together with the secret visions of his inner life. When those visions emerged, they emerged with a feminine cast upon them.

The romantic dictum that the child is father of the man may well be considered proven by modern psychology. Sharp's father died when Sharp was twenty, and thereafter the pressures that came from his family could not have been in any real sense binding. But psychologically Sharp had by that time already been made. As he grew older he still fought in his imagination the shadows of tyrannies his feelings had warred with as a child. Shelley, also profoundly sympathetic to women, became his poetic idol, and his fictional heroes became surrogates for his own victimization. They made an entire gallery of disinherited sons: Charles Cameron of *The Sport of Chance*, urged by his father to disappear after a mysterious and unexplained besmirching of the family name; Alan of *Green Fire*, an adopted son, sent away because he was unwanted; Jim Ruthven of *Silence Farm*, turned into a monster and deprived of his patrimony by a fiercely vengeful father. It is hardly a surprise to come upon an entry for about 1890 in Sharp's fragmentary journals, where he speaks of someday writing a "blank verse tragedy— a terrible modern instance of the scriptural warning as to the sins of the father . . . an instance where the father himself shares the doom and agony."[41]

When Sharp left Scotland for Australia in 1876, he was already a moral exile. For him there was no place called home, and no roots he wished to acknowledge as his own, except the vaguest of ties with the gypsies, themselves a wandering and expatriated race, and along with these a dim sense of being bound by ichor if not by blood to another race which was not of this world. Clearly he did not consciously identify himself as a Scot—a member of the race of his father. His few Scottish intellectual connections were with the university, and were not markedly different from those any hopeful young man might have made in the search for guardianship and guidance. Even these were soon to be replaced in London by the exciting avant-garde of the Rossetti circle.

2

CLIMATE AND LANDSCAPE

Early Work

It is, practically speaking, with Sharp's entrance into the Rossetti circle that we begin in any way to be provided with details concerning his development and the influences upon it. It is also at this point that Sharp's development can be said to assume anything like the independence of character that he and his wife required for their reading of him. He had failed to make anything respectable out of his trip to Australia in 1876–77, and was still paying sufficient lip service to those same old "prospects for his future" to come to London in 1878 in order to attach himself to the bank business. But it is evident that the remission of parental pressure was making it less and less difficult for him to eschew the Philistines, who came to want him as little as he wanted them. His wife takes characteristic delight in telling how William's casual attitude toward working hours, and his penchant for slipping out to the country to hear the cuckoo on pleasant spring days, caused him to be fired from the London Branch of the Melbourne Bank.[1] The sirens of springtime were not, however, his only distraction. By late 1879 he had been introduced to Dante Rossetti through the good offices of his friend Noel Paton. From the moment of their meeting the young poet spent many hours with his literary idol, some of them, owing to Rossetti's nocturnal habits, cutting well into the time a good prospective banker would have spent in bed.

Perhaps no circle was more calculated to satisfy Sharp's young craving for nonconformity than that which gathered about the declining Rossetti. The glamor had not completely departed from his presence, and, still seeking occasion to bask in it, or certainly aware of it, were many celebrated late Victorians. Through Rossetti Sharp came to know almost every important literary figure of the time, including Swinburne, Morris, Pater, Meredith, and Browning, and was gradually admitted to their circles and to those of artists like William Bell Scott, Ford Madox Brown, and Holman Hunt. He was joined by other aspiring poets and writers like Philip Marston and Hall Caine, who were among Rossetti's young protégés. Sharp's successful admission to this group would have been heady enough potion in itself. But ever since Robert Buchanan, the eminent Scot and infamous rebuffer of poets, had dealt Sharp the terrible blow of advising him to leave the writing profession altogether, Rossetti's encouragement had acquired a special lure.

Under this bohemian influence, Sharp's tendency to the life-style of protest flourished. In the flush of his new-found freedom from the inhibitions of home, his earlier appetite for privacy and brooding seclusion was all but forgotten and the changeling garb laid aside. For the moment he could fulfill two equally strong, but opposing desires: to belong to a significant literary and artistic movement, and to indulge his craving for uniqueness, convinced that the members of the group to which he belonged were themselves outsiders with regard to the establishment. Having little perspective and no cynicism, he was able to direct his wholehearted enthusiasm toward what he understood to be the principles of the Pre-Raphaelites, and he made himself their spokesman. Thus, the biography Sharp hastily scribbled after Rossetti's death in 1882 was as much an apology for the movement as the man. Making free use of Ruskin's insights and misapprehensions, Sharp justified the boldness (if not capriciousness) of Pre-Raphaelitism on the basis of its dispensing with imitation and derivativeness, and urged the increased application of its principle of "native inspiration." This made him observe with special emphasis in his biography that Rossetti "seemed always to me an unmistakable Englishman."[2] His initial reaction to Rossetti, documented in a letter to Elizabeth, had perhaps been more sound "I was not in London," he had then mused rhapsodically. "The blood of the South burned in my veins, the sky was a semi-tropical one. The river rushing past was not the Thames but the Tiber."[3] It would not be the last instance of Sharp's altering the memory of an actual experience in the passion of new insight. Yet regardless of which reaction was valid, it is apparent that this attachment to the Pre-Raphaelite movement gave him the first opportunity for seriously applying a theory that equated creative inspiration with nationality or the national best self.

The theory itself he had stated somewhat earlier. Geographical determinism had in fact been the theme of one of Sharp's earliest articles, "A Note on Climate and Art" (1881), the very title of which would become a kind of subtitle for all his future work. In that essay, Sharp spoke of the "determinate law" that rules the productions of science (a branch of learning he had not yet relegated to the limbo of things not to be achieved in one lifetime), literature, music, and art. Each poet, he asserted, was not "an individual aberration from the lower levels of the commonplace, but . . . literally the product of his time."[4]

> Nature knows no such things as wholly separate links: she is made of an infinite multitude of connexions, that form one chain . . . An enquiry into the influences which art, or music, or belles lettres, or philosophy, exercise upon the community of nations, must be based upon an understanding of the actual surroundings and material agencies existing in and operating upon each race and country.[5]

This concept is entitled to exclusive place as the central philosophy of his life's work. Whether directly derived from Ruskin's notions of the organic relationship between great art and the time and place of its creation, or from the Darwinism that had filtered its way down into intellectual commonplace, this concept merely reflected an intellectual "climate" that had been forming for at least a century, and in which many a nationalistic storm had gathered. Drawing a distinction long familiar to Europeans between the sense experiences of northern and southern peoples, Sharp suggested that the "artificialism" in the work of many English and Dutch artists was due primarily to fabricated experience or imitation of the work of others, to the expression, in other words, of a false identity. Whatever success these artists have achieved, he said, is in landscape, and that success is in direct proportion to the sincerity with which they have tried to catch the nervous, fluctuating variety of their own climate. But northern art, he concluded, will find its true self—and has already done so in the Pre-Raphaelites—in the study of man, "not so much historically as emotionally . . . [in] the portrayal of all the human passions."[6]

Because Sharp felt the Pre-Raphaelites so cogently illustrated this doctrine of cultural relativism and truth to experience, the London circle influenced his future development; and it is worth evaluating his first volume of poetry, *The Human Inheritance, The New Hope, Motherhood and Other Poems* (1882), dating almost entirely from the early London period, for its prefigurations of his later, more important work. The great diversity of theme and form and the unevenness of conception evident in these poems might seem to indicate many false starts. Yet Sharp's seemingly very diversified poetic motives are really only different aspects of certain central premises of contemporary esthetic though and thus possess a fundamental unity.

One of these central premises is a focus on perception itself, a concern with the relativity of experience. It expresses the convergence of scientific and artistic attitudes found, for example, in the painting of the French impressionists. These painters, although highly subjective in their vision, worked nevertheless from the axiom that the self is a quasi-scientific medium of experience through which data can be gathered for the expression of relative truth. Autobiography and autobiographical forms of writing represent in literature a similar kind of applied scientific sensibility. Such genres, so characteristic of the nineteenth century, were capable of appearing brooding and evocative in tone at the hands of certain writers. But they were gradually inclining more and more to a studious, half-clinical scrutiny of subjective emotional experience. It was Sharp's sympathy with this movement that led to his admiration for George Meredith's "Modern Love" and Rossetti's "House of Life," both of which revolutionized the sonnet-sequence tradition by submitting the poets' own erotic and conjugal experiences, happy and unhappy, to a ruthless poetic analysis.[7]

There is psychological coherence, then, to the heavy autobiographic emphasis of this first volume of poems. Seven of them are in the form of the conventional sonnet, traditionally a subjective lyric, and a form in which Sharp had such a passionate interest that he later wrote three critical essays on the sonnet's history and function as companion studies to his three sonnet anthologies.[8] Twenty-six other poems in The Human Inheritance, together entitled "Transcripts from Nature," are written in a form called the "ispetto" that has distinct affinities with the sonnet, and that Sharp, borrowing from John Addington Symonds, considered its forerunner.[9] But the current of autobiography, or "autopsychic" poetry, prevails even outside of the sonnet and related forms. Though Sharp occasionally borrowed Shelley's practice of using the third person instead of the first to camouflage the personal strategy, he was clearly fictionalizing his own experience. This is equally true of both the long, serialized narrative "The Human Inheritance" and the poetic essay of symphonic proportions called "The New Hope," a work that attempts to come to terms with a large and puzzling variety of past and present religious philosophies and beliefs.

There are, of course, marks of obvious derivativeness. Indeed Sharp seems to have modeled his own image of poetic self on Shelley. Wordsworth's presence is identifiable too, especially in the first part of "The Human Inheritance," with its theme of the happy child, and its tone of narrative recollection in tranquillity. That spasmodic, poetic bildungsroman *Festus* was undoubtedly effective in providing a model for Sharp's panoramic historical purview in "The New Hope."[10] And in both these poems, almost overwhelmed by all the heavy formal machinery of English romanticism, was a transcendental vision of the natural world, part of the residue of his favorite readings in Emerson. Finally Walt Whitman, whose vitalism Sharp shared throughout this work and in all his serious poetry thereafter, provided the ebullient epigraph for the entire volume, a fragment from "Starting from Paumonok" beginning "I will make the poems of materials, for I think they are to be the most spiritual poems."

But the fundamental, unifying principle of these poems can be seen as characteristically Sharp's, the fascination with the variety and relativity of subjective experience. Thus "The Human Inheritance," divided into four parts or "cycles," one for each of the ages of man, may be classed as a series of case studies in human emotional development. The first cycle, "Childhood's Inheritance," is of peculiar interest as background: it is set in Scotland and discloses a child growing almost wildly on the moors, in union and communion with his natural surroundings, and developing in spirit through the beneficent agency of nature and clean living. He is in some ways like the later "Peterkin" of Fiona Macleod without his visions, and both pieces show the same tendency to romanticize childhood, though in the earlier work Sharp has not yet developed the wistful vocabulary of wonder so idiomatic in Fiona Macleod. Not surprisingly, the child of "Childhood's Inheritance" manages to be "sunny" in spite of being motherless, and almost in spite of being fatherless, for his father, his only surviving guardian, is really only a functional link with the adult world, and appears vaguely and fleetingly just outside the undefined boundary of the child's immediate consciousness.

But one fact related to Sharp's development as a poet of environment must be made clear. Though we are told the child is a Scottish child, and the landscape he gambols in a Scottish landscape, such knowledge is not sustained through any evocative power of the description itself. The scenery used as background is generic natural scenery, and has little, if any, of the distinctive quality of Fiona Macleod's later Scottish landscapes. But there is already evident the poet's ability, exercised through his child-surrogate, to identify with and project himself into his natural surroundings. This has great significance for the direction of Sharp's future growth, and suggests one way that contemporary esthetic thought was beginning to be incorporated into his imaginative equipment. Henri Frédéric Amiel, whose *Journal intime* was enjoying great popularity in these years, entered in that journal a statement that might have been the title to a study of ninteenth-century painting: "un paysage est un état d'âme." It might also have been the working hypothesis behind much nineteenth-century poetry. Certainly it sanctioned a great deal of Sharp's own literary practice. Some of Baudelaire's esthetic utterances were of an equally congenial kind. "What is pure art according to the modern conception?" asked the French poet in "L'art philosophique." "It is to create a suggestive magic that can hold both object and subject, the exterior world to the artist, and the artist himself."[11]

Sharp is highly representative of the British mode of assimilating and expressing this outlook. His trip to Australia and back again through the South Pacific, abortive though it may have been as a family investment, bore fruit of this imaginative kind. The Australian landscape was eventually to find its way into "Old Age's Inheritance," the fourth cycle of the "Inheritance" series, and again into "Australian Sketches," part of Sharp's second volume of poems, published in 1884.[12] But the Pacific Islands provided the background for the second cycle of "The Human Inheritance," on youth. The young hero of this cycle has gone to sea in a merchant ship. His foreshortened odyssey consists of enjoying a romantic adventure with a Haidée-like native maiden when his ship is forced to make a short stopover on a Pacific island. The actual experience of visiting the islands seemed to have awakened in the poet, already receptive to natural scenery in an extraordinary way, a response to the great variations in landscape and climate which nature is capable. Nature here is shown in its raw, tropical force, and the hero responds to it by dint of a special faculty for seeing

> beyond and deeper—every clod
> Of earth that holds a flow'r root is to him
> The casement of a miracle.[13]

The youth's love affair with the primitive girl is passionate, brief, and fatal. Her grassy hut is struck by lightning during a violent tropical storm, and she and her family are discovered as charred bodies. The poet is making a clear attempt to draw a symbolic correspondence between the inexorably self-destructive force of the fatal passion, and the natural phenomena themselves. This particular correspondence, though in one sense merely illustrative of a pattern of correspondences ("correspondances"—a key concept for the French symbolist), is interesting as one which Sharp was to exploit again in a later novel, *The Children of To-morrow* (1889). In that story, a pair of lovers divided by religion and social convention, and nothing else, is struck by lightning while engaged in a furiously passionate embrace which they have had the temerity to attempt in a wooded grove, at the edge of the sea, during an electrical storm.

It is not really a digression here to point out that Sharp's fascination with love in its extremes, either of violent passion or overwhelming tenderness, is something he shares with his contemporaries by virtue of the fundamental semi-scientific curiosity about human nature of which something has already been said. In the area of human sexual behavior, it was by the examination of extremes, of unconventional behavior, even of aberrations, that many later Victorians saw the possibility of negotiating the entire range of the emotional life of "the human animal." The interest in feminism and in sexual inversion expressed by men like Havelock Ellis, Edward Carpenter, and J. A. Symonds, is representative.

Still, in exploring these extremes, Sharp made an effort to rely as far as possible on his own experience. Thus, the love that is expressed as overwhelming tenderness in the "Manhood" cycle of the "Inheritance" series has in many details close points of contact with Sharp's real romance with Elizabeth; one instance is the name of the woman herself, Lillian, "Lill" being the familiar nickname Sharp used for his wife. The *Memoir* offers no factual basis for the veiled allusion to a love triangle in "Manhood," but it does provide the data behind other inclusions—the London background, the meetings in public parks (in actual life necessitated by the clandestine nature of Lill's romance with a ne'er-do-well first cousin), and the sense of singular mental and spiritual affinity to which Mrs. Sharp often discreetly alluded and which undoubtedly helped them to survive the many vicissitudes of their lengthy engagement and frequent separations of time and distance during their marriage. Sharp's attempt, however unsuccessful, to reproduce the experience of absolute soul-harmony in love, is something he persisted in, and for which as Fiona Macleod he finally found the proper medium—myth. In this fairly realistic early effort, however, he is dependent upon effusions of eternal devotion, and unconvincingly glorifies the woman as a medium of heavenly exaltation. The result is the creation of a kind of divine troubadour ideal, distinctly misplaced in nineteenth-century London. Stopford Brooke, writing to Sharp about his newly published work, prophetically observed that Sharp possessed too much faculty for reporting nature, and too little "humanity": "The poem in the midst of *The Human Inheritance*, Cycle III," he wrote, "is nearest to the human heart and yet the least well-written of all the cycles."[14] But Sharp was not to give up trying.

The poem then leaps many years to the most hypothetical (for the young poet) of the ages of man, and an Australian wilderness is the desolate setting for another "autopsychic" narrative, this time the obverse of the first. Here an old man is living out his last days in devoted contemplation of his wife, now dead, and the sons, now grown, that she bore him. His salutary meditations on his own impending death consist in his being

> not glad to leave the earth,
> Yet wishing not to shun the soul's rebirth
> Through the dark womb of death.[15]

The piece is really no more than a concoction which permits Sharp to express some of the eschatological opinions that had emerged from a deep concern with death and immortality during the period of his alienation from his family religion.[16] He had set out to explore the human inheritance with dogged dedication of purpose, and produced a dogged and unsatisfying exploration.

Once again, the underlying unity of impulse behind Sharp's early work is illustrated by "Motherhood," the most striking, as it was certainly the most controversial, of Sharp's poetic attempts in this first volume.[17] Three kinds of mothers are portrayed, in Sharp's own words, "the brute, the savage, and the civilized woman."[18] The poem is another instance, in a different area, of the poeticized sociological data-gathering of some of "The Human Inheritance." It comes as no surprise that at about this time Olive Schreiner, author of *Story of an African Farm*, and an active feminist as well as close London friend of the Sharps, was making a study of the social laws behind female subjection that included precise parallels of Sharp's three categories. Sharp was clearly as fascinated with the moral implications of the birth experience as he was with the moral implications of man's outlook on death. Manifest in this poem is his interest in the physical and physiological components of the birth process itself, and how these were related to its significance as a spiritual and moral event. The union of science and poetry is inherent in the sequential, documentary structure of the poem, which is on the one hand dramatic, and on the other an invitation to spatial and chronological comparison or contrast. It sets up, objectively and without commentary, a confrontation of different states or attitudes that suggests both the unity and the relativity of experience. The point is clear: in essentials, the experience of motherhood is the same for all forms of life. It supplies a unifying principle for all the phenomena of creation, despite wide variations of sensibility and culture. But another note is struck here that will tend to become permanent with Sharp: at all three levels of increasingly sensible and conscious experience, a moment of crisis is suffered in which, dimly but perceptibly, the suffering female recalls the past experience of her predecessors in the line of evolution. Sharp is asserting the persistence of racial or animal memory throughout the evolutionary process—a subliminal knowledge of generic past experience in each individual creature at her particular level of developed consciousness.

This concept was not new with Sharp, for a similar kind of unconscious or race memory had been one of the resources of Alton Locke in Charles Kingsley's novel of the same name published in 1850. In greatly varying degress of explicitness, in fact, it was to be found in many Victorian writers, shadowily in Meredith's *Egoist*, more solidly in Hardy's *A Pair of Blue Eyes*, and quite directly in Butler's treatise *Unconscious Memory*. Butler's work, appearing as it did in 1880, may have had a direct effect on Sharp. For Lafcadio Hearn, in this as in so many other respects parallel to Sharp, it was the core idea of his literary philosophy.[19] The theory lay squarely behind much of the myth-making of the Celtic movement, and had a strong formative influence on the imagination of Fiona Macleod.

Increased consciousness, as the feature that distinguished one higher form from its lower predecessor, was one of the axioms of those theorists who looked upon evolution as convincing illustration of natural progress. Sharp seems to have adopted this principle too, one which would receive strong support a few years later from the redoubtable mathematician-philosopher W. K. Clifford, in his *Cosmic Emotion*,[20] a work that influenced the young revolutionary writers of the late eighties. But Sharp had been assisted also, as surely the theorizers themselves had not been, by a sense, derived from his studies of spiritualism and folklore, that spirits of the past could and did dwell in men of the present, with the cumulative effect of giving some men, of sufficiently high sensibility to perceive their presence, a more complicated spiritual life than others.

"The New Hope" is a longer and more outright first-person disquisition on the same theme of increased consciousness, and of racial memory progressing through evolution. Here the basis of man's link with the past, and with other men of varying cultures and ideologies, is religion and not maternity. "The New Hope" is too palpably an essay on religious philosophy to be a very good poem, and somewhat too rapt in its tone to be very good philosophy. Reconstructed, however, the essential message is fairly clear—that centuries of religious institutionalizing have blinded man to "the glory of life," and have turned his attention to the rewards or punishments due him in the hereafter rather than to his compatibility with nature in the here-and-now. Though the philosophy is a rather patent compound of pagan wisdom, Stoic and Epicurean, Sharp emphasizes its modernity. The greatest of nature's laws being death, modern religious thought has shown its superiority to the teachings of the past (presumably, the Christian past) precisely in its assertion, as Sharp sees it, that death must be faced with hope instead of fear. Once again, as in "Motherhood," Sharp proposes that the recrudescence in history of similar religious forms and myths is evidence of a racial or generic consciousness, along with an inexorable religious need. But modern man, besides recognizing the instinctual basis of religion, has also come to recognize the basis of true religion as the acceptance of change, both in the experience of the individual and in that of the race. Thus within his own lifetime a man may undergo a series of moral deaths and regenerations, finding in these reason for the acceptance of the process of flux, and realizing thereby the "new hope." On these same grounds he may also find the "new charity," so to speak, for the underlying unity of all creation in its manifest diversity is the most prominent feature of this entire philosophy; when acceptance and joy replace reluctance, resistance, and fear, the result ought to be a general love of all creation. The man who recognizes the beneficent purpose of death may thus see

> A vision of life in some divine new birth . . .
> Beyond himself, beyond the human soul . . .
> [Which] blooms into the flower of praise
> . . . for . . . that mighty love, whose breath,
> Whose gift to life is never-lying death,—
> Eternal change.[21]

Sharp was unaware at the time that around this same philosophy would grow the essential, distinguishing form of Fiona Macleod's Celtic art. The source of all the thrust she gave to the Celtic movement lay in her conviction that the very passing of the Celtic races would be evidence of a "spiritual rebirth" that could move the world.

Again, the link between science and poetry, even in this species of esthetic fatalism, cannot be overemphasized. A limited scientific education might well have assisted Sharp in the very phrasing of notions that so absorbed into intelligible harmony death, love, and beauty. One contemporary biological treatise had it that

> admitting the theory of evolution we are not only entitled to the hope, but logically compelled to the assurance that . . . [the] rare fruits of an apparently more than earthly paradise of love, which only the forerunners of the race have been privileged to gather, or it may be to see from distant heights, are yet the realities of a daily life towards which we and ours may journey.[22]

The treatise quoted here was published some years after Sharp's poem, and is not therefore being cited as a source. Curiously, however, its authors, Patrick Geddes and J. Arthur Thompson, were to become close partners of Sharp later on as founders of the Scottish branch of the Celtic movement, and their similarity of views must have played its part in sealing their association. Their community of mind is one of the most interesting and characteristic phenomena of this period. Scientific thinkers moving empirically, and literary thinkers moving intuitively, were able, for possibly the last time in history, to travel simultaneously the same lines. Butler's theories (and indeed his quarrel with Darwin over getting credit for them) are another pertinent illustration of this phenomenon. Perhaps Geddes and Thompson's book, *The Evolution of Sex*, was, to their fellow empiricists, a dramatic thesis on the development of sexual differentiation in living organisms. But to nonscientists it could only have served as useful confirmation of what they had for some time imagined. Certainly it worked in beautifully with their views, and is striking evidence, ignored by casual critics of "decadence," that the union of love and death was not a mere contrivance of morbid minds but the scientifically documented conclusion of respected biological evolutionists. Geddes and Thompson based their work entirely on the thesis that reproduction is a function of "katabolic crisis"—a crisis of decline—and is an expression of the consequent and contrary desire for vicarious immortality. Still almost untouched by the divisive force of specialization, they were not averse to drawing the same metaphysical conclusions as the poets, that love and death were thus inextricably associated.[23]

An exuberant optimism, then, a romantic "wonder," and not a decadent impulse at all—a profound social, scientific, and artistic curiosity, finding itself upon an opening frontier—is the key to all of Sharp's responses to his world. That same exuberance provided one of the several reasons for his choice of the traditional romantic child as correlative of the proper attitude toward life. Undoubtedly the Victorian Blake revival, so much advanced through Rossetti, had a great deal to do with the quantity of brief childlike lyrics in Sharp's early poetry. But the Blake tradition seems only to provide literary sanction for what is essentially Sharp's personal psychological need to justify his rebellious resistance to any authoritarian pressures, and to restore himself to an imaginative state of freshness, independent of ties to people, dependent only on nature itself.

Thus a passion for the primitive, the vital, the unconventional, the unspoiled, the unsophisticated, and the untrammeled is characteristic of these early poems. Sharp rests his sympathy in the "natural" man, as well as in the natural landscape, as pure and raw as possible. The Scottish moor in cycle I of "The Human Inheritance," the Pacific Island of the "Youth" cycle, with its brown maidens swimming naked in the sea, the Australian wilderness of "Old Age's Inheritance" —all these are of a piece with the simple, bold nature-sketches of the "Transcripts from Nature" and the glorification of the child. They all form part of a view of life which consistently favors innocence, and which is already more than half-way toward damning experience. It is a thoroughly conventional romantic attitude, yet one with ramifications of a special kind for Sharp as an incipient form of a dual view of life. For the moment, nature and civilization are merely juxtaposed. An invidious contrast may be implied, as in "Motherhood," or in the "Manhood" cycle of the "Inheritance" series, but it is not spelled out. In the latter poem, no invidious criticism of the city is offered beyond the cliché that cities are the "busy haunts of men," but even there Sharp does not seem to take much pleasure in describing civilized human relations, nor, as Stopford Brooke pointed out, does he do it especially well. Though present here only in embryonic form, the polarity of the civilized and the primitive will later come to be an intrinsic part of Sharp's vision, partially defining his artistic personalities as he conceives them. There are represented here other devices in the craft of the mind that opposes itself—sudden contrast, interior dialogue, ironic comparison—but these are present to no greater extent than they would probably be in many, if not most, young writers with a limited range for interpreting experience.

When all is considered, at any rate, Sharp reveals himself as an exponent from the start of a highly functional, nonpathological narcissism. He is fascinated with himself, with his own personality, as a trustworthy and fundamentally interesting medium of experience, whose vision ought not to be violated by fiction. He is, of course, predisposed to thinking of that "self" as a natural, unprejudiced, and unconventional man. Precisely how this conviction was to be set forth in artistic form is a problem. The special use he makes of nature as a moral and emotional equivalent for his internal experience is his characteristic strategy for groping after that wished-for self. The following extracts from "Transcripts from Nature" are good examples.

41

The furtive lights that herald dawn
 Are shimmering mid the steel-blue firs;
 A slow awakening wind half stirs
And the long branches breathe upon;
 The east grows clearer—clearer—lo,
 The day is born! a refluent flow

Of silver waves along each tree
For one brief moment dazzlingly.

   . . .

Between the salt sea-send before
 And all the flowing gulfs behind,
 Half lifted by the rising wind,
Half eager for the ungain'd shore,
 A great green wave of shining light
 Sweeps onward crowned with dazzling white:

Above, the east wind shreds the sky
With plumes from the grey clouds that fly.[24]

Not great poetry by any means, but observant to a high degree, and bearing a suggestive resemblance to impressionistic painting in its focus on sheer visual experience and on light. Yet there is here, and even more in later poetry of similar form, an attempt also to define and isolate such visual experience by a fine process of selection, to the point that it becomes no mere neutral description of matter, but evokes a precise, self-contained emotion. In this, a primitive form of expressionism, and in his total reliance on a sensitive, almost scientific response to natural phenomena, Sharp largely departs from the manner of some of the literary influences of his early career, alleged by his critics to have been so overwhelming. He widely misses the prevailing hothouse quality of Rossetti, Swinburne, and Pater, to whose esthetics he was otherwise so susceptible. The Rossetti who described nature with the eye of the painter, of whom Sharp himself ruefully observed that only one of his poems "was composed in the open air,"[25] the Swinburne whose descriptions were woven into a tapestry of human emotional experience, the Pater whose stained-glass faculties hardly seemed designed to invite clear and unimpeded perception—none of these could have instructed Sharp in his perceptual strategy. A professor at Glasgow University named John Veitch, under whom Sharp studied the logical methods of science, could have done so, for he published a work entitled "The Feeling for Nature in Scottish Poetry."[26] It is rather probable, however, that in devising this strategy Sharp was responding to new esthetic movements superseding these older influences, and to which he was highly attuned by his early vagabondage.

Indeed, those same great men of Sharp's London experience appear to have received their private translation through Sharp's eyes. It was the man Rossetti who, from the evidence of Sharp's critical and biographical essays on him, certainly touched him most deeply, and who, as Sharp saw him, showed even in his decline a deep receptivity to the natural world. Swinburne's childlike pleasure in the sea was the source of Sharp's greatest delight in him.[27] He characteristically worshipped Pater's *Renaissance* as "a gospel of joy"; yet it was Pater the man, and not merely the appreciator, who left his most profound mark on him. Within that strangely elusive human being, Sharp was able to perceive a student and observer of natural phenomena, whose response indeed carried a height of feeling amounting nearly to mysticism, but who could also dispel self sufficiently to say to Sharp on their first meeting in 1881 how delighted he was at the prospect of hearing the adventures of a man "who had travelled much and far, and experienced not a few strange vicissitudes."[28]

Whether or not the Pater of Sharp's perception was the true Pater, the Sharp of Pater's perception was certainly an insight into the true Sharp. His own confession that one of the happiest moments of his life was the discovery that Rossetti "liked" him, is another.[29] An ebullient and rosy "Viking in build," eager in proportion to his social naiveté, vain of himself in proportion to his hunger for the affection of men, overflowing with an abundance of experiences he had so far only enjoyed alone and was impatient to relate to others, yet clearly no glib courtier ready for the casual barter of such experiences, Sharp was bound, amid the highly unstable artistic life of the London eighties, to make enough social and literary mistakes to require the construction, eventually, of a strategy for protecting the sacred sphere of his imaginative life from violation by the profane.

Indeed, from the point of view of Sharp's development, the only fault with the London intellectual and artistic circle in which he moved was that it was breaking if not already broken. It was owing partly to a habit of isolation acquired early, but also partly to the fact of finding himself in an artistic atmosphere decidedly in flux, that he was compelled to grope as frantically as he did for an artistic modus operandi. New circles were opening and closing around him everywhere and every day. But they would prove either too tight to include him, or too loose to provide a real basis for shared artistic feeling and experience. By the time the Celtic movement captured him in the nineties, Sharp had so systematized his loneliness that he could not absorb from that movement the kind of inspiration provided by mutuality of artistic life. Actually, that movement, particularly its Edinburgh phase (as Sharp himself saw with such penetration later on), did not possess the vital stuff on such mutuality. Had even such sympathies as later generated by shared Celtism existed earlier, however, he might have developed quite a different—and stronger—artistic voice. But so too would many another artist of his generation. From the standpoint of art, for those who have not the stamp of inexorable genius, there is not only safety but vitality in numbers. The sense of artistic community was lacking for others as it was for him, and he may for this very reason be more typical than isolated and autonomous luminaries of the doubt-filled, floundering quest for identity that characterized his generation.

3

LONDON

The City as Countertype

Sharp's first attempt at popular biography, *Dante Gabriel Rossetti: A Record and a Study*, marked the beginning of a long period, though not a completely unbroken one, of potboiling and hack work, of city life and literary editorships. Some idea of this maelstrom of activity can be suggested by a summary of the work that engaged his energies between 1882 and 1890. The life of Rossetti was published late in 1882. By 1885 this inconspicuous beginning as a biographer had been expanded by the enterprising young writer into a lucrative portfolio. Hired by Eric Robertson of the Great Writers series, he was already at work in that year on a biography of Shelley, with two more, of Heine and Browning, in the offing. He became a contributor to Ernest Rhys's Camelot Classics, and an editor of the Canterbury Poets series, writing numerous introductory essays for that comprehensive, though uneven, five-foot shelf of Victorian "culture." He was a member of the staffs of both the *Glasgow Herald* and the *Art Journal* in the capacity of art critic, these posts providing him with the opportunity in 1884 for a subsidized fling in Paris, where he was sent to report on the Salon exhibitions.

Late in 1882, while he was still trying to find his footing in the London publishing quagmire, the gifts of some considerate friends allowed him another bit of travel for which he had long been yearning, and he took his first trip to Italy. Though it too was a kind of junket required by his apprenticeship as an art critic, he turned it to his own uses, and Italy, true to its Victorian reputation, left its mark permanently on his character and his work.

Meanwhile, he continued exercising his imaginative talents to the extent permitted by time and energy. After *The Human Inheritance* in 1882, he produced two more volumes of poetry, *Earth's Voices* in 1884, and *Romantic Ballads and Poems of Phantasy* in 1888. The second of these marks a shift to folkloristic subject matter, but a tentative one only. By the date of its publication he had already begun to write, under the stimulus of a fresh look at Walt Whitman and at the free verse of Ernest Henley, one or two of the poems later included in a very different kind of work, the *Sospiri di Roma*, a volume that would be filled out during a second stay in Italy in 1890. Two novels also saw completion in this period, *The Sport of Chance* (published in serial form in 1887, as a book in 1888), and *The Children of To-morrow* (1889). Among his other prose were several short stories and a bundle of travel sketches.

Some years later, Arthur Waugh described the Sharp of this hectic writing and publishing circuit as one who had adapted himself well to the demands of such a life. He was, says Waugh, "a familiar apparition in editorial offices and literary gatherings":

> With his Olympian stature, bright complexion, full head of hair, and well-kempt beard, he attracted attention at once, and took good care to retain it. His manner was a mixture of suavity and aggression, and he knew (no man better) how to overcome the hesitation of editors. He was at the birth of every new literary journal, and comfortably absent at its death. He knew whose money was behind every fresh venture, and exactly how much money there was. He was early on the scene with a string of suggestions, and editors found it more convenient to accept two or three of them off-hand than to await the outburst of a fresh barrage . . . He knew all the big men, and could quote their judgments at first hand.[1]

Ernest Rhys, one of Sharp's closest acquaintances and an editor in his own right, bore Waugh out: "Thanks to his large and imposing presence, his sanguine air, his rosy faith in himself, he had a way of overwhelming editors that was beyond anything, I believe, ever heard of in London, before or since."[2] Rhys amplified this characterization in *Everyman Remembers* in 1931, with Rhys himself playing the overwhelmed editor:

> [Sharp] burst in impetuously one summer morning as I was having a bath. . . . His fine figure and exuberant contours, set forth in unusually resplendent clothes, suggested a stage Norseman. He talked very fast and excitedly, his bright yellow hair brushed up from an open brow, under which blue eyes, rosy cheeks, full red lips, and a pointed yellow beard suggested a staring picture by some impressionist painter.

Then came the pitch:

> He had been editing the Canterbury Poets, in which series my George
> Herbert volume appeared, and had heard from the publishers of my
> prose argosy [the Camelot series]. Here was an opening after his
> own heart. In half an hour he had proposed half a dozen books
> which he would like to edit for me, and De Quincey's *Opium-Eater*
> was there and then allotted to him.[3]

As though something were driving him despite himself to achieve
the "success" his family had desired for him, Sharp seems to have
cultivated every manner that would make him popular and "well-liked."
But this image of himself was acquired at great cost. If one is to believe
his wife's testimony, this suavely aggressive literary hack was not the
true Sharp at all, or rather was an affectation that succeeded eventually
in dividing him irrevocably from himself—the self, that is, that longed
for true artistic glory and the fulfillment of his creative dreams. The
picture she gives of her husband even at this time, when he appeared
to others so happily cast in the role of publishing entrepreneur, is that
of a man profoundly discontented with city and publishing life, despis-
ing all the subjection to others' opinions that is the price often exacted
by worldly success. Sharp's writing reveals his exacerbated awareness of
the dilemma of such success. Very often in his fiction, an artist-hero is
found in the midst of a crisis of choice between the demands of
success and those of the genuine artistic self. And, probably owing to
his private turmoil on this issue, many of the subjects of his criticism
and biography seem to have been presented with the same choice,
and resisted the same temptation. Apparently Sharp came to see how
naive were any expectations he might have had of second-rate fame as
a bright light in publishing. He felt the longing, the often frustrated
longing, to give them up. After the death of Rossetti, and later of
Marston, his remaining friendships began to pall, the constant reminder
of his own charm and personal success to seem a hollow kind of glory,
the need of turning every pleasure into profit to take the pleasure even
out of those trips abroad other men might consider diversions. He
could not have been totally unaware that, in the eyes of friends like
Richard Le Gallienne, the "disappointing inadequacy" of his work "was
a secret source of distress."[4] He could hardly, in fact, have helped being
aware of all this and growing to hate the atmosphere that encouraged

him to create for himself a personal image that was shallow and commonplace beside those of his idols.

In 1894, Sharp worked into his memorial essay on Walter Pater many parallels between himself and the mentor of the aesthetes, and he was undoubtedly thinking of his own experience when he said of Pater that "for a time, London gave him a fresh and pleasant stimulus; but later it began to weary, to perturb, and at last to allure him into even deeper despondencies than his wont."[5] The statement provides a succinct, though if anything understated, equivalent to a reversal of feeling in himself that by 1894 Sharp could thoroughly document from personal experience. In the years preceding that article he had certainly recognized his own urban malaise, even to the point, in 1890, of rejecting city life and the pace it required to make a trek through Europe. What the statement also makes clear is that Sharp had waited too long to make that break. A deep resentment toward urban life had already taken root in him and become a permanent part of his creative vision.

In order to trace the development of Sharp's attitude toward the city—the first major realization of the "place" mentality in his work— we must go back not only to London in 1882 but perhaps still further, to that uncertain time in his London life when he began drafting *The Sport of Chance*, a novel he must have worked on sporadically until its completion in 1887. It is based in part on his experiences "down under," but also on his life in Scotland before them and his life in the city after them.

The *Sport of Chance* is the longest of the novels Sharp wrote in his lifetime, comprising the three standard volumes of Victorian fiction. It is also the most surcharged with adventure, containing a bewildering variety of those "vicissitudes" about which Pater, in 1881, had been so eager to hear.[6] The hero, Hew Armitage, like Othello almost damned in his fair wife, suffers unbelievable torments at the hands of Charles Leith, an Iago-like villain whose pointless malevolence wrecks his marriage. Armitage's alienated wife, Mona, spirits away their only child to the Isle of Arran for seventeen or eighteen years' safekeeping, and the hero himself is sent off on the wildest of wild-goose chases to track the villain through endless miles of Australian desert.

Several features of Sharp's treatment of this unpromising material indicate the permanence of some of his thematic interests. His eagerness to make the novel marketable no doubt accounts for his padding it with layer upon sensational layer of accident and happenstance. But there is much in his handling of the material to suggest that Sharp was also inspired by a sincere belief in fate.[7] Numerous appeals to destiny and fate, and even to some occult superior power, are in harmony with the determinism prefigured in such early pieces as "A Note on Climate and Art." These forces cause the rootlessness and scattering of all the central characters. And it is Armitage's suspicion that Charles Leith (alias Charles Cameron, Mona's brother) may himself be operating his evil will through some kind of occult magnetism, for there seems almost no other way of explaining his extraordinary powers of persuasion. Nevertheless, Leith is also the traditional romantic villain. One of Sharp's typical disinherited sons, he has been cut off by his father from his natural share in the joys of family and the peace of home, and seeks his perverse consolation by denying them to others.

Sharp's emerging consciousness of place is apparent in various ways— in the desolate Australian landscape, background for Armitage's nightmarish journey of vengeance, and in the primitively beautiful isolation of Arran, where the lovely daughter Lora is raised. It is also present in the significant role the Cameron-Armitage home, Fern Place, plays in this overacted drama.[8] Leith attempts to burn it down just as Lora, rediscovering her parentage after many years, has reinherited it. Fern Place is, in fact, a Poe-esque symbol for the continuity of the family and forms the setting for the maudlin final scene in which the long-lost Armitage at last dies peacefully on the front porch, his young granddaughter playing at his heels. There may also be a hint of the occult in Sharp's frequent use of the word "atmosphere," a technical term for the force exerted by place in the jargon of the spiritualism for which he had so strong a sympathy.

Amid all of its use of the English countryside, Arran, and Australia as background or "atmosphere," however, *The Sport of Chance* contains an undercurrent of subdued animadversion upon the city that provides a form of antiphony to its larger bucolic setting. The city is the scene for some of the characters' most terrifying experiences. It has also nurtured the viper who destroys the happiness of an entire generation, for Leith is a city slicker cut from the most obvious of molds. And finally, in the tale's significant and appropriate epilogue, this same villain receives his overdue comeuppance at the hands of American justice during a final debauch in New York. The irony of Leith's being taken in exile and receiving his due from a relatively impersonal and distant power is undoubtedly intentional. But it is even more interesting that, at this early date in the chronicle of the birth and death of American cities, New York could function as a last pit of infamy for the outcast and derelict. When he wrote, Sharp had not yet been there himself, and he probably would not have employed it thus in his novel if he had, for he came later to associate New York with some of his closest friends and most fervent admirers. Until such time, however, it could be used to convey a moral judgment that the novel had already frequently urged, and could function as a convenient (and probably common) type for the corrupt and corrupting city—no longer for Sharp merely the "busy haunts of men," but a sink of iniquity, a bed of chaos and degeneration.

The mood of this implicit attack was one long familiar to romanticism. From the time Rousseau had cried, "The breath of man is fatal to his fellows . . . Cities are the burial pit of the human species,"[9] and Blake had decried London's "charter'd streets" and "charter'd Thames," the loudest anti-urban screeds since Sodom and Gomorrah had been delivered to the civilized world. "The city as vice" had found its image in Wordsworth's carnival:

> What a shock
> For eyes and ears! What anarchy and din,
> Barbarian and infernal—a phantasma,
> Monstrous in color, motion, shape, sight, sound!
> . . . All out-o'-the-way, farfetched, perverted things,
> All freaks of nature, all Promethean thoughts
> Of man, his dullness, madness, and their feats
> All jumbled up together, to compose
> A Parliament of Monsters . . .
> Oh, blank confusion! True epitome
> Of what the mighty city is herself . . .[10]

The image had been altered, but not in intensity of disgust, by Keats's "the weariness, the fever, and the fret" and Arnold's "disease" of modern life; such cries, amid growing grime and poverty, had echoed their way through the increasingly industrialized nineteenth century.

Sharp's progress to utter sympathy with these lamentations in *The Sport of Chance*, probably the effect of the later London years of the novel's long gestation, is not very devious. He came to it by the same deductive logic as the romantics: if nature is right then civilization must be wrong. Perhaps he also came to it by the same inductive logic, as a result of the sheer physiological discomfort he suffered amid the "noise and confusion"[11] of London. It may not be too literal-minded to suggest that possibly all the anti-urban romantics possessed extremely high auditory sensibilities.[12] Certainly Sharp did—witness his passionate fondness for music and his almost obsessive attraction to the whispering sounds of wind and water. "What noise there was"—a reaction he attributes to Mona Cameron in Glasgow—is a summary of the many reactions to London and other cities with which his prose work is filled at this time. In one of his short stories, "Madge o' the Pool," London's Pool evokes an opening passage pervaded with contrasts between sound and silence. These are the sounds, catalogued with almost excruciating accuracy:

> the dull roar of omnibuses and cabs on the bridges, the muffled scraping sound of hundreds of persons moving rapidly afoot, and, from the banks, the tumult of indiscriminate voices and sounds of all kinds round and beyond the crank-crank of the cranes on the grain-wharves and the bashing of the brick and coal barges against the wooden piers.[13]

A little further on:

> The wharf-rats are so fat that they make a stone-like splash when they plunge through the grain-dollops; but only a practised ear could recognise the sound in the rude susurrus of the current, or "spot" the shrill squeaks, as of a drowning and despairing penny-whistle, when a batch of these "Thames-chickens" scurries in sudden flight down a granary-slide and goes flop into the quagmires of mud left uncovered by the ebb. But at the Pool there is never complete silence. Even if there be no wind, the curses of the Poolites . . . would cause enough current of air to crease the river's dirty skin here and there into a grim smile.[14]

Among Sharp's travel sketches is a curious report on a faraway place that is very close to home, the old veterans' hospital in Chelsea. Here the hospital garden's

> very air of remoteness has a special charm for eyes and ears weary of the noise and confusion of the dusty streets . . . At noontide is

51

heard no other sound than the long caw-caw of a restless rook, the drowsy toll of a bell, or the chiming of the hours from the clock in the grey old spire.[15]

A sketch entitled "A Memory of Verona" from the log book of his first Italian journey contains these details:

> Somewhere, not far away, a curious flute-like hooting betokened the presence of one of those small owls . . . which Shelley loved to hear; and from the hollows in the quarry, dark with shadow, came intermittently a blithe echo of the song, lessening as the singer passed into the distance, of a labourer or peasant, " 'lla 'talya! Oh Italia-a-a! Oh, bell-la, bell-bell-la!"[16]

But Sharp does not require twilight in Italy to augment his sensitivity to sound, as demonstrated by this vivid auditory description of the Verona marketplace at midday:

> With what appalling shrillness yon good-wife recommends her *fragole*, *uva*, *limoni*; with what stentorian voice the vendor of oranges proclaims their speculative worth! Everybody shouts at once, apparently indifferent to audience, scales clash, merchandise falls with a clatter, dogs bark, donkeys bray, and below all there is a kind of whispering sound of laughter and the indescribable *susurrus* of actively moving human beings.[17]

And similarly, in an introductory essay for a collection of short stories by P. B. Marston, an essay in which the communion of spirit between himself and Marston is conveyed with fervid intensity, Sharp says of Marston—who was blind—as he would say of himself, that he had a horror of "the noise and bustle of the city."[18]

Sharp's other senses must also have been irritated in the city, for "the storm cloud" Ruskin saw had rolled inexorably over nineteenth-century London, and cast its shadow upon many other British cities. "Dust and Fog" is, in fact, the title of one of Sharp's earliest articles, published in *Good Words* in 1883.[19] This article sheds light on the development of Sharp's attitude toward the city and shows that the city engaged him early as a subject of concern.

"Dust and Fog" is not a thoroughgoing diatribe. Possibly drafting it in 1880 or 1881 under the supervision of some of his university professors, the young poet—still, indeed, poet-scientist—struck in the article a tone of scientific detachment that excluded the rhetoric of personal feeling. Thus, with a generous breadth of outlook that the city's first "fresh and pleasant stimulus" had not yet discouraged, he deplored the presence of increasing fog in northern cities, but at the same time credited "bearable fog" with having some "highly antiseptic properties."[20]

But the story of "Dust and Fog" does not end there, for a good deal more than Sharp's scientific curiosity was awakened by the subject. Early in the article he alludes to a "recent" and "well-known" work entitled "The Doom of the Great City,"[21] which he briefly and casually describes as prophesying the "dismal ending" of London. And indeed it did. Published as a pamphlet in 1880, W. D. Hay's *The Doom of the Great City; being the narrative of a survivor written A.D. 1942*" provided a deliciously horrendous account of how a fatal fog, one terrible day in 1882, settled down over London and caused "the greatest calamity that perhaps this earth has ever witnessed."[22] The story is laced with generous amounts of jeremiad, the event having been for the author more than just a technical fluke, a failure of the city to get rid of its industrial waste products. It was a fit punishment dealt out to London's degenerate populace by the just hand of God. The fog is merely a symptom, if not a symbol, of "the black enormity of London sin."[23] London, growls Hay, "was foul and rotten to the core, and steeped in sin of every imagineable variety." Even as a mercantile center, a model for other nations, it was declining, overwhelmed by "the avaricious selfishness that had supplanted the old British feeling." "Republicanism," says the author with terrible foreboding, "whispered." "Socialism . . . was not unknown."[24]

These are scarcely the words of a great social prophet, though the great social prophet John Ruskin was shortly to scan with larger vision the same dismal scene. Yet they do suggest with a certain crude strength the desperate horror with which the simplest man might survey the dark spectacle of the modern city. Even Ruskin, perceiver of *The Storm-Cloud*, or James Thomson, creator of "The City of Dreadful Night," might not have gone untouched by some of Hay's lurid descriptions:

> Everything was wrapped in murky gloom, though it wanted quite an hour of sunset, and the gas lamps that were alight all day were wholly insufficient to penetrate the cloudy atmosphere with their sickly lights . . . A London fog was no mere mist . . . Its density turned day into night, and clothed night in impenetrable obscurity.[25]

The intuitive leap from the pollution of the atmosphere to the pollution of the human soul is not a long one. Romantic anti-urban sentiment, already strong, thrived on it, and the fog itself became its own demonic advocate during the so-called "Black Winters" of the eighties. All this, combined with Sharp's gradual psychological breakdown under the stress and demands of his frenetic career, eventually had its subverting effect on his imagination. By 1889 he could say "a great city is a great ulcer";[26] and by 1896 the anguish was complete: "God need not send poets to Hell: London is nearer and worse to endure."[27]

It was during the years in London after Rossetti's death, his wife tells us, that Sharp began conceiving his one short story exclusively about the "great city." Although it did not come to be published until 1895, "Madge o' the Pool: A Thames Etching"[28] is clearly a result of first-hand observations of the waterfront life of the poor that Sharp could not have gathered except in those lean early years of his struggle to make literary headway in London. Perhaps Dickens too had played a part in impressing the more sordid facts of city life on Sharp's imagination, for in many ways the story is remarkably similar to *Our Mutual Friend*. Both make use of the river and its slushy scenery as setting; in both the "river rat" and his unwittingly-begotten, noble-minded daughter are dramatis personae; and in both river intrigues assist the basic action. But there the similarity ends. Sharp's Madge and Dickens' Lizzie have quite different fortunes, and Madge's is in some ways closer to the fate of Stephen Crane's "Maggie, a Girl of the Streets" than to that of Dickens's heroine.

Madge's failure of respectability, however, in no way impairs her nobility in her creator's eyes. Quite the opposite: respectability, for Madge, is an irrelevant standard. When Madge questions the virtue of matrimony for its own sake, the narrator explains that "she was one of those rare natures to whom the thing was everything and the symbol of no moment."[29] Basically one of the simple, naturally innocent souls of whom Sharp was so fond, Madge remains impeccably faithful to her lover, a river policeman, but resists agreeing to marry him even when she is five months pregnant with his child. Fate does not allow him to realize his honorable intentions; he is killed in a river feud. She comes near drowning in the Thames, suffers a stillbirth, and eventually drowns herself in the Pool whence she came.

Although, as with many of Sharp's plots, there is some conflict here between the melodramatic and the naturalistic, Sharp does attempt to mediate between them by stressing the union of the heroine's surroundings and her fate. His description of those surroundings is thus both graphic in its unpleasant detail and impressionistically beautiful in its total effect—much like a Turner painting. It is as if Sharp meant to create a scenic metaphor of unsavory beauty for the same strange composite of these qualities in Madge herself:

> When the January fog hangs heavy upon London it comes down upon the Pool as though it were sluiced there like a drain, or a mass of garbage shot over a declivity in a waste place. The Pool is not a lovely spot in winter, though it has a beauty of its own on rare days when the sun shines in an unclouded frosty sky, or when a northwester comes down from the distant heights of Highgate and Hampstead, and slaps the incoming tide with short splashes of waves washed up by the downward current, till the whole reach of the Thames thereabouts is a jumble of blue and white and of gleaming if dirty grays and greens. On midwinter nights too, when the moon has swung up out of the smoke, like a huge fire-balloon adrift from the Lambeth furnaces, and when the stars glint like javelin points, there is something worth seeing down there, where the forest of masts rises sheer and black, and where there is a constant cross-flash of red and green rays from innumerable bow-lamps and stern-windows and tipsy lanterns trailed awry through the rigging . . . A disjointed passenger-boat, with spelican funnel darting back to perpendicular, shoots from under a bridge, and paddles swiftly down-stream like a frightened duck; a few moments, and it is out of sight, swallowed in a haze, or swung round a bend. A trio of barges, chained to each other like galley-slaves, passes up-stream, drawn by what looks like a huge bluebottle-fly. The bluebottle-fly is a tug-boat, a "barge-bug" in river parlance; and as it flaps the water with a swift spanking smash of its screw, the current is churned into a yeast of foam that is like snow against the bows of the first barge, and thin as dirty steam when washed from the sternmost into a narrow vanishing wake.[30]

Madge, the product and human symbol of this atmosphere, undergoes her crisis, and foreshadows her doom, when her love for Jim Shaw becomes inextricably bound up with a totally different atmosphere from that in which she has been bred. Sharp has already described how that love has been an exaltation, a source of discriminative judgment between the tawdry and the beautiful. Now Jim has decided to take her on an outing up the Thames, and the discriminative power has a real chance to work.

> The beauty even of the winter riverscape affected her painfully. That great stillness, that indescribable calm, that white peace, that stainless purity of the snowy vicinage of the Thames near Windsor, was an overwhelming reproach upon life as she knew it, and upon herself.[31]

Sharp persuasively conveys how deeply and fatally Madge's Pool upbringing had marked her nature, and sensitively expresses the emotional confusion caused by so jarring a rejoinder to all her previous experience. The complication and resolution of the story consist entirely of Madge's fruitless struggle to extricate herself from the sordidness that clings to her soul like the rust and slime of the Pool:

> She had nothing to distract her from her inner self, nothing to ease her from the dull perplexity and pain of that incessant if almost inarticulate soul-summons of which she was dimly conscious. More than once, even, a great home-sickness came upon her; a bodily nostalgia for that dirty, congested, often hideous, always squalid life, to which she had been born, and in which she had been bred.[32]

The sentimental prolongation of Madge's distress, as she suffers the death of her lover, the stillbirth and water-burial of her child, and the anguish that precedes her own suicide, tends to obtrude on this developing theme by turning our attention from the symbolic nature of Madge's experience to the poignancy of these events in all their uniqueness and particularity. But Sharp recaptures his theme at the end, providing a strong closing picture that represents his final revulsion from the city river—described earlier with such ironic poetry, seen fully now as setting and cause of awful human suffering and disintegration. "For an hour or more thereafter, till the river police discovered it, a woman's body was tossed to and fro in the Pool, idly drifting and bumping against the slimy piers, along the gaunt, deserted wharves."[33] The coldness of distance is definitive: here is a life wasted in every sense. Madge's very womanhood, her own "woman's body," like the body of the child she had borne and seen deposited into the river, has now become the refuse of an impersonal and indifferent urban civilization.

"Madge o' the Pool" and *The Sport of Chance* display several close parallels that testify to their contemporaneous composition. The heroines themselves both wander off after premature childbirth, though

Madge's has been fatal to her child, and Mona's has not. There is also Sharp's emphasis on the "irresistible attraction of the river," though in the novel the river is in Liverpool, not London. This attraction corresponds especially to a state of emotional despondency—a state that could well have been similar to Sharp's own in those years. It leads Madge to drown herself and nearly has the same effect upon Mona. The descriptions of the city rivers are themselves alike, those in *The Sport of Chance* being only more definitive, if that is possible, in their indictment of the life of the city. This scene is in Liverpool:

> There is, at low-tide, at a certain part of the eastern side of the Mersey, a stretch of muddy ground whereon is generally to be seen, by the bargemen, water-police, or street —, who know the dismal spot, a collection of broken tin and china vessels, dead cats and dogs, the nameless and foul refuse which such places attract, and during tidal intervals retain. On the same night that Mona Armitage arrived in the great city, a mixture of frost and malodorous fog brooded above the river, and along this dreary stretch of mud the former had caused a glittering sheen, which had the same kind of evil sparkle that may be seen on a toad's back, or in the repellent gleam of stagnant ditchwater.[34]

Mona's flight northward takes her to Glasgow as well, a city with whose failings Sharp was even more familiar.

> [She] was at once submerged in the dense and fast flowing human stream, and even as a broken flower is swept along by some current, so was she carried Eastward in the direction of the Trongate as if she had no volition of her own. What noise there was, what glare of lights, what brutal faces and brutal words, and brutal laughter, what evil and hollow mockery of gaiety, what drunkenness, what loathesome and omnipresent vice. In the midst of this human maelstrom, Mona felt as if she were in some dreadful nightmare.[35]

These vicious pictures were reinforced by the somber testimonials of Sharp's biographical studies. His *Life of Heine*, published in 1888, is pitted with evidence of his acid urban discontent. There is much of the biographer in his guess that, to Heine, Hamburg seemed "a town of automata, machinery, and grim facts, with nothing of what makes life beautiful."[36] There is peculiar pleasure in his repetition of Heine's opprobrious epithet for that city, "bedammtes Hamburg"; and he triumphantly observes that for Heine, as for himself, the escape from such

57

a city to the seashore was the fulfillment of a profound and urgent desire, and the return to the true source of "native inspiration."

Only in his essay on Browning (1889), where the nature of his subject made it essential that he sympathetically delineate a highly urban temperament, does Sharp hold fire. But even there the hesitancy and qualification of his remarks suggest a failure of real sympathy. Typically, of course, Sharp attributes to the place of Browning's birth the most permanent and important influences on his character. For Browning to be born in London, he says, was "singularly appropriate: it would seem as though something of that mighty complex life, so confusedly petty to the narrow vision, so grandiose and even majestic to the larger ken, had blent with his being from the first."[37]

But as the same passage continues, Sharp more and more betrays the reluctance of his sympathy. First he reveals the provincial's resentment of the city-dweller's arrogant belief that the city and the city alone is the breeding place of genius. "A man may be in all things a Londoner and yet be provincial. The accident of birthplace does not necessarily involve parochialism of soul. It is not the village which produces the Hampden," he goes on, "but the Hampden who immortalizes the village." Then, while striking a further blow for the country cousin, he retreats again: "Though the strongest blood insurgent in the metropolitan heart is not that which is native to it, one might well be proud to have one's atom-pulse attune from the first with the large rhythm of the national life at its turbulent, congested, but ever ebullient center."[38] Later Sharp pauses imaginatively at one of the places Browning must also have paused in his walks through the city. He cannot entirely enjoy the large vista, but he makes a vigorous attempt:

> The coming and going of the cloud-shadows, the sweeping of sudden rains, the dull silver light emanating from the haze of mist shrouding the vast city, with the added transitory gleam of troubled waters, the drifting of fogs, at that distance seeming like gigantic veils constantly being moved forward and then slowly withdrawn, as though some sinister creature of the atmosphere were casting a net among all the dross and débris of human life for fantastic sustenance of its own— all this endless, everchanging, always novel phantasmagoria had for him an extraordinary fascination.[39]

The "fascination" is, in effect, a weird compound of beauty and horror. The light over the city is "dull," the haze "shrouds," the waters are "troubled," the presiding genius of the city is "some sinister creature," casting among the "dross and débris" of life. And only the allure of novelty mitigates the fundamental terror of this extraordinary "phantasmagoria."

When for a moment, however, the city vista takes on an emotionally definable character, we can see Sharp discovering one means of validating through his own perception the attraction the city holds for temperaments unlike his own:

> There was something ominous in that heavy pulsating breath: visible in the waning and waxing of the tremulous ruddy glow above the black enmassed leagues of masonry; audible, in the low inarticulate moaning borne eastward across the crests of Norwood. It was then and there that the tragic significance of life first dimly awed and appealed to his questioning spirit, that the rhythm of humanity first touched deeply in him a corresponding chord.[40]

Herein lies Sharp's fleeting sympathy with Browning's passion for the city, for at this moment Sharp too can recognize "the rhythm of humanity" in its "tragic significance." But, paradoxically, herein may also lie the reason for his distinct and pitiable alienation. There is absolutely no joy in this perception. The city is "tragic," and the source of the tragedy urbanization itself—the crowding of human beings among those "black enmassed leagues of masonry." Sharp shared with many others of his time this axiom of the socialist revolution and most insistent argument of urban critics—a simple moral and physical revulsion from the damage done to human nature by the misery and crowding of the city.

But there is another kind of city feeling not necessarily a logical judgment based on observation, suggested by Sharp's sense of London's "heavy, pulsating breath," a feeling that comes of investing it with powers beyond the sum of its human and material parts and giving it an effective life of its own. For us today the idea is a commonplace— such a commonplace that we are scarcely aware of it. But for the nineteenth century the idea must have been tinged with the awe and wonder of discovery. We might take Ernest Rhys as a convenient and appropriate test of how compellingly this discovery was working on the minds of the young men of the eighties. Rhys's memoir, *Everyman Remembers*—one might be inclined to say his life—has as its prevailing theme "the spirit of place." The episodes he collects and recollects he intended quite consciously to represent a "London log-book": "London indeed, when all is said, is the chief character, the real protagonist of the drama . . . It was with some hope of becoming its interpreter, and with Dickens and William Morris to point the way, its ideal citizen, that I turned Londonward."[41] That Rhys was looking on London from the retrospective vantage point of 1931 does not alter the conclusion that his wonder was a Victorian remnant. Indeed, if anything, it supports it. The twentieth century has been so sated with characterizations of place that no man of Rhys's sophistication would so naively warm them over unless his youthful sense of discovery had overwhelmed him to the extent that it overflowed into another era. Before the Victorians, of course, there had been no lack of London-lovers, nor even evokers of its infernal horrors. But for these—among them, Nashe, Defoe, Gay, Hogarth, Johnson—London might have been a smorgasbord of human virtue and vice or, even at its most symbolic, an apocalyptic, biblical vision of sin. It took the Victorians to eschew the traditional categories, to discover the living and actual symbolism of the London atmosphere, as it took a Dickens to evoke one of its numerous faces with the piercing expressionism of the opening pages of *Bleak House* and a Thomson to label it "the city of dreadful night." Nor did they stop with London— and perhaps there lay the clue to their new kind of vision. Was Paris really the "city of light" before it had undergone its full philosophical enlightenment and could stand for the luminosity of French culture itself? Was Venice the city of death before Ruskin came to see in its opulent decadence a metaphor for the moral decay of an entire civilization? The clichés of modern tourism indicate how the most common sensibility has been schooled in a technique born of the romantic "peculiar" and the "pathetic fallacy" and bred of Victorian cosmopolitanism, a talent for travel that led Victorians to see themselves anew because they had seen the differences in others.

Rhys was one such traveler and had proved travel's inevitable effects. Yet for Rhys, quite clearly, the "spirit" of London was the antithesis of what it was for Sharp. A colloquy with a "red-faced cabby" could leave him "with a delicious feeling that . . . London was a grand adventure and every public house a side door into Paradise."[42] And it could inspire him with a sense of mission:

> The spirit of place, that subtle essence which first enters the fibres of
> man like the sap in a tree, was gaining on me daily. London, in its

smoky sunshine, its myriad streets, its colours, noises, and specific odours, its individuality, held me with a spell. How was I to get its equation into art, its expression into verse or prose?[43]

Obviously Rhys was one Victorian who had inherited an outlook quite different from that of the Brahmin caste of romantics. The enlightenment-bred doctrine of the city as the vital center of man's civilizing power had, like its opposite, grown strong amid the Victorians—was "surely," as one historian has said, "the unspoken assumption of the great middle class of the nineteenth century,"[44] even the assumption of the same Wordsworth who decried its stifling frivolity. This was the tradition of Rhys, and, though he might not have wanted to express it as such, of his socialist mentor Morris, who could well see the sordid pathos of the city, but who could translate this perception into a desire, not to excise the city from the life of the nation, but to shape it into new and beautiful life—to make it the best possible representative of the national life for which it stood.[45]

This is where the extremes meet. For both schools of thought as represented by Rhys and Sharp, the city was the core, the palpable expression of the national life as it appeared to the nation-conscious Victorians,[46] though one thought it vital and the other diseased. From both points of view the city, equated with the national spirit, was sufficient to characterize it, whatever the temperament and tradition of the spectator. For a man like Sharp London was "the national life at its turbulent, congested . . . center," it was the materialist Philistine spirit, it was the name for urban gravitation, for the calloused crowding, the industrial exploitation, the moral parsimony. Its facts as hard as its "enmassed masonry," London was the whole Gradgrind civilization of England trying to proselytize the "uncivilized" world.

It was thus that Sharp, like others of his era, gave a name and a character to the repelling qualities of the city. Yet this character was only obliquely connected with the real source of his private distress—the city's indescribable variety, its unnameable chaos. Anyone who has lived for any length of time in an urban center might document the paradox of feeling from which Sharp suffered. The city's "individuality" begins to blur. It becomes, possibly, a place of "contrasts," a form of characterization abused by travel literature to the point of insufferable insipidity. Yet to the alert this device is all too simplistic. After a time, no means of generalizing remains sufficient to handle the city's diversity; any such means decreases in efficacy in proportion to the increase in time spent there.

Such a response to the city is more characteristic of Sharp's psychological make-up than any efforts to handle that response with which he may have temporized. The ordinary city-dweller, conscious of the city's diversity, may become content not to care about its character, at best limiting himself to identifying with his particular smaller community within the larger, wavering, and unidentifiable entity of the city itself. But this does not seem to have been the case with Sharp. His mind, oversensitive to impression, could not relax into a state of insouciance before the urban "phantasmagoria."

In his essay on Heine, Sharp had tried to describe, through his subject, the sort of mind he possessed. He called it "the genuine poetic temperament of swift respondence to the mood of whatever companion he might be with, and of intense susceptibility to all extraneous influences."[47] His wife, well aware of a similar variability in her husband, quoted Ernest Rhys's judgment on it as valid and acceptable:

He had quite peculiar powers of assimilating to himself foreign associations—the ideas, the colours, the current allusions of foreign worlds . . . The same susceptibility marked his intercourse with his fellows. Their sensations and emotions, their whims, their very words, were apt to become his, and to be reproduced with an uncanny reality in his own immediate practice.[48]

In response to this same impression of Sharp, Rhys in 1908 published a memorial poem on his friend, entitled "Proteus":

> Is he a part with wind and morning light?
> His ashes lie far south in Sicily,
> Not far from Etna; but the flame they spent
> It is a spirit, one with day and night,
> Changed with the changes of the earth and sea,
> And wrapt about with fire's old element.[49]

Such evidence of Sharp's "protean" temperament may fall short of being conclusive, yet it is fairly persuasive. It was apparently well within Sharp's nature both to approve and to convey in himself a tendency to play any and every role offered to him. If we are therefore justified in deducing anything from this fact, it would have to be that when this role-playing nature confronted some configuration of facts in city or landscape, its human dynamic required something sure and yet flexible in the surroundings themselves, the flexibility to demand his control, and the sureness to control him. In the city Sharp could find no equal balance of both. The city's clumsy variety was too "turbulent" to control, too "complex," too "ebullient," too shifting to permit him to dominate it. In its interminable novelty—a result of impressions not slowly giving way to one another, but all crowding in at once—it became instead the source of physical, emotional, and psychological distress. On the other hand, when for an evanescent moment that city might present a single face, it was too "mighty," too "sinister," too "ominous," too "tragic," too overpowering. Instead of attracting him, its force was sufficient to alienate and revolt. The result was a series of breakdowns that by slow degrees depleted Sharp's resources for withstanding the city's disintegrating effect upon him.

It is thus hardly surprising that a travel essay on the Isle of Arran (1885) should open with these words: "The writer is one of those persons on whom the sense of the sublime in nature is most borne where there are vast spaces . . . He feels the grandeur of mountains to be less impressive than that of boundless sea or limitless desert."[50] Vast spaces, the sea, the desert—and in his other writings, the sky, the wind, clouds—vague and amorphous entities that control, but do not overwhelm, that evoke a describable emotional state, but may also be imaginatively peopled, imaginatively wrought, imaginatively controlled— these are "impressive." If the city was hateful, it was thus paradoxically because it lent itself to neither of these uses, being too elusive in its phantasmagoric variety, too oppressive in its might.

One wonders if Sharp's "peculiar" susceptibilities were really quite so peculiar as Ernest Rhys would lead us to believe. H. G. Wells thought that a tendency to self-dramatization and role-playing, the adoption of what he calls personas, was one of the most striking characteristics of his generation of writers and thinkers toward the turn of the century.[51] Lafcadio Hearn, whose mind and career bear an almost uncanny likeness to Sharp's at certain points, found occasion in a letter (1889) to express a psychological and physical distress remarkably similar to Sharp's, from the sense of lost, confused identity to the explicit equation of the city with all that was hateful in the civilization. He had been trying to meet a friend in New York and records his failure in words that evoke a surrealist nightmare.

The moment I get into all this beastly machinery called New York, I get caught in some belt and whirled around madly in all directions until I have no sense left. This city drives me crazy, or, if you prefer, crazier; —I have no peace of mind or rest of body till I get out of it. Nobody can find anybody, nothing seems to be anywhere, everything seems to be mathematics and geometry and enigmatics and confusion worse confounded: architecture and mechanics run mad. One has to live by intuition and run by steam. I think an earthquake might produce some improvement. The so-called improvements in civilization have apparently resulted in making it impossible to see, hear, or find anything out. You are improving yourselves out of the natural world . . . This is frightful, nightmarish, devilish! Civilization is a hideous thing . . . I came in by one door as you went out the other. Now there are cubic miles of cut granite and iron fury between us. I shall at once find a hackman to take me away. I am sorry not to see you,— but since you live in hell, what can I do?

He seeks emotional relief in representing the landscape in which his spirit might be clear and free:

I want to get back among the monkeys and parrots,—under a violet sky among green peaks, and an eternally lilac and lukewarm sea . . . Blessed is savagery . . . Surely a palm 200 feet high is a finer thing in the natural order than seventy times seven New Yorks.[52]

Perhaps the "protean" uncertainty Rhys ascribed to Sharp might account not only for a record like this, but also for the insatiable travel hunger exhibited by Victorian journalism everywhere and for the frenzied quest by writers of every stamp for a place they could endure. Indeed, had Rhys been reflexive enough to turn his analysis upon himself, he might well have seen how far it went in accounting for his own susceptibility to the power of London.

4

NORTH AND SOUTH

The First Italian Journey

<hr />

Like his reflections on the city after the experience of Australian wilderness, Sharp's article on Arran (1885), written after his first trip to Italy, is an excellent illustration of the contrapuntal effect of travel upon the Victorians. This and other writings dating from the period following his first excursion to Italy in 1882-83, and those following his second in 1890, are evidence that his sensitivity to the distinguishing character of the north was a direct result of comparison with the experience of the south.

Such comparison admitted many degrees of intensity. Sometimes Sharp could be merely general and geographical, as on one occasion during his first trip to Italy when he observed that the bleakest Italian landscape had "nothing of the grandeur and beauty of the barrenness and desolation of the north."[1] Or he could be simply invidious, as when, in the Arran article, he chaffs the devotee of the south: "See Naples and die—unless you have not yet seen Arran."[2] But he is also capable of being quite specific and refined, revealing how much his travels had realerted him to the familiar topography of his own land. While describing the peculiar "mountain beauty" of Arran, Sharp reminds his readers that "mere altitude alone" is not sufficient to capture the imagination, and chooses an illustration from his own recent experience:

> Many an Alpine mass is less impressive than a Scottish Ben, and this because the former frequently mounts from a series of wave-like plateaux, and rises into an atmosphere serene, sometimes for weeks without intermission; while the latter lifts its granite flanks sheer from some still, dark loch, and takes on mysterious beauty and stern grandeur from the mists that so frequently trail along the pines on its mid-way slopes, or tear themselves into thin shreds against the scimitar-like boughs of windy larches, from the sudden rains that sweep over separate heights.[3]

Phyllis Bentley's study, *The English Regional Novel*, bears out the theory that such sharpening of sight as that represented here was in the nineteenth century the common experience among English writers returning home from their travels.[4] Yet there is more at work in Sharp's case than mere intensified perception. Behind his apparently simple geographical distinctions is an attitude of allegiance, a form of personal identification with one kind of atmosphere. Sharp was already thinking in a deterministic vein as early as 1881, and his travels increased not only his awareness of the climate and geography of his origin but also his sense of their implications for his own character and temperament. "I never so fully recognize how intensely northern I am," he said finally, "than when I am in the south."[5] Although this remark dates from a later period in his life, it has many predecessors in kind and reveals how much more influential was his trip to Italy than any other he had previously made for his development as a Celtic writer.

Sharp's observation rests on a dichotomy between north and south that could have become directly and personally available to him only through his Italian experience. But the theoretical concept of a determining cultural division between north and south was a readily accessible formula for comparison that had long achieved currency through the thinking of earlier cosmopolitans. When in his *Literary Geography* years later Sharp revealed a long acquaintance with Charles Bonstetten's *L'homme du midi et l'homme du nord* (1827), he was also showing his direct line of descent from a classic European document in the environmental school of social studies, one that had as its thesis precisely his own favorite distinctions between northern and southern climate and psychology. Actually, by 1827, Bonstetten was already something of a descendant himself. As early as 1800 Mme. de Staël's *De la littérature* had developed the environmental interpretation of art, religion, literature, and culture. Bonstetten and later relativist critics rising in the wake of mid-century evolutionary theory merely popularized, diffused, and reinforced what was by Matthew Arnold's time a deeply entrenched critical tradition. Matthew Arnold was, of course, its English popularizer, but the genealogy of Arnold's racial and national sense was, like Sharp's, European. Behind it was Renan's, behind Renan's Chateaubriand's and Mme. de Staël's, and behind theirs a romantic conviction deriving from one of the firstborn of modern cosmopolites, Rousseau, who has been described as the prime mover behind the gradual effacement of boundaries between real and internal landscape in the literature of the nineteenth century.[6] From this encouraging "climate," Sharp's personally-observed distinctions between north and south took nourishment and grew in number and significance.

Another important motivating factor behind Sharp's new "northernness" was the especially powerful force for him of personal acquaintance. A growing sense of fraternity among Scots and Northerners (and Irish too) expatriated to London must have had its share in restoring Sharp to his Celtic allegiances. His early career leaned heavily on the good offices of Donald Macleod, editor of *Good Words*. He was also indebted to the North-Country publisher, Walter Scott, and to Joseph Skipsey, the editor from whom he inherited the Canterbury Poets series, and a balladeer in his own right. It may well have been Scott and Skipsey who encouraged Sharp to edit and introduce his first contribution to the Canterbury series, an anthology of Walter Scott's poetry; if so, they can lay claim to being among the first to foster a renewed nationalist spirit in the young poet. In the tentative assurance of his fraternity in the same Scottish cause, Sharp wrote in this introduction that "the freshness, vigorousness, genuine manliness" of Scott's poetry were its Scottish qualities.[7] The Arran article, meanwhile, revealed that he had begun to carry his research into his native culture well beyond the limits of such impressionistic adjectives. There, for the first time in his work, appear references to Gaelic etymology and folklore.[8] Finally, as though to give concrete proof of the patriot in him, he began his own *Romantic Ballads and Poems of Phantasy* (1888), a fairly large group of poems almost entirely in the form of narrative ballads in the Scottish and North-Country tradition.

Among the other friends and connections who may have helped awaken this renascence of Celtic spirit in Sharp were Edward Dowden and Ernest Rhys. Dowden, though Irish, had connections enough with the broader Celtic fraternity to remark to Sharp after the publication of *The Human Inheritance* in 1882 that he might do well to look for "some heroic old Scottish story to brood over and make live."[9] This is precisely what Sharp, a little belatedly, tried to do with *Romantic Ballads*. Ernest Rhys's influence was that of colleague and (at the time) mutual admirer. Rhys had a "Celtic strain": his mother was partly Irish, and he had spent some time in Wales and the North Country. The "fellowships" of like-minded men and women Rhys organized, like the "New Life," attracted many uprooted Celts. Among them was Yeats, who, with Rhys and T. W. Rolleston, was one of the founders of the Rhymers' Club. Though Sharp never achieved membership in that exclusive assembly, he fraternized in its friendly antechambers, meeting many of its members, including Yeats, and continuing with Rhys along closely parallel avenues of activity. These resulted, during the nineties, in their association with the Celtic Library series and their collaboration in a series of scholarly articles on various folk literatures for Warner's Library.

Yet the part of Sharp's enthusiasm for Celtism encouraged by these personal influences of the eighties was seemingly less deep-rooted than that which found its source in his cosmopolitanism. His real Celtism, represented by Fiona Macleod, was separated from this early spurt by several years, a very un-Celtic novel (*The Children of To-morrow*, 1889), a very important second trip to Italy, and a volume of poetry completely of Southern inspiration (*Sospiri di Roma*, 1891). The trip to Italy—as Rhys later recalled with some sarcasm—was the occasion of a crucial and "wonderful encounter with an exquisite maiden, who was enjoying a sunbath on the banks of Lake Nemi," and Rhys was left with no doubt that it was she who inspired Sharp to new bardic heights.[10] The implications of this fact are clear: whatever might have been the quirks of hindsight that made Sharp diminish the role of other influences in restoring his Celtic identity, he caused it to be unequivocally understood that nothing led him to dramatize in his own personality the classic variations in racial and national temperaments as much as his Italian journeys. As Rhys's remark suggests, it was the second of these that produced the great illumination of his career, but Sharp's reactions to his first journey are full of their own smaller illuminations. Indeed these, submitted to slow modification and reinforcement in the intervening years, led inexorably to that "wonderful encounter" with an exquisite maiden, real or symbolic.

The experiences Sharp underwent on that first Italian trip are effusively recorded in his letters to Elizabeth, as well as in several pieces of art criticism for the *Art Journal* in 1884 and in travel sketches published in *Good Words* from 1885 to 1890. A group of casual jottings, accurately entitled "Random Impressions from an Author's Notebook," appeared in 1889, sometime after their composition, in the unhappily shortlived journal known as the *Scottish Art Review*.[11] Examining all of these, one cannot help noticing how complex was the effect of Italy upon him, for by no means are all Sharp's reactions evidence that his new allegiance with the "north" grew directly out of distaste for or dissatisfaction with the "south." Despite their many expressions of distress and discomfort, Sharp's reflections on Italy are not without their moments of ecstatic contentment and, as usual with him, total identification with the Italian scene. He was as sensitive as any of his contemporaries to its magic. Often, in the very process of denigrating, he gave signs of wanting merely to avoid the fashion of being in love with Italy, but even this he could not totally resist. He went a long way toward becoming thoroughly Italianized, as testified by the titles of many of the poems included in his second volume, *Earth's Voices* (1884). Among these are "Gaspara Stampa," "Sospitra," "Madonna Natura," and "Sonnets on Paintings by Bazzi." Also in that volume appear a characteristic group called "Graffiti d'Italia," impressionistic translations of some of the experiences recorded in his letters and travel sketches. These bear striking witness to Italy's effect in increasing his consciousness of place: "Rome," "Siena," "Val Mugnone," "Maremma," "Volterra," "Campagna," "Cascine, Florence," and "Old Protestant Cemetery, Florence."

All of these writings together demonstrate the profound effect of the Italian "atmosphere" and Sharp's fresh awareness of the power of place, at times overwhelming. This power was no vague magnetism, but a compound of very specific forces. He reflected, for example, that in Italy geographical space was not merely space alone, but space and time. The spectacles of city and landscape that offered themselves to him aroused an often uncomfortable sense of the relentlessly longlived influence of the Italian past upon its present. Unlike the ordinary travel writer of the period, Sharp invariably speaks of the "melancholy" of Italy.[12] "There is a monotony in its beauty," he could say of Umbria, "at variance with the prevalent conception of 'the sunny South.' "[13] He is making no simple dismissal. There is something about the atmosphere that commands his response, and he must put forth the effort to explain this sincere and ineradicable sensation:

It is as though the land were far more ancient than the remotest human traditions, as though it had seen too much of the change of ages—too much of the rise, the greatness, the oblivion of successively dominant races—ever again to be joyous with the joyousness of youth.[14]

But the effort to explain could not explain away. The landscape, he continues to insist, has a "strange sombreness," "a keenly pathetic note."[15] He notices the "absence of that exuberance which farther North, and perhaps in England preeminently accompanies the regenerated youth of the spring." The scenery carried a fascinating appeal to the "inner vision," possessing in its melancholy a kind of "magic." But still the "magic" and the "melancholy" were irresistibly the cause of a "sometimes oppressive emotion." He could not put off a response to "this strange historic mystery, this monotonous sense of a barely-recorded antiquity, shrouding an even more shadowy and ancient past."[16] The presentness of the past came to characterize the Italian scene: "The pathos of the past permeates the whole landscape." Even Rome became oppressive, burdened with this paradox of past and present coexistent and coterminous. There he experienced "a feeling as if life would become intolerable unless all sense of the past were put away." Later he would come to "put away" these words instead, but now he vociferously rejected Rome. "I hate death, and all that puts one in mind of death—and after all Rome is only a gigantic and richly-ornamented tomb." His distaste for cities in general did not help. He wails, "How I hate large cities! Even Florence is almost too large."[17]

From the tone in which it is repeatedly expressed, Sharp's discovery of the inexorable will of the past working itself permanently and "mysteriously" into the landscape of the present obviously came as a profound shock. Nevertheless, the distress associated with the shock gradually wore off, while the insight represented by the discovery gradually sharpened and finally transformed itself into a joyous celebration of the Roman Campagna, ruin-scattered and historic, in the *Sospiri di Roma*. Still another transformation, and the same insight became part of the essential vision of Fiona Macleod. Her work, seeming on the surface to have so different an inspiration, arises in fact from the identical perception and conveys almost more than anything else the grandeur—even the joy—certainly the power—of such a burden of tradition lying upon the land. Italy, in effect, forced the developing poet to see, and in fact to seek, this same indwelling tradition in his own Scotland. "Wonderfully impressive are these ancient monumental stones by moonlight," he was able even by 1885 to say of the druidic remnants on Arran's Machrie moor, or "during an autumnal thunderstorm, when from the blue-black lowering clouds the broad white flashes of lightning seem like fiery swords thrusting hither and thither amidst petrified figures"[18]—an early prefiguration of the way the "oppressive" past was to be transfigured into wonder.

Yet it is no surprise that Sharp's immediate impulse was a desire to protect himself from the past's painful influence. Whatever joy he derived from his first response to Italy was almost entirely limited to childlike observations of the curious nature phenomena he saw and heard around him. He was "electrified with delight to see a large eagle shining gold-bronze in the sun . . . such a swarming of lizards . . . the funniest fly . . . What surprised me so much about the flowers was not only their immense quantity, but also their astounding variety."[19] Even in Venice, where he does not specifically refer to its architectural delights, he tells his wife-to-be that he is infinitely relieved to find "life, joyousness, brightness everywhere." He is ecstatic about the Lido: "There were hundreds of butterflies, lizards, bees, birds, and some heavenly larks—a perfect glow and tumult of life."[20]

This focus on nature was a curious, even if momentary, limitation of vision amid all of Italy's man-made splendors, and was evidently intended quite sincerely as a means of expressing a simple and healthy desire merely to enjoy himself after having found so much to lament. It was, nevertheless, somewhat self-deceiving. The line between pleasure and pain was seldom quite so clear for him as he may have liked to believe. A kind of excitement, for which these nearly fatuous effusions may have provided his only simple and normal means of expression, seems to pervade all of his experiences in Italy. His nature readily delighted in its own range and capacity for experience, deriving a subtle, perhaps even perverse pleasure from what was ostensibly unpleasant and "oppressive." No matter how great the recoil of his Protestant soul, for instance, there is evidence of some delectation in his declaring that while assisting at a Good Friday ceremony in Florence he himself "felt the agony of the pierced hands and feet."[21]

His response to Italy's natural delights—that they were filled with an "astounding variety"—might thus be extended to explain the basically pleasurable effect which, though mainly in retrospect, characterized his entire Italian experience. In Tuscany Sharp could find the simplest of sincere devotions to the girl-saint Santa Fina,[22] in Rome the most cynical of religious hypocrisies, "blind with blood and lust and hate."[23] In art, the purest restraint and asceticism of Giotto or Cimabue could be hallowed side by side with the sensuality and morbidity of Ghirlandaio or Orcagna, who he says had "a horrible imagination, poisoned by horrible superstitions."[24] The primitive and the sophisticated, nature and artifice, the ebullient presence of life amidst so many reminders of death—these must have yielded the thrill of paradox. And unlike the overwhelming turbulence of the city, Italy's varying images came one after another in colorful alternation, and each offered the separate possibility of identity to Sharp's responsive temperament. He was, long before Thomas Mann, a willing victim of the strange influence of Venice's sirocco. He records how he had been contemplating Tintoretto's Satan, then his Bacchus, in an attempt to grasp the spirit that had been capable of producing them both. There was momentarily, he reports, a magic in the atmosphere that made one half expect to "see Dionysus pass from out the green leafland behind." Then,

> just as Venice seems to merge into Naxos, a tremor in the North has spread southward . . . In a few moments all is changed, and Bacchus is again a dream, a beautiful unreality. But as the flying shreds of mist and streaks of flame above Fusina and Mestre shine like crimson flames, as scarlet and purple and gold burn above Venice in splendour wholly indescribable, suddenly the beauty of Tintoretto's plumed and triumphant Satan dominates my imagination. This glowing splendour, this terrible glory, is one with *his* magnificence of beauty, with *his* power and dominion.[25]

Venice, however, was only one among many places in Italy that commanded Sharp's imagination and provided counterparts for entire and sometimes overpowering states of mind. Assisi, like Rome, "oppressed" him with its aridity and sense of death. "Barren and desolate and colourless, with neither shade of tree nor coolness of water . . . hideous to the eye, inexpressibly dreary, dead, and accursed."[26] Even his otherwise pleasurable reception of Giotto's frescoes was, he says, destroyed by this atmosphere's control of his imagination. "They are overweighted in my memory with the *hideousness* of the immediate hill surroundings," he reported to Elizabeth, and added further proof of the depth of his reaction: "It made me feel almost sick and ill."[27]

It is marvelous how Sharp could rejudge his experience with hindsight. Consistency seems to have carried much less weight with him than the new wisdom of the moment, added evidence surely that the *kind* of reaction he had mattered infinitely less than the extent of his own sensitivity. This same visit to Assisi came to be recorded again in the work of Fiona Macleod, but there the author says that, at the very moment "a friend" was pointing out to her the barrenness and desolation of its landscape, Assisi was for her suddenly "transfigured" with the beautiful light of the religious mystery that had taken place there centuries ago.[28]

The "transfiguration" of Fiona Macleod was, of course, the result of the new design Sharp was to give to his perception of the immanent past. Perhaps, indeed, there is something quite honest in his remembering later on that he was already giving it that new design at the time, for certainly Italy had the effect of throwing him into a tense and turbulent process of change. At the moment, nevertheless, the perception took the only form then available and familiar to him. It provided occasion for the exercise of his theories on the formative role of place in the course of life and history. To this part of the Umbrian landscape itself he attributed the shaping power behind the mysticism of Assisi's thirteenth-century saints, a mysticism with which he was not yet, as Fiona Macleod would be, in total sympathy:

> I can well understand how either the ecstasy of religious delirium, or a very passion of faith, must have dominated any soul who should long dwell between these echo-haunted declivities; and still more, when I look from the heights northward, where abides a very desolation of barrenness, I realize that penitence in such a place, in those strange, pathetic middle ages, must have meant absolute renunciation . . . or else have impelled the passionate spirit to the license of despair to the extremest tyranny of the lusts of the body.[29]

One can hardly help noticing here, as in so much of Sharp's first response to Italy, how he estimates the effects of this landscape upon the human spirit in terms of none but the most exaggerated oppositions.

Among Sharp's "astounding variety" of experiences in Italy, however, there was one that by itself provided an almost absolute correlative for his own temperament and that substantially assisted him on his way toward the "transfigured" perception of Fiona Macleod. Etruria, with its scant and tantalizing remains, aroused him to complete and passionate sympathy and proved for him that the ancient Etruscan civilization had recognized and reconciled the conflicts that so beset him—sense and spirit, life and death. Even beyond this, there was something in its nature as a lost, disinherited culture, but somehow a culture that seemed still to survive, that gave Sharp a means for dealing with the strangely disquieting presence of the eternally existing past. What had most disturbed him in Italy was the past's so often spectral presence—as though a dead hand were laying its weight upon the efforts of life to refresh itself. The Etruscan civilization seemed not to have had this effect. The civilization, as a historic fact, might well be lost and "dead." But its fragmentary remnants could somehow be invested with life, its religion with all the virtues of a religion as he would have conceived it. At nearly every point anticipating D. H. Lawrence, Sharp claimed for the Etruscans a palpable recrudescence— not in the forms of modern civilization, but in the surrounding earth itself and in the peasants that arose from and were closest to that earth. Sharp dramatized this insight in his "Random Impressions," where he sketched

> a girl of eighteen or twenty, carrying a bundle of reedy grass upon her head, and walking with an exquisite poise and sway of body. Her eyes, large and of that lustrous velvety darkness visible in twilit waters, turned upon me . . . Such passion, such pathos, such an inheritance of yearning, such an inheritance of regret, dwelt in their depths. The oblivion of Etruria gleamed therefrom; and the vanished Etrurian grace fulfilled itself again in that perfect body.[30]

An intellectual sympathy for a philosophy of recrudescence had been prefigured in Sharp's earliest poetry. But here for the first time in his work, though hardly for the last, he located that truth in an actual race. Here for the first time it was felt. The ancient, vaguely naturalistic religion of the Etruscans was a vessel already partially shaped, but because of the crudity of its remnants, he could complete that vessel as he chose. To the Etruscans he could attribute a prevision of man's true and essential nature, an acknowledgment of the sanctity of both body and spirit. This semi-real, semi-legendary race he could make, as he would of the Celtic race later on, the truest symbolic expression of his own feeling that somehow the primitive and prophetic knowledge of an ancient people could survive, and perhaps newly inspirit, the civilization that had overwhelmed it and beclouded its wisdom.

The depth of this insight even Sharp himself could not appreciate at the time. Beyond this one magnificently evocative passage, he used the Etruscans merely as a convenient foil for his animadversions upon

Christianity, especially the deathful and joyless Catholicism he claimed to have hated in Florence and Assisi. "The comparative joyousness . . . of the Etruscans," he wrote to Elizabeth in 1883, "contrasts greatly with the joylessness of the Christians, who have done their best to make death repellent in its features and horrible in its significance, its possibilities . . . Not till the gloomy precepts of Christianity yield to something more akin to the Greek sense of beauty will life appear to the majority lovely and wonderful, alike in the present and in the future."[31] A measure of Sharp's growth and change is to be found in the strange echo of these words that reverberates in the work of Fiona Macleod. There only Northern Protestantism, not Christianity in general, is scorned as alien to the true Celt, and ritual Catholicism ironically becomes the expression of the true spirit of her race.

If the Etruscans failed, despite the pleasurable sympathy they aroused in Sharp, to remain a permanent metaphor for his temperament, the reason was assuredly that none could be perfect—and certainly none in Italy. There, of course, if anywhere, he could find correspondences for his fluctuant and all-appreciative self; he could just as well, if inconsistently, participate in a Good Friday ceremony to the point of identifying with the crucified Christ as leap with pagan joy at the glance of a peasant girl on an Umbrian hillside. He could be enraptured at the enchantment of Venice, that epitome of civilization at its artificial best, and overcome with the sense of ages of human effort expended in the making of so many of Italy's cities and monuments. He could have all this and still long for "some loch with the glory of morning upon it, some mountainside flecked with trailing clouds";[32] for as always with Sharp the excitement and variety were themselves self-defeating. Just as the city had provided a "fresh and pleasant stimulus," so too did Italy, but also like the city it aroused in him finally a need for rest, for escape, for self-control; and at such times his wearied spirit would become "northern" and something in him would recoil from the attraction of the south. Nor was he, in his keen perception of exterior phenomena, unaware that a particular kind of natural scenery existed that could not be found in Italy. This awareness often caused a part of his personality to be disengaged, even in his most sympathetic moments of joy at the happy Etruscans or in the Lido sunlight. There was, in other words, one variety of landscape of which even multifarious Italy was incapable, that of "the cool north"; and the emotional equivalent for that missing landscape was, for him, in distinct conflict with the Italian spirit of place.

Of course it is not always easy to deal with Sharp's quick reversals. After the excited reactions to the Etruscans, it is disturbing to come once again upon a reflection like the one in an article on San Gemignano, where Sharp records meeting an Ayrshire woman, the wife of a local antiquary. The pathos is indubitably his own when he says, "and much, I think, she yearned to see once more the land she loved better than the alien country in which her lot was cast."[33] It is even more disturbing to come upon the striking and carefully deliberated parallels of this feeling in his short story, "Fröken Bergliot," like "Madge o' the Pool" part of the later retrospective collection, The Gipsy Christ (1895). Reechoing the Ayrshire woman, the Norwegian Bergliot, also living in Italy, "felt as though she would die if she were to stay much longer in this foreign land, among this alien folk." Sharp thoroughly explores her consciousness, filling it with the passion and pain of the gulf between north and south: "She now hated this glaring, burning south that had appealed to her so much at first, hated this stifling heat, this inland weariness, this malaria that everywhere brooded as an invisible beast of prey." She became, like the Sharp of one of his many moods, "consumed by an abiding passion for the lost north. To be away from Norway seemed to her a fate to sympathize with; to be away in the far south, with a northern soul, and see no more the dark mountains and the wild, beautiful Scandinavian seas."[34] At times she would look down upon Lake Albano,

> and dream of green fiords and precipitous rocks . . . Her nostalgia for the beloved north became an abiding pain . . . She felt . . . conscious of her overmastering desire to see the north once more, to feel its cool breath in her mind and in her spirit as well as upon her body; to hear the lap-lapping of the waves, to watch the white seahorses leap in the sunlight when, at the fiord mouth, a mountain wind tore against the tide race. If, in these moments of intense longing, she descried, trailing across the sky like a thin Japanese eyebrow, a flight of northward-winging birds, she would turn away sobbing in bitter pain, or throw herself upon the ground and seek relief in tears.[35]

Bergliot was to find her soulmate in a young painter who provided, in this same tale, another surrogate for Sharp's own condition, and who confessed "that while winter, spring, and summer in Rome and its neighborhood, were delightful, the early autumn lacked both solace and joy for a northerner. 'Oh, for a breath of the Blue Fiord!' he cried again and again, filled with longing for his sea-swept home."[36]

Could this scene of agony and anguish be the same Italy into whose bosom Sharp rushed with joy in 1890, and then again and again for all the years remaining to his life? Could it be the same "beautiful, living, pulsing South" of which he spoke later on? And, indeed, could this north be the same whose "fierce cold and gloom" he was to describe as "mentally benumbing"?[37] The only possible answer, of course, is yes, in actual fact the very same, though in psychological fact they could be poles apart. To know the vicissitudes of Sharp's temperament is to know that such despondencies and exaltations were inevitable, that the despondencies, when they came in Italy, were easily to be translated by his opposition-seeking mind into moods of utter alienation from the spirit of the south. Though Italy in its abundant variety and Etruria in its rich paradox corresponded in high degree to his personal fragmentation, they had to yield in the face of the clearer duality represented by north and south. Each of the poles could at different times evoke a sincere and deep allegiance in him. But he needed their conflict: he was committed to ineluctable, irreconcilable differences within himself and seized and rejected in turn every symbolic reconciliation he found for them.

This half-conscious knowledge of his own interior division constituted a partial self-discovery that bore almost immediate fruit in Sharp's poetry, fiction, criticism, and biography. Perhaps the biographies yielded the most concentrated opportunities for applying his tense and ambiguous cosmopolitanism. All of the subjects he chose during the later eighties, Shelley (1887), Heine (1888), and Browning (1890), exemplified to varying extents his own mixed sensibility, and in none of them did he fail to exploit it.

Shelley, of course, had long been his passion, and many of the emphases in the biography were therefore throwbacks to his own childhood and adolescent conflicts, particularly his focus on Shelley's desire to liberate body and spirit from the bonds of conventional authority. Shelley also gave him the first broad opportunity to express in something resembling sociological terms his own compassion for women, and the biography largely dwelt on Shelley's women, rather than on Shelley's experiences of place. Then, too, as the first of his volumes in the Great Writers series, *Shelley* was essentially an exercise, adhering abjectly to the Great Writers formulas, and venturing with little freshness or daring into areas of Sharp's own peculiar concern. It was, moreover, produced under the enormous burden of competition with Dowden's major work on Shelley, which appeared in 1886.

By the time Sharp had been through *Heine* and come to *Browning* in 1889, his biographical finesse had matured considerably. Now writing more freely within the biographical formulas, he was able to express the provocative effects of his cosmopolitan thinking, and devoted an enormous amount of space to the travel and place influences that went into Browning's making. As has already been pointed out, the city, itself called "cosmopolitan,"[38] was given major emphasis. But Sharp did not by any means scamp other place influences. He termed England Browning's first passion of "race and country," found it necessary to observe that Russia had little enduring effect, and finally and copiously dealt with Browning's experiences of "the mystic Orient" and "the glowing South." Of these, especially Italy, he said, the poet "oftenest thought and dreamed."[39] As far as Sharp was concerned, they effectively formed and controlled Browning's imagination.

It was with Heine, however, a poet whom the English could know less well than their own, that Sharp perhaps felt more free to range among his materials, to select and emphasize as he chose. Of all Sharp's biographies, this one emerges as having the most permanent strength. To it he seems to have brought the freshness of discovery, and there is evidence in specific borrowings from the German poet in Sharp's later work that the encounter was an influential one.[40] Considerably more important, however, than such specific borrowings was the extent to which Heine could function for Sharp as a parallel for all his cosmopolitan predilections and could, for the time being at least, satisfactorily resolve them. Indeed *Heine*, coming as it did before the Browning biography, was really the first to broach effectively the questions of race and nationality. The interpretation of the man and his work that resulted was based substantially on the premise that race and country were, more than any other influences, those that formed him; every earlier effort to cope with such issues—and even the later one in *Browning*—pales beside the lengthy passages devoted to them in *Heine*.

Not surprisingly, Sharp takes particular pleasure in finding Heine a kind of national catch-all, a man who combined all the contrasts that Sharp had himself perceived in his European travels. In Heine, as in himself, he saw "the swift respondence to outside influences" that accounted for his remarkable variations in temperature.[41] A note of exhilaration informs his testimony that Heine was "essentially one of the men of no nationality," "a typical cosmopolitan."[42] And what most seemed to appeal to Sharp was Heine's ability to express through such cosmopolitanism an enormous variety of opposing attitudes, to be constrained in his literary strategy by no limitation of personality. Heine was mercurial, flexible, various, and he was this, significantly, not because of any special fluke of temperament, but because he was a barometer of sensitivity to "the troubled spirit of the times."[43]

To be in harmony with the times (in Sharp's determinist philosophy, a fate the true artist could hardly avoid) was to be, in short, a man without a country—not German, not French, not Italian, not northern, not southern—capable of being all these, but belonging to none. Yet Heine, despite his variety, was a "northerner" by birth, and he could and did share some of Sharp's special and reserved love for the "cool north." An inordinate amount of space in the biography is thus devoted to poetry reflecting a passion for northern seas and piney landscapes. That booming, dominating sea of Sharp's own early experience, the same he constantly missed in Italy, was there in Heine's *Nordsee* poems. They gave expression to precisely those feelings for the northern seascape which Sharp had already attempted to express in his own "Transcripts from Nature" and *Romantic Ballads*, and was working into "Fröken Bergliot." One of Heine's poems, "Ein Fichtenbaum steht einsam" (A pine-tree stands lonely) peculiarly realized for Sharp the "unbridgeable gulf" between north and south. It gave vent, he says, to a "vague, informulate yearning,"[44] which he undoubtedly valued as the emotional counterpart of his awareness of the same gulf in his own personality.

The cosmopolitan slant of Sharp's interpretation of Heine may perhaps seem falsified by his simultaneously strong emphasis on Heine's Jewishness. He spoke of Heine as "an early Hebrew" in soul, studied the poet's Jewish origins, and explored with fascination his "apostasy"— Heine's renunciation of Judaism to enter the practice of law, like all German professions at that time restricted to Christians. But Sharp was fully aware of the social conspiracy against Jews that had led to Heine's betrayal of his race. In speaking of him as "an early Hebrew," he was attempting to give a larger dimension to Heine's conflict than mere personal suffering. He was translating into new terms the same homeless, divagating spirit elsewhere construed as characteristic of the cosmopolitan Heine—and of himself. And he was shading the characterization with the moral and emotional depth of tragedy. In Heine, the Jew and the man of no country coalesced; he was dislocated from a homeland he could conceive only in desire, a true national of a nation existing only in spirit.

But Sharp's interpretive mood was not always tragic. Heine's "Bimini," the poet's fanciful transformation of the Caribbean Island, suggested a happy and affirmative way of expressing an allegiance to a land conceived in imagination.[45] In cooperation with every other similarity Sharp found between himself and the German poet, the concept of using such an imaginative land to realize such an imaginative allegiance had immediate and durable effects upon Sharp's art and thought. Heine thus became a main force behind the creation of the "informulate" country of the work of Fiona Macleod—the unearthly land presaged by Celtic myth as Silis, Avalon, Tir-N'an-Og, and the Land of Heart's Desire.

5

THE PROMISED LAND

Zion and the American Eden

Though Heine's "apostasy," which figured so prominently in his personal as well as his public life, was hardly something a biographer could ignore, there were other reasons why Sharp would have devoted so much space to this event in Heine's life and to its consequences. England had lately shown a marked popular interest in Jews, Judaism, and Jewish national aspirations. The reasons for this were complex. Ever since the Jews had been enfranchised, true-born Englishmen had worried themselves into hysteria about whether or not such "tribal separatists" could really be patriots. A measure of our own difference from the Victorians is the candor that characterized the controversy. Jew and Gentile quite openly tore at one another even in the most sophisticated of popular journals.[1]

Two events served to exacerbate this quarrel in the late seventies and early eighties. One of them was a large immigration of Ashkenazian Jews into England, the exodus from persecutions then occurring in Poland and Germany. These Jews, allegedly more clannish, more exclusively devoted to Hebraic ritual, and poorer than many of their Sephardic predecessors in England, disturbed a status quo in which the existing Anglo-Jewish community had by and large socially and economically assimilated into English life, while at the same time maintaining a quiet sense of Jewish identity.[2] The battle was joined anew, motivated not so much by racial difference itself as by fresh fears that a race "secretly" aspiring to its own nation could not be trusted to submit itself to common British interests.

The other event to bestir popular concern about Judaism was the publication in 1876 of *Daniel Deronda*, George Eliot's fictional portrayal of Jewish life and Jewish hopes. Eliot's reputation and popularity were at their height, and the novel, which appeared just prior to the large Jewish immigration, received a great deal of attention as a partisan statement in the controversy that arose so soon after its publication.

Yet Eliot's novel was so impassioned in its apology for Jewish national aspirations that it seems ironically to have served a function opposite to its sympathetic intention, providing added ammunition for critics of Jewish patriotism. Not that everyone misunderstood her purpose. Edward Dowden was well aware that Eliot had been using Deronda's mission to reinforce a theme already long familiar in her work:

> The higher, the religious life, is that which transcends self, and which is lived in submission to the duties imposed upon us by the past, and the claims of those who surround us in the present, and of those who shall succeed us in time to come. To be the centre of a living multitude, the heart of their hearts, the brain from which thoughts, as waves, pass through them—this is the best and purest joy which a human creature can know.[3]

But not many were as fully equipped as Dowden to reach beyond Eliot's immediate concern to her transcendent one. A flood of articles, then a stream, and finally a persistent trickle followed Deronda's Zionism for years after the novel's publication, accompanied by a steady wash of essays intended to enlighten the newly aroused British public about Jewish history, tradition, ritual, and family life.[4]

Sharp was not one to leap unprepared into this perilous battlefield. Before writing Heine, he armed himself with formidable amounts of research, something he had not done before with any of his biographical subjects, substantially thickening the little volume with a long addendum of sources. He was indebted to many, but particularly to Katie Lady Magnus, one of the more widely-read and respected commentators upon and apologists for Judaism in the later part of the century. She had published an essay on Heine in 1882, as well as one on Eliot's Daniel Deronda in 1877, including both of them in a volume entitled Jewish Portraits that appeared in 1886. For Sharp's purposes the earlier essay on Eliot was fully as important as the one on Heine, for in it Lady Magnus clarified what she saw as the nature of Jewish tribal separatism and national aspirations. Her Heine essay, meanwhile, laid special emphasis upon the scar that Heine's apostasy left upon him. Both studies, as well as the fervent tone of the authoress herself, poignantly conveyed the depth of Jewish racial loyalty. Sharp's sympathy for Heine's suffering, and his understanding of Heine's attempts to be reconciled with his race, may be traced almost directly to her.

When Sharp closed his biography, however, he liberated his imagination. Certain seminal phrases and expressions about Jewish nationalism encountered in his reading had fallen upon ground thoroughly prepared for them and were to flower into a rich and splendid vision in his fiction. Lady Magnus, speaking of *Daniel Deronda*, had, for example, succinctly defined the scope of Eliot's understanding of Jewish national aspirations:

> There is more validity to Eliot's portrait of Mordecai in that novel, who *dreams* of a future Jewish nation, than in Daniel, who seeks to realize it. While a sense of a national ideal does exist in the average Jewish mind, that sense is more a hope of spiritual dominion than an actual habitation.[5]

Perhaps this was not quite so true as she thought, but Lady Magnus had been reared in that older Anglo-Jewish society which had added such luster to the Victorians. She could not yet see the Zionist movement that would come partially to characterize subsequent Jewish generations. To her, the Jew saw "the unity of his people [as] a symbol of the unity of his God." She concluded in agreement with George Kaufmann, another of Eliot's Jewish reviewers, that the fulfillment of the Jews' national ideal might actually lie in "dispersion."[6]

Dowden had spoken along similar lines. To him Eliot had chosen to make Deronda's mission a Jewish one "because the Jewish race is one rich with memories, possessed of far-reaching traditions, a fit object for satisfying that strong historic sympathy which is so deep a part of Deronda's nature"; but also because the Jews were

> a sad, despised, persecuted race, and so much more dear to one whose heart is the heart of a saviour; a race whose leaders and prophets looked longingly for no personal immortality, but lived through faith in the larger life to come of their nation; a race not without some claim to be . . . "the heart of mankind"; a race, finally, which though scoffed at for its separateness, implied in its confession of the Divine Unity, the ultimate unity of mankind.[7]

And Hermann Adler, patiently parrying the cruelly anti-Semitic thrusts of Goldwin Smith in a duel that for several years sent sparks flying from the pages of the *Nineteenth Century*, reminded his antagonist with quiet irony that the Jewish religion taught all men "to be kin."[8]

These eclectic resources, and a cosmopolitanism already tending to the status of full-fledged philosophy, Sharp brought to the making of his first book after *Heine*, and his first genuinely serious novel, *The Children of To-morrow* (1889). The title itself gives some indication of the novel's theme. It is an apology for an avant-garde younger generation of artists and thinkers, who live in the hope that a new social dispensation will compensate them for their present disinheritance. Among its other aims, *The Children of To-morrow* had a palpable social object. It advanced the freedom to love and asserted the often damaging and inhibiting effects of marriage. It was one of the first of Sharp's forays into the battlefield of sex and marriage mores. But this theme significantly took its place as merely one of several embraced by the broad symbol of racial and national allegiance.

The novel's hero, Felix Dane, is a reembodiment in modern terms of Browning's Andrea del Sarto. He is in this case a sculptor who, at the time the book opens, has reached an impasse both in his work and in his marriage. Both Dane's wife and his art, in their slick, superficial appeal to conventional taste and shallow class values, are "successful," and both are the source of his unhappiness. Lydia Dane is passionless and coldly beautiful; she has for years either totally ignored her husband's work or encouraged him only insofar as it might contribute to his fashionable success. Sharp's initial handling of this painful failure of sympathy between two people who had believed in love, and of the tedious continuum of a relationship gone stale—"the slow wear and tear of uncongenial intimacy"[9]—is sensitive and real.

It is not unlikely that Sharp's sympathetic insight into this domestic situation had been influenced by the penetrating social criticism of Olive Schreiner, a contemporary feminist and friend. Lydia Dane is the embodiment of Schreiner's "female parasite," the degenerate product of the long cultural subjection of women in western civilization.[10]

As for Dane, social and commercial respectability have not fulfilled his real artistic ambitions, and a sense of having betrayed his original talents has invaded his morale. But the sources of Dane's self-disgust are not all within himself. In admiration of his earlier work, and in a spirit of admonition for what she hints is a falling-off in his achievement, a poetess appearing under the pseudonym "Sanpriel" has sent him a copy of her writings. One of her poems, especially marked for him to make note of, contains a good deal of Browningesque philosophy about a man's reach exceeding his grasp. Beyond that, however, it also hints at the special principle of resurgent human unity that will later be revealed as guiding her self-chosen mission:

> How wonderful the Spring
> That with regenerative power
>   Swept round the earth—how vast, how great
>   Humanity confederate . . .
>
> What mattered each small life was vain
> When all in one great whole were blent,
>   When all were links in one vast chain
>   That rose from earth's remotest sod
>   And passed the stars and reached to God.[11]

It is at this point in the first chapter, unfortunately, that Sharp deserts the credibility—and one might add, the pathos—of a true human crisis. Despite his admiration for Meredith, it was not in the nature of Sharp's fictional talents to have passions spin the plot. The book carries its own excuse for this weakness in its subtitle. There we are reminded that it is "A Romance," and we are not permitted to forget this through its many disquisitions on the "romantic spirit" in life, literature, and love. In his preface to *Romantic Ballads*, Sharp had already equated that spirit with freedom of fantasy and the license to dream.[12] In the case of the present plot, this license is not only advanced, it is taken. This means that Dane will by coincidence meet the young poetess at a concert given by her father, a half-mad violinist. It also means that he will fall in love with her on the spot, unaware until much later that she is, besides the love of his life, the authoress of the catalytic poems. It means too that there will be a villain in the piece, Gabriel Ford, a banker, a weasel, and a man with a conviction, damaging per se for any Sharp character, that the city is by far "the best place to live in." It is an indication of how far Sharp had come from the spirit of the later Rossetti circle—and by extension the spirit of the city—that he also chose to make Ford a painter in the "decadent" school, a creator of Liliths, with a fixation on death and decay.

Each of the major characters in the novel represents some shade in the spectrum of possible attitudes toward art, the whole giving us a fairly clear reproduction of Sharp's aesthetic thinking at the time. Dane himself, of course, is in transition; he is open to suggestion, a seeker of truth, examining all those modes of art the various characters make available to him. He instinctively rejects the facile super-realism of Ford, who seems to have exercised his talent only to shock human sensibilities and expose the weaknesses of the flesh. Adam Acosta, Sanpriel's wild violinist father, though more ostensibly insane than Ford, is also more sympathetic. There is a bardic, prophetic strain in his artistry that achieves a level of creation beyond the capabilities of ordinary mortals. Sanpriel herself is the true romanticist, her work conceived and executed in the spirit of "new" faith and "new" hope. Her vision, most sympathetic of all to Dane, though to the modern reader perhaps somewhat vague or confused in expression, rises from a commitment to the special conditions of what she calls "modernity." It is a reaction to the lost traditional faith of past generations, and the effects of that loss in producing "the partial eclipse of hope." As a romanticist, in Sharp's terms, she finds her new hope (as her creator did himself in an early poem of that title) by discovering "wonder" in all phenomena, no matter how apparently insignificant or mundane— the only hope, she says, of "the true genius." Sanpriel looks to science, especially, to quicken the artistic spirit rather than to deprive it of vitality. "Science," she says, "will bring us to a goal whose far shining we do not even descry as yet."[13] Here again, the curious partnership of science and art that was for Sharp and his contemporaries a truism.

Sharp's presentation of this esthetic philosophy can illuminate the artistic atmosphere of this period. Indeed, perhaps the single most characteristic motive behind the new romanticism of the later nineteenth century is the sense of wonder opened to the artist through modern science. The power of delicate, sensitive observation, in itself so much underlying Ruskinian esthetics and what Ruskin admired in the Pre-Raphaelites, joins the scientific and artistic temperaments at this time unequivocally to one another. The measure of "modernity" and relevance is the extent to which the artist admits and rejoices in the discoveries made by scientific inquiry.

Sanpriel is, then, an esthetician whose vagueness to us not only reflects our distance from this outlook, but also suggests the degree to which words like "modernity," "science," and "wonder" were then loaded with meanings they no longer evoke. Without making the effort to reconstitute such meanings, we would find her statement that "the typical romanticist looked forth and beheld all things in that light whereby alone genius can reach the heights whereto it strives"[14] no more than inflated rhetoric.

Yet it is indicative of how many seemingly distinct movements worked toward a corporate effect in Sharp's imagination that he conceived of Sanpriel not only as an avant-garde poet alert to science and discovery, but also as a person expressing through that outlook a distinct racial character and mission; thus she is an existential embodiment of all Sharp's recent influences. Sanpriel is Jewish—or rather, in Sharp's characteristically equivocal terms, half-Christian, and half-Jewish. Her father (whose name, Acosta, Sharp undoubtedly took from Uriel Acosta, the seventeenth-century Jewish philosopher considered an apostate and heretic) has been driven by the fatalistic compulsion of a family curse to marry a Christian, then to torment her with cruel recriminations, and finally to lead her to suicide and himself to perpetual remorse. The beautiful young woman who is the offspring of this strange union finds her aspirations for humanity totally at one with the aspirations of the Jewish race in which she has sought her identity.

Thus Sanpriel functions as the agent through whom Sharp exploits the concepts offered by Lady Magnus and others to express his own views on the future directions of art and of human relationships. The proto-Zionist group called "The Children of To-morrow," of which Sanpriel is a representative, carries as its banner "our inevitable triumph," "the consummation of our national hope."[15] Yet, though it seems to be speaking specifically of Jewish political nationalism, behind these words echo those of Lady Magnus, "the hope of spiritual dominion," and something of that broader, less political goal is amply revealed when Sanpriel exclaims, "We are the torchbearers of the moderns."[16] "We who live more intensely and suffer more acutely than others, are the Children of To-morrow, because in us the new forces of the future are already astir or even dominant."[17] "Intensely" is another one of those characteristic catchwords of this period. To live "intensely" was the Paterian admonition that avant-garde artists and writers of the time found attractive in such a variety of ways. The concept of "intensity" is carried forward with special insight when Felix Dane further observes that the Jews "are the intensive form of any nationality whose language and custom they adopt."[18] The statement, in itself an argument in favor of the "dispersion" of which Lady Magnus spoke, demonstrates how the Jewish race could form a perfect metaphor for the earnest, forward-looking, and enlightened artists and thinkers with whom Sharp sympathized. And these same artists and thinkers, by virtue of their own "disinheritance," would obviously share with the Jews their historical condition as the outcast and the exiled.

In Sanpriel herself, of course, lies the key of the metaphor. Her artistic integrity and her faith in the future dominion of her people are interchangeable. Both require that she sustain hope for a coming triumph and resist the temptation to succumb to the world of fashionable success, moral convention, and loyalty to mean values—the world, in short, of the Philistines. Gabriel Ford is the foil that sets her off. He is, in keeping with the racial metaphor, an apostate Jew, constantly attempting to hide his race. The characterization was undoubtedly the result of Sharp's study of Jewish society, its internal intrigues as well as its external debates. His analysis of those intrigues was probably accurate:

> The Fords, the Montagues, the Despards, and a few other wealthy families occupied a strange position. They were not Christians, nor were they Jewish, in faith; yet they never intermarried save with the sons and daughters of Israel. The orthodox Semites regarded them jealously, hating them because they mixed mainly in Christian society, and made their wives and children cease from attendance at the synagogue, but eager not to offend them on account of their paramount influence and also, to no slight extent, because of their reputed earnest though disguised sympathies with Judaic federation.[19]

Sharp, however, leaves no doubt in Ford's case as to the earnestness of those "disguised sympathies." Ford is both an artistic and a religious fraud. In his longing for acceptance into the present establishment, he has falsified himself and his talent and forfeited his claim to a share in that "dominion" to which his race would otherwise have entitled him.

Thus "The Children of To-morrow," whose ranks Dane, though not a Jew, wishes to join—whose ranks Sanpriel, though passionately requiting his love, will not and cannot desert—are all those who dare beyond the boundaries of convention, or who do not permit themselves to be constrained by those boundaries.[20] These "torchbearers of the moderns" act out of a spirit that lays no real claim to some small earthly plot. Theirs is indeed the spirit of "dispersion." Their supranationalism is their protest against any alliance with values that have no sanction but tradition and have not been submitted to inquiry. Such values, touching every area of life either directly or by extension, including art, sex, self-expression, and even national loyalty itself, "The Children of To-morrow" can and will dare to overthrow.

Sharp's *Life of Browning*, written in 1889, the year of the appearance of *The Children of To-morrow*, throws a curious sidelight on the novel's predominating interest in Judaism. Several of the early pages of *Browning* are devoted to speculations that had recently been bruited as to the poet's racial origins. Among these was the widespread notion, clearly not always well-meant, that he was a Jew. Sharp offered his own conjecture in the matter, supporting his opinion with a lengthy genealogy. "I can find nothing to substantiate the common assertion that, immediately or remotely, his people were Jews."[21]

Sharp might just as well have left the whole issue alone, or dismissed it briefly. Instead he devoted considerable attention to it, unconsciously revealing more about himself than Browning. The curious aspect of Sharp's discussion of Browning's background is its tone. After what seems in *The Children of To-morrow* so fervent a statement in behalf of Judaism, Sharp's fastidiously detached study of Browning's ancestry is unsettling. One is tempted to ask why he should dignify in this way a notion that has no basis in fact, and that can serve no better function than to become some sniping critic's weapon of derogation. The answer to this question may lie in the very different stylistic demands of biographer and novelist, and Sharp's corollary pleasure in playing the appropriate role. To dignify the prejudice by the strategy of serious study is cannily to avoid embarrassing the common reader who may have shared it. If this was Sharp's strategy, it should follow that after establishing his psychological advantage with cool research he will conclude with a barrage of fresh and reversed feeling. And this quite unabashedly, even a little sardonically, is what he does:

> If those who knew [Browning] were told he was a Jew, they would not be much surprised. In his exuberant vitality, in his sensuous love of music and the other arts, in his combined imaginativeness and

shrewdness of common sense, in his superficial expansiveness and actual reticence, he would have been typical enough of the potent and artistic race for whom he has so often of late been claimed.[22]

But Sharp's rhetorical motives were not his only ones. In a man who is a biographer, but wants to be a literary artist, it is the artist who finally prevails. Browning's putative Jewishness was in Sharp's artistic consciousness as useful a means for interpreting his Browning as the Zionism of the Children of To-morrow was for interpreting his social and artistic philosophy. And it was an identical metaphor in both cases: Judaism, an extraordinary race and religion, the vehicle for expressing transcendence of any common ordinations of race and religion. Browning might be thought of as Jewish: for Sharp, via a typical imaginative syllogism, this is the same as saying that he is an artist—that he is vital and volatile in his sympathies—that he is cosmopolitan. Sharp permits Browning to share with the artist-cosmopolitan Heine the spirit of his race, if not his race itself, because Sharp's equation of artist and Jew is his means of driving home the more significant equation of art with transcendent, or ideal, rather than real nationality.

From this period onward, Sharp became more and more preoccupied with this generic or ideal nationalism, as distinct from and indeed opposed to any narrower nativism. In his eagerness to experience fully the enormous diversity of national kinds, and in his desire to appreciate the best of each, he reached out to touch every variety accessible to him. The study of Heine introduced him to German literature; his jaunts to Paris brought him into contact with the turbulent esthetic world of French literary and artistic intellectuals—Mme. Blavatsky, Paul Bourget, François Coppée, Daudet, Zola, and others—and he joined the debate then raging over the possible demarcation between science and art, between dispassionate analysis and evocative power. His passionate interest in modern literatures led him to contemporary Italian writers, and it was not too long before he began writing substantial articles on them for two of the most reputable British journals, the *Fortnightly* and the *Quarterly*. As early as 1890 he was commissioned to write the preface to the English translation of Sainte-Beuve's *Essays on Men and Women* in the Masterpieces of Foreign Authors series. From 1892 on came a rash of articles that testified to his growing reputation as an authority on the recent Belgian literary movement.

This broadly cosmopolitan criticism, principally coinciding with a later period in Sharp's development, will be given fuller treatment in a coming chapter. But his writing on one other literature is especially pertinent here, having engaged his energies in the late eighties. At this time, almost by accident, he was brought into full awareness of the literature of the United States; and America, rising on the horizon of his imagination, though it did not wholly replace Zion, reinvested the concept Zion embodied with new and clearer supra-nationalist significance.

Sharp's first contact with America was the result of an exchange of letters in 1887 with the noted American critic, scholar, and entrepreneur, Edmund Clarence Stedman. Stedman was preparing a volume of "Victorian Poets," and had thought Sharp's two volumes of verse of sufficient value to permit his inclusion. Sharp was naturally delighted by this evidence of American appreciation. For two years the friendship warmed, and Sharp reciprocated Stedman's favor by devoting himself to an intensive study of American literature.

So far he had really been impressed only by Emerson and Whitman. Now his interest and study broadened and deepened. He chose to approach American literature first by means of the sonnet, a form in which he had become something of an expert. The result was "The Sonnet in America," published in April 1889 as an article in the *National Review* and used later that year as the basis of a critical introduction to a volume of American sonnets for the Canterbury series.

Sharp's initial reaction to American literature was as enthusiastic—and as vague—as might be expected from a writer who hoped to be indebted to the Yankee market. But there was a note of discovery, too, that could only be genuine. Though he concurred with the general opinion that there was not "a sufficiently strenuous literary tradition in the U. S.," Sharp also extolled the youth, the energy, and—again—the "modernity" of the American school. "It is almost incredible to those who have not closely studied, and who do not continuously watch the course of American literary affairs," he exclaimed, "how electric the nation is, how quick to respond to the first spark of emotion." He praised the immediacy of inspiration in America, its passion for contemporary subjects, its lively, if undisciplined, artistic life. There is, he says, "no wave of national sentiment . . . no heroic impulse, no calamity, no great national thrill that does not immediately find its echo in song."[23]

By the late summer of 1889 Sharp's wanderlust was thoroughly aroused. On Stedman's invitation he planned a tour of Eastern Canada and the United States which his wife says he "looked forward to . . . with keen delight."[24] He arrived in Canada in late August and was in Boston by mid-September. A visit to Harvard was the beginning of a long, informal friendship with the university; he was invited to deliver a lecture on contemporary literature in 1892. Though Sharp's chronic heart and nervous condition forced cancellation of that lecture, the relationships he made then paved the way for the eager reception of Fiona Macleod, Sharp's alleged protégée, by later Harvard undergraduates, who adopted her as their own discovery and vigorously fostered her American reputation.[25]

Sharp's genial charm combined with Stedman's well-placed introductions to make Sharp many American literary friends, among them William Dean Howells and an imposing host of publishers. But he was particularly drawn to one young bohemian couple, Thomas and Catherine Janvier, who became lifelong and devoted friends. The Janviers, several years later, left New York "for a summer's stay in Europe" and remained in France, at Rémy de Provence, for seven years.[26] There Sharp often visited them during the Fiona Macleod years, and they were among the first and the few to be in on the great secret of the author's career.

Sharp and the Janviers obviously had one very important thing in common—a passion for travel. "Both have travelled much in Mexico," Sharp wrote home to Elizabeth of them when they met. "We dined together at a Cuban cafe last night. He gave me his vol. of stories called 'Colour Studies' and she a little sketch of a Mexican haunted house."[27] Both gifts they inscribed to Sharp in Spanish. By sympathetic instinct, Janvier understood perfectly Sharp's preferred image of himself. In an introduction to a combined American edition of *Romantic Ballads* and *Sospiri di Roma* (1892), Janvier observed that, "while born of substantial Paisley stock, and bred for half his lifetime in Scotland, his years of journeying and residence in foreign countries have made him very much a citizen of the world."[28] He dwelt on the diversity of Sharp's talent, as demonstrated by the two markedly different bodies of work represented in the volume. These, he said, "might pass for the utterances of two men of different races." Here, "joined but not blended, is the poetry of the South and of the North."[29]

Sharp's visit to that "fortunate Eden," as he gallantly called America in a letter to Stedman,[30] had indeed served perceptibly to heighten his sense of his role as the missionary of cosmopolitanism. Almost immediately upon his return to England, "A Note on the Aesthetic Development of America" appeared under his name in the *Scottish Art Review*. He opened the article with a characteristic round of applause for the spirit of self-confident protest that had recently made Americans tend to exaggerate their claims to literary repute: "Better thus—better the exaggerations of independence than subservience to critical formulas." He discerned the genres that were the Americans' peculiar forte—the episodical novel, the short story—but added, with an ardor forgivable because prophetic, "the poetic renascence in America is as remarkable in the present as it is significant for the future."[31]

These observations were, however, only secondary to the polemical keynote of his article. The butt of attack was the British "misapprehension" of American esthetic development and its cause: "At the base of our misunderstanding is the *idée mère* that the Americans are Anglo-Saxons, even as we are. Our kindred oversea are essentially continental, as we are essentially insular . . . It is this factor . . . of continental influence, which is so profoundly affecting American art, and impelling it towards developments altogether independent of Anglo-Saxon art proper." Sharp does not neglect the influence of "climate," which is characteristically deployed in defense of his thesis, as are also "widespread intellectual and aesthetic education and . . . geographical and political advantage." But he returns inevitably to his core idea that the American character is, more than anything else, the result of "incessant and complex racial admixture": "This perennial invasion of the States by hordes of Swedes, Norwegians, Germans, Russians, Italians, French, Spanish, Irish, Scots, and English—what can it lead to, what has it led to, but a vital reorganization of the nation at large?" The American nation, he continues—and in his tone is a note of triumph that invariably accompanied any animadversion upon British insularity—the American nation "is new in its amalgam, just as England was new when Pict, Celt, Frisian, Angle, Jute, Norseman, Dane and Norman all mingled their tributary strains in one national river of race."

And, he adds, "we are one people now," perhaps even an "old" people, because we have developed "a greater homogeneity." To be "old," however, was not a Sharpian virtue. Sharp loves America because, in these terms, it is "new." Its "incessant influx of multiform European race and sentiment" brings with it a vital "spirit of change, 'mutations infinite.'" He strikes one more blow at the myth of Anglo-Saxon supremacy and domination: "Few seem to have recognized the vital Latin element in the great continental nation overseas. But the Italians and the French, with their northern allies in spirit, the Celts, have had and are exercising an enormously potent influence in the evolution of the American race." This "enormously potent" diversity of influence will realize in America, and nowhere better, what Sharp calls "the cosmopolitan dignity and freedom of art."[32] Nothing should be allowed to inhibit that realization.

Sharp is led by his tendency to interpret artistic history and development in terms of "that potent, subtle, mysterious factor of climate" to foresee, with some acuteness, a growing regional division among the various parts of the United States. "Fortunately," he comments, "the climatic factor now works harmoniously to one great end." Yet perhaps his readers "do not readily apprehend the significance of this climatic diversity. It is," he observes with delight, "as though all Europe, from Valencia to Tobolsk, from Spitzbergen to the Ionian Isles, were subject to one central government." In its comprehensiveness, America is able to produce "poets so radically distinct as Poe and Emerson, Longfellow and Walt Whitman, and novelists so widely unrelated as Hawthorne and Howells, Fenimore Cooper and Bret Harte."[33] Sharp's tone of rejoicing reflects how close the longing exile had come to his cosmopolitan paradise. America was the palpable realization of Sharp's ideal nation. It both embraced and liberated every form of expression in western culture; it realized the triumphant "dispersion" of the Children of To-morrow.

The implicit union of America and Zion in Sharp's vision was not unique in him. The special character of his vision lay only, perhaps, in its residing in the mind of someone who was not a Jew. A measure of Sharp's sense of his own alien condition is the extent to which he could equal the compassion for the disinherited, and the hope for their reinheritance, felt by the Jewish writers of his day. Israel Zangwill, the Jewish local-colorist, author of "Children of the Ghetto," looked to America for an answer to the Jew's need for a nation in which to resolve his identity. For Zangwill, too, America embodied "the harmonious diversity" of "the true cosmopolitan concept."[34] For him, as for Sharp, every "alien" could, in the American "melting pot," purge his sense of exile. "Into the crucible with you all!" was the command of his American dream. "What is the glory of Rome and Jerusalem where all nations and races come to worship and look back, compared with the glory of America, where all races and nations come to labour and look forward?"[35]

But Zangwill came to synchronize his visionary hopes for America with practical efforts to territorialize the Jewish people. Sharp was not motivated by such a sense of racial need; his was stringently personal, and he lacked resources of practical instinct to supply it. Though his celebration of the "fortunate Eden" did not entirely end with his article in the *Scottish Art Review*, its fervor could not survive his own restlessness. In 1891, in an article in the *National Review* called simply "American Literature," he continued to applaud the various and opposing strains in American work, but there was an almost painful urgency to his plea that Americans free themselves once and for all from the English tradition.[36] It was as though his imagination feared the failure of an American cosmopolitanism his intellect had earlier described as inevitable. Or was it perhaps that his intellect had not really operated independently in seeing in America the realization of that cosmopolitan dream? For in these articles, as so often elsewhere in his work no matter how merely critical or informative it might purport to be, Sharp had let slip past him a spirit of creative fabrication. Hope was validated into belief because of the author's need to have it so. "We are all seeking a lost Eden," he had written sometime during the late eighties: "It may be that, driven from the Eden of direct experience, we are being more and more forced into taking refuge within the haven guarded by our dreams."[37] America was only another inchoate, yet-unformed Israel of desire, a promising if not a promised land. "The Celt went forth to battle," a medieval poet had once written, "but he always fell." Perhaps here in Sharp's dream was a misplaced Celt's last chance to go forth, and not to fall.

6

ITALY AGAIN

The Second Self

Mrs. Sharp says in her *Memoir* that her husband's hopes of devoting himself finally and exclusively to independent creative work led to his taking the bold step, in the fall of 1890, of "burning his ships" as he put it—giving up his London associations and editorial obligations completely—and leaving England for a second trip to Italy.

The step was taken and the trip made, but the rupture with the past was bolder in appearance than in reality. The Sharps's financial means were not yet sufficient to permit the sacrifice of all his usual projects. He continued working on a biographical study of Keats and Joseph Severn, drawn from the Severn papers and ultimately published in 1892. Work on this book required visits to William Severn, W. W. Story, and John Ruskin, all in their various provincial habitats, and thus prevented Sharp's departure from being quite so sudden or complete as Mrs. Sharp suggests. In addition he was planning another undertaking that was not independent, even if it was imaginative. This was an epistolary novel to be written in collaboration with the American author Blanche Willis Howard: *A Fellowe and His Wife*, also published in 1892. Miss Howard, now Frau Hof-Artz von Teuffel, was living in Stuttgart. To meet with her the Sharps traveled through Germany, and Sharp alone paid her another flying visit on his return to England the following year.

Nor did Sharp turn over all his editorships. He retained his post with the Canterbury series, or at least gave it up only temporarily: in the mid-nineties and later he was still editing and introducing for that series such volumes as the poems of Matthew Arnold and Eugene Lee-Hamilton. He did jettison the literary editorship of the *Young Folks' Paper* and relinquish his positions as art critic on the *Glasgow Herald* and the *Art Journal*, but the extent of his recklessness is shown by his passing the art criticism on to his wife.

Yet there remains some justice to the impression of turning point that Mrs. Sharp conveys. However cautious and shrewd the pruning, Sharp succeeded in cutting away much, if not all, of the tangled variety of his London activities. From one point of view, of course, there had been no variety to them. His editorial burdens had all had something of hackwork about them. The real element of variety in his life he did not give up. His reading had been developing breadth and diversity—Meredith, Browning, Swinburne, and Patmore, among the English; Balzac and Sainte-Beuve among the French; and among the Italians, Fogazzaro and D'Annunzio. Ibsen and Poe were thrown in for good measure, and he was soon to know Maeterlinck and other Belgians so well that he could allege himself "the only specialist [on them] among English men of letters."[1] This heady mixed potion was working its effect on him. He was burgeoning with new ideas—so many, in fact, that only a fraction of them would come to fruition within the remaining fifteen years of his life. The break with London, even if qualified and temporary, was an expression of a growing sense of his own potential and of a hope for sufficient freedom to realize it. This hope was not to be entirely disappointed.

After their short visit to Stuttgart the Sharps went quickly to Rome. Curiously enough, even the romantic journey down the Rhine failed to strike any strong chord of response in the usually responsive Sharp. He longed to get on to "the beautiful, living, pulsing South."[2] The Sharps remained in Rome from December 1890 until the spring of 1891 and probably used it as their home base during the rest of that year, though Mrs. Sharp does not make the matter quite clear. She does say that he visited the Janviers in Provence and she went to Florence in March 1891, and she recalls that in September Sharp returned to Stuttgart to compare notes with his female collaborator.[3] In any case, before the year was out he was already back in London consolidating his literary gains, and by 1892 he was caught in a feverish new round of activities.

Anyone might then have observed something different about Sharp. His creative voice was stronger, all his work more passionate and vital. And those who knew him intimately knew also that it was in the years immediately following his return from Italy that Sharp began, quietly but steadfastly, to produce the work later to be attributed to the pen of Fiona Macleod.

The stay in Italy, brief though it was, must loom great in any

97

examination of Sharp's development. He himself spoke of its influence in large though vague terms, terms which suggest that it was complex, a result partly of the new sense of liberation, partly of new personal acquaintances, and partly of reading in new areas. Mrs. Sharp lists that reading without attempting to define its effects, yet it is possible to see links (as will be shown) between the work of men like Elie Reclus, Pierre Loti, and Restif de la Bretonne and Sharp's work thereafter. Added to these was, of course, that influence best described as the reciprocal operation of all these factors, which makes the effect of the whole greater than the sum of its parts.

By far the essential circumstance surrounding the second Italian trip was the climate of relative liberty in which it was realized. Sharp owed this excursion to no means but his own. It was not necessary this time, as it had been in 1883, to see himself as an art critic being seasoned for his chores with sightseeing and travel. He was not required to visit galleries or cathedrals or to follow slavishly a fixed itinerary. He recalled with fervor the interlude during that first trip spent admiring the "enormous variety" of natural life on the Roman Campagna, and it was to the Campagna he returned. Memory had not betrayed him:

> Oh Italy, Italy! . . . not Rome, but "greater Rome," the Agro Romano . . . the ever new, mysterious, fascinating Campagna. I love North Italy too, all Umbria and Tuscany: and to know Venice is to have a secret of perpetual joy: and yet, the Agro Romano![4]

No doubt the lizards and bees still caught his attention, for Sharp never lost his naturalist's eye. But even in this brief outburst there is evidence of a new focus in his vision. It is now the "mysterious, fascinating Campagna," and this Campagna, the Campagna of vagrant winds and fragments of ruin, was to leave its permanent impression on Sharp's work. The solitude and suggestiveness of the landscape liberated him both physically and imaginatively. The several manuscripts he had taken with him to work on in Rome were laid aside until he had finished an almost completely new volume of poems, *Sospiri di Roma*— "sighs," or as Sharp himself translated it, "breaths of Rome." Sharp's private affection for these poems, written in free verse and deriving their principal inspiration from this capacious landscape, is demonstrated by his having them immediately printed in Anzio in 1891, at his own expense. They were the first and most important publication directly resulting from his second Italian experience.

Sharp had made some straggling efforts at free verse earlier in his career, dictated by his own need for undisciplined form as well as by his familiarity with Whitman. Henley's *In Hospital* had served to give him fresh incentive. But powerful feelings newly aroused to overflowing by the Italian landscape were more than anything else the source of the *Sospiri*, and their vigor and spirit found an immediate British audience. With their publication, Sharp came to be considered one of the leading exponents of free verse in his own day: Richard Burton coupled his name with Whitman's and Henley's in an article in the *Atlantic Monthly* in 1894.[5]

As Burton suggested in that article, not altogether without censure, the *Sospiri* were notable for employing the "free" form in combination with "free" themes. For Sharp such verse provided a perfect vehicle for expressing all liberties—sexual, social, and poetic. He marred the poems occasionally by an unnatural and self-conscious diction—as though Henley had gone through the poems making, as Yeats once said, a "hath" out of every "has." But their unequivocal outbursts of sexuality were often breathtakingly successful, and their near-symbolic use of natural phenomena to express such sexuality sometimes remarkably suggestive of D. H. Lawrence's *Birds, Beasts, and Flowers*. Here is "The Wild Mare":

> Like a breath that comes and goes
> O'er the waveless waste
> Of sleeping Ocean,
> So sweeps across the plain
> The herd of wild horses.
> Like banners in the wind
> Their flying tails,
> Their streaming manes:
> And like spume of the sea
> Fang'd by breakers,
> The white froth tossed from their bloodred nostrils.
> Out from the midst of them
> Dasheth a white mare,
> White as a swan in the pride of her beauty:
> And, like the whirlwind,

Following after,
A snorting stallion,
Swart as an Indian
Diver of coral!
Wild the gyrations,
The rush and the whirl;
Loud the hot panting
Of the snow-white mare,
As swift upon her
The stallion gaineth:
Fierce the proud snorting
Of him, victorious:
And loud, swelling loud on the wind from the mountains,
The hoarse savage tumult of neighing and stamping
Where, wheeling, the herd of wild horses awaiteth—
Ears thrown back, tails thrashing their flanks or swept under—
The challenging scream of the conqueror stallion.[6]

Meredith, commenting on this poem after publication, called it an "unrivalled" example of "impressionistic work" and noted that such work "surpasses all but highest verse" if written "where the heart is hot."[7] Sharp also wrote sexuality into the cooler and quieter rhythms of the fountain in "Sorgendo La Luna," though with less success:

No sound,
Save the hush'd breath,
The slowly flowing,
The long and low withdrawing breath of Rome.
Not a leaf quivers, where the dark,
With eyes of rayless shadow and moonlit hair,
Dreams in the black
And hollow cavernous depth of the ilex-trees.
No sound,
Save the hush'd breath of Rome,
And sweet and fresh and clear
The bubbling, swaying, ever quavering jet
Of water fill'd with pale nocturnal gleams,
That, in the broad low fount,
Falleth,
Falleth and riseth,
Riseth and falleth, swayeth and surgeth . . .

> Up from the marble fount
> The water leaps,
> Sways in the moonshine, springeth, springeth,
> Falleth and riseth,
> Like sweet faint lapping music,
> Soft gurgling notes of woodland brooks that wander
> Low laughing where the hollowed stones are green
> With slippery moss that hath a trickling sound:
> Leapeth and springeth . . .[8]

Not surprisingly, many of the poems severely shocked Mrs. Grundy with their unabashed sex and their exposure of bare flesh, among them "The Naked Rider," "The Bather," and "Fior di Memoria."[9] From "The Bather" are the following lines:

> Silent she stands,
> And looks far seaward
>
> . . .
>
> Beautiful, beautiful
> The sunlit gleam
> Of her naked body,
> Ivory-white 'mid the cyclamen blossoms.
>
> . . .
>
> As a water-lily
> Touched by the breath
> Of sunrise glory,
> Moveth and swayeth
> With tremulous joy,
> So o'er the sunlit
> White gleaming body
> Of the beautiful bather
> Passeth a quiver
> Rosy-white, as a cloud at the dawning . . .[10]

One can't resist speculating that this September-Morn image is the original of the "exquisite maiden on the banks of Lake Nemi" to whom Ernest Rhys later half-jestingly attributed the inspiration for Sharp's new poetic prowess. Rhys was probably, perhaps deliberately and for sensation's sake, identifying her with the mysterious "friend" Sharp repeatedly credited with that inspiration.[11] Of course, circumstantial evidence was on the side of Rhys's malicious wit. Sharp's new life in and around Rome was bohemian enough to have encouraged his joining the pagan water activities suggested by "The Bather." He and his wife counted many resident artists among their friends—Theodore Roussel, Charles Holroyd, and others—as well as several literary people on their holidays. Sharp's reading of Reclus' *Primitive Folk* and Loti's *Le mariage*, combined with the momentum already provided by many radical London friends, was, moreover, inclining him to an earnest reappraisal of what he called "the sexual morale."[12] It is also true that his wife was rarely with him on his exploring expeditions over the Campagna, where the inviting solitudes might well have tempted his sensual side.

Yet to look for Sharp's inspiration in such putative sexual daring is to ignore the quality of tentative and romanticized lust that makes poems like "The Bather" resemble the wish-fulfillment dreams of adolescence. It is also to ignore how much they reveal of Sharp's imaginative life. Even as a mere figment "The Bather" supplies a shorthand symbol for what was happening to Sharp psychologically as a result of the new freedom he had given himself to divagate in the cloudless dazzlement of the hills and plains around Rome. In keeping with his characteristic technique for applying perceptions about the external world to his internal life, he had accomplished a "return to nature" that was more than just a physical and poetic return to natural surroundings. It was a "return" to some basis of actuality, to what he later called "the wastes of the imagination,"[13] a symbolic stripping-down to the essential self in an effort to realize it.

As a means of expressing Sharp's need for physical and creative freedom, the metaphor of nakedness had great directness and simplicity. Possibly in his association with Yeats, begun in 1888, he had already become acquainted with the concept of the "mask," to which his own bears a resemblance. The figure had appeared in Sharp's work in the essay on Browning, where he spoke of the dramatic monologues as an ideal means of handling the "masks" or postures of human variety, especially, as he put it, the variety of modern times. But the influence of the second Italian experience is observable in the figure's increasing significance from the *Sospiri* onward. Stories like "The Oread," which appeared in Sharp's *Pagan Review* (1892), and impressionistic dramas like "The Passion of Père Hilarion" and "The Black Goddess," later incorporated into *Vistas* (1894), all make use of the uncovering or stripping of the hero physically as he emerges into a new kind of life.

It is thus possible to draw a direct line from the *Sospiri*, through the *Pagan Review*, to the "psychic dramas" published together under the title *Vistas*. The *Pagan Review* undoubtedly originated as a device for baiting the prudish critics who had responded so archly to his *Sospiri*; it bore on its front cover the motto "Sic transit gloria Grundi." But the satirical tone of this inscription, the review's guiding principle, and some of its introductory preface was tempered by a strain of high seriousness. Under the guise of the editor "W. H. Brooks," Sharp advanced in that preface the movement called "the new paganism," describing it as "a new inwardness," a scrutiny of the hidden human life, of which sexual mores were a significant part. And using the familiar metaphor, he spoke of wanting "to withdraw from life the approved veils of Convention."[14]

Indeed the entire magazine expressed a growing "mask" or "veil" fixation. Its single edition, published in September 1892, did not merely disguise its editorship. Its full contents were composed by Sharp under seven different pseudonyms. Not once, in fact, did he use his own name;[15] and he chose mostly French pseudonyms, like Gascoigne, Verlayne, and others, revealing his alignment with esthetic movements on the continent. The *Pagan Review* was not the first example of the use of a pseudonym on Sharp's part; he had, in desultory fashion, employed an anagram of his own name, "H. P. Siwäärnill," to designate a certain profoundly wise Dutch philosopher to whom were attributed epigraphs to poems in *Romantic Ballads*, and oracular fragments quoted by Sanpriel in *The Children of To-morrow*. Nevertheless the *Pagan Review* represented the first broad and more than whimsical use of a pseudonym.[16]

This burst of pseudonymous writing coincided with Sharp's interest in the drama: the *Pagan Review* contained his first attempts at dramatic writing, "The Black Goddess" and a fragment called "Dionysos in India." Like his own "Oread" in the same *Pagan Review*, Sharp in Italy had paused "in contemplation of [his] second self."[17] The congruence of drama and "mask" in Sharp's creative work thus defines the full effect of the self-examination which the trip to Italy had prompted and which that trip represents in the chronicle of his development. Both were means of expressing the fragmentation and variety Sharp had discovered within himself—the drama or dramatic monologue in universal terms, and the pseudonym in personal, internal terms—though the line between these was not always clear.

In this connection Sharp's essay on Browning, produced just before the Italian trip, merits further examination as a work of criticism in which the principles of drama and "mask" were first outlined in proto-type and examined in terms Sharp would thereafter apply to himself and to his own method. The portents are readily visible. Browning was "a type of the subtle, restless, curious, searching modern age." He was, in other words, as Sharp believed himself to be, a form of summary representative of his times. "The Victorian era," says Sharp, "is characterized by vast, Titanic struggles of the human spirit to reach . . . Truth . . . by piling Ossas of searching speculation upon Pelions of hardly-won positive knowledge." Browning, he continues, "is the profoundest interpreter of [this era]. To achieve supremacy [he] had . . . to fashion a mentality so passionately alive that its manifold phases should have all the reality of concrete individualities."[18] In a similar vein, Sharp credited Browning with recognizing "the value of quintessential moments,"[19] a concept in itself dramatic. And emphasizing the "autopsychic" nature of Browning's individuations of attitudes and "moments," that is, their function as extensions or projections of his own flexible internal personality, Sharp drew attention to Browning's ability to identify, as Sharp himself did, with any external phenomenon:

> Those who know and love "Pauline" will remember the passage where the poet, with that pantheistic ecstasy which was possibly inspired by the singer he most loved [Shelley], tells how he can live the life of plants . . . or . . . of the bird . . . or be a fish.[20]

On this basis, Sharp debunked the critical view that celebrated Browning as a subtle thinker. He believed Browning's eminence lay not in the content of his "philosophy" at all, but in his having successfully dramatized the conflicts of his time. This was his true "message." "Through a multitude of masks, he, the typical soul, speaks and delivers himself of [that] message which would not be presented emphatically enough as the utterance of a single individual."[21] Browning's great contribution, Sharp therefore concluded, was as a dramatic poet who, besides adding "a wealth of poetic diction" and "new symbols" to the language of English poetry, set the conditions for a total reappraisal

of the tools of criticism "involving our construction of a new definition" around the concept of the poet as dramatist.[22]

On the score of these observations alone Sharp should be credited
with a high degree of critical and historical insight. Perceiving this
one vital direction of modern literature, he was led to remark, on encountering the work of Maeterlinck in October 1891, "I believe that
much of the imaginative writing of the future will be in dramatic prose
of a special kind."[23] It was to this future that he proceeded to dedicate
himself in his own work, providing not so much an instance of the
"poet as dramatist" as of the self as drama. Needless to say, in his
application of this latter concept he produced results of an eccentric
kind by attempting to create separate artistic tasks for his personae.

"Fragments from the Lost Journals of Piero di Cosimo," an imaginative work Sharp published the same year as *Browning*, is also interesting as a link between the London and Italian Sharps. The technique
Sharp employed in this story comes from the tradition established by
W. S. Landor, Browning, and Pater in which the life and character of
a historical figure are dramatized and given a fictive context. Though
not intended as a literary ruse, "The Lost Journals" had the effect, as
such things sometimes will, of calling out the occasional fool among
critics, who in this case complained that Sharp's "translation" was not
sufficiently literal, "probably from lack of knowledge of medieval Italian," a defect he claimed to have discerned by comparing Sharp's
version "with the original."[24] Success like this might easily turn anyone to a life of deception.

"The Lost Journals," which first appeared in the *Scottish Art Review*
in 1889 and was later subsumed with a group of other stories under
the title *Ecce Puella* (1896), exemplifies as a whole and in some of
its particulars Sharp's increasing tendency to focus on the self as drama.
The piece is, as its title suggests, a form of dramatic monologue in
prose. Piero di Cosimo was a painter of some interest to Walter Pater;
and the form of the narrative, as well as the nature of the personality
and life with which Sharp chooses to invest his subject, show strong
indications of the influence of Pater's *Imaginary Portraits*. Like so many
of the *Portraits*, "The Lost Journals" follows Piero day by day through
a series of events peculiar to the life of an artist, and therefore a man
of special sensibility. Notwithstanding its derivativeness—and its melodramatic climax—the work is worthy of consideration as a tour de

force in a genre significant for its popularity in this period. There is vigor and originality in its detail and psychological plausibility in its central character.

Beyond the drama inherent in the form, however, Sharp has given Piero some interesting characteristics of internal drama. Even his art is in conflict with itself, for Piero is a seeker of "the real in the occult."[25] He is prone to paradoxical responses to nature, which he claims is his subject: she is both "Madonna Natura" and "a beast of prey."[26] He is possessed by the idea that virtue and vice, love and hate, beauty and horror are contiguous and coexistent. He is called "the mad painter"[27] because his personal temperament varies from hilarity to despondency. His devotion to his art is fitful: he is both industrious and inclined to periods of paralyzing idleness. Though scrupulous in his personal habits, he cultivates a jungle-like garden, overgrown with weeds and tropical plants. When asked to participate in a local Florentine festival, joyful in its theme, he contributes a float called "The Car of Death."

The drama of paradox, of total oppositions, is of course the drama of the self in its simplest and most obvious form, but also, in a sense, its most fascinating. This may explain why Sharp did not progress much beyond it. He had quite early developed a predisposition to seeing character in oppositions. This limited mode of confronting external and internal complexity merely underwent a gradual clarification and translation into the fictionalist's vocabulary. It had its beginning as early as Sharp's first biography, his Rossetti study of 1882. Sharp's Rossetti, just like his Piero, had been grindingly industrious—at times— and at other times submerged in ennui and lassitude. Sharp expressed fascination with Rossetti's "Hand and Soul," a tale painstakingly rendering the split between artistic perception and realization.[28] In his work as art critic, he had found a similar paradox in Sodona, or "Bazzi," a Sienese painter also of some interest to Pater. Sharp described Sodona as both hedonist and industrious craftsman. He attempted to rationalize the combination in terms that suggested his personal acquaintance with the fault: "Like many men similarly endowed, the hedonistic tendencies of his nature came too frequently and too forcibly into contest with his powers of prolonged application and continuous study." And very much like the Piero of "The Lost Journals," Sodona was "more heedful of the softly-toned autumnal hues, and drooping of over-burdened vines . . . than of the stretched canvas or half-o'erfrescoed wall." On this fact could be blamed his failure to attain "those heights which were surely to him possible of achievement."[29]

This particular duality, it may well be argued, is a common, often imaginary preoccupation of every artist, who knows full well the difference between the excitement and pleasure of conceiving a work of art, and the rigor and discipline of executing it. But in discerning dualities, Sharp had gone well beyond the division between soul and hand, even in his earliest work. Rossetti had inspired his often-expressed fascination with the doppelgänger legend.[30] And an extension of this concept, the werewolf, wraith, or "weird," the specter of oneself whose visitation is a portent of death, Sharp had effectively used in *Romantic Ballads*, especially in "The Weird of Michael Scott." Furthermore, his memoirs of Philip Marston had dwelt on the blind poet's youthful "dual existence," a penchant for romanticizing himself in the role of swashbuckler and taking "imaginary voyages."[31] Sharp claimed also to have been the recipient of a sonnet in which Marston asserted his belief in a previous existence.[32] Nor was Shelley spared Sharp's habit of vision. It was, Sharp says, as though the poet, a moral visionary, and the man, defeated in all his high intentions, "were a distinct identity, united by no other bond than a literary partnership."[33] Sharp added George Meredith to this eminent tribe of divided minds by describing the conflict between his scientific and his poetic visions.[34] Heine's variegated personality as seen through Sharp's eyes—not a simple duality, but a combination of many oppositions—has already been discussed.

The instinct for division so prefigured in this early work intensified from 1890 on. Evidence of Sharp's and Fiona Macleod's similar fascination with doubles and double personalities should indeed have been clue enough for any enterprising literary detective of the day to establish Sharp's identity with Fiona Macleod, whose employment of the folkloristic "wraith" or other self is frequent. But more than the "weird" of Sharp's *Romantic Ballads*, which is used strictly qua folklore, the "other self" as employed by Fiona Macleod has an intensely felt reality. The author's voice seems to quaver even behind the mask of omniscience. This increased intensity of feeling is anticipated in the period of the early nineties by one work written under the name of Sharp. This work was "The Gipsy Christ," written and published as a short story, though, interesting to note, conceived originally as a drama.[35] The full autobiographical impact of this story may only be felt if it is

107

placed beside some private remarks Sharp made at the time of its composition. The first of these gives some corroboration to the theory advanced in Chapter I regarding Sharp's self-image as "changeling" or member of another race; it also provides evidence of the intense self-scrutiny Sharp was at this time undergoing. Writing in his diary for September 1891, he mused, "I suppose I was a gipsy once; a 'wild man' before: a wilder beast of prey before that."[36] Speaking more publicly of the story in question, but not much more, Sharp confessed to Robert Murray Gilchrist that "the story goes back to my own early experiences," though he is quick to add "—not as to the *facts* of the story of course."[37] The *Memoir* leaves us to guess what he meant, but that is not too difficult. The "early experiences" to which he alludes were those youthful, truant wanderings among the gypsies, when in feeling, if not in "fact," he saw himself as their "sun brother." "The Gipsy Christ" is no more than a full articulation of Sharp's fantasy. The central character, half gypsy and half English, is haunted by the more compelling gypsy self, and is finally forced to lead a separate existence as messiah and sacrificial victim—"Gipsy Christ"—of the race to which he is half-brother.

The inspiration for this tale, however, came from no mere casual recrudescence of Sharp's past. His varied and esoteric reading was bringing him to exciting self-discoveries and rediscoveries; his new self-confidence was providing the occasion for realizing these discoveries in his art. There is no way of knowing precisely what led him to read Elie Reclus's *Primitive Folk* at this time—perhaps it was sheer curiosity. But it is tempting to imagine his enthusiasm at finding so much in the book to reawaken private visions and fantasies so long laid asleep by hard facts and hard times. Reclus's anthropological technique was as primitive as his folk, but through the colorful pages of his narrative, with their vivid and affecting detail, the youthful Sharp who had felt himself "allied" with the prophets and seers of "other lands and other days"[38] was reborn. How curiously like Mrs. Sharp's characterization of her husband in those days of childhood and adolescence, wandering off to the hillsides because he must be alone with his visions, is this description of the *angakok* among the Konyagas, the tribal figure gifted with mystical and healing wisdom:

At an early age the novice courts solitude. He wanders throughout the long nights across silent plains filled with the chilly whiteness of the moon; he listens to the wind moaning over the desolate floes;— and then the aurora borealis, that ardently sought occasion for "drinking in the light," the *angakok* must absorb in all its brilliancies and splendours . . . And now the future sorcerer is no longer a child. Many a time he has felt himself in the presence of Sidné, the Esquimaux Demeter; he has divined it by the shiver which ran through his veins, by the tingling of his flesh and the bristling of his hair . . . He sees stars unknown to the profane; he asks the secrets of destiny from Sirius, Algol, and Altair; he passes through a series of initiations, knowing well that his spirit will not be loosed from the burden of dense matter and crass ignorance, until the moon has looked him in the face, and darted a certain ray into his eyes.

And, the *angakok* must surely have corroborated Sharp's own experience of his second, elusive self:

At last his own Genius, evoked from the bottomless depths of existence, appears to him, having scaled the immensity of the heavens, and climbed across the abysses of the ocean. White, wan, and solemn, the phantom will say to him: "Behold me, what dost thou desire?" Uniting himself with the Double from beyond the grave, the soul of the *angakok* flies upon the wings of the wind, and quitting the body at will, sails swift and light through the universe. It is permitted to probe all hidden things, to seek the knowledge of all mysteries, in order that they may be revealed to those who have remained mortal with spirit unrefined.[39]

"The Gipsy Christ" is here, though without the added dimension of Sharp's own experience. His story is the tragedy of an *angakok* misplaced in a civilized world—indeed residing in the flesh of a normal, civilized Englishman, an ordinary "mortal with spirit unrefined." Only among primitive folk may the *angakok* unite himself "with the Double from beyond the grave," and fly "upon the wings of the wind . . . swift and light through the universe." The fate of the seer who has walked long in the ways of civilization—undoubtedly Sharp's bleakest prevision of his own fate—remains instead suffering and self-destruction.

Also beyond Reclus was the racial division of the "Gipsy Christ." Sharp's early sensitivity to differences of race and culture had become more intense with time and with the experiences of Italy and the

United States. In nearly everything he wrote he consciously reflected through parallel dualities the dual racial strain in his own blood (Celt and Scandinavian) and in his education and literary training (Scottish and English). A racial tension similar to that of "The Gipsy Christ," though somewhat less dramatically treated, had formed an important part of the characterization of Sanpriel, heroine of *The Children of To-morrow*. Half-Christian and half-Jew, she came close to being "cursed" as her father had been with affinities for both Jew and Gentile; but she had, both idealistically and quixotically, dedicated herself to that part of her origins which, like the Gipsy's, might be considered the "outlaw" race.

At the same time that racial duality was becoming a more insistent motif of Sharp's fiction, it was developing into a near obsession in his criticism and biographies. Racial oppositions were worked into almost every portrait. There is the Belgian Maeterlinck: "his literary inheritance is markedly English . . . A strain of English blood, I understand, runs in [his] veins."[40] Walter Pater: "In that serene, quiet, austere, yet passionate nature of his, so eminently Teutonic, so distinctly Northern, there was, strange to say, a strain of Latin savagery."[41] Edward Burne-Jones: "He expressed his own conviction that in nature and temperament he was Celtic and not English."[42]

Other nonracial dualities persisted in Sharp's writing through the nineties. In the case of his brief study of William Morris,[43] it was not surprising, of course, that he should emphasize his subject's obvious double life as creative artist and active socialist. But Sharp's reappraisal of Rossetti at the end of the decade was so overwhelmed with dual terms that it revealed little more than the writer's relentless habit of vision:

Winsome, lovable, perverse, irresistible, weak, brilliant, moody, robust, morbid, visionary, shrewd, fitted to excel among his fellows and a recluse almost monastic in his isolation, sane in his vision of life and insane in his application of the principles of life, an ideal lover and at the sway of lesser emotions, an indifferent loyalist in love and yet dominated by one passion, a follower of ideal beauty and heedless of that comeliness which is her outward approach, a moralist who had few morals, a wit who was tired of wit, a humourist who was tired of humour, and yet whose wit and humour made so many hours bright for himself and others, a man strong to endure and yet the impotent slave of a drug, the most powerful temperament of his time and yet shattered by his own weakness, morose to a degree on occasion and yet habitually so lovable that not one of his intimates took thought of resentment, sweeping in denunciation and yet generous to everyone and to a foe most of all, impassioned with the romanticism of the most subtle and sensuous imagination of his time and yet with his chief delight in the novels of Dumas, an epicurean by temperament and in practice at all times heedless of the first principles of the epicure, agnostic in most matters of common faith and yet superstitious to a degree, gifted with superb energy and the most subject of all men to the prostrations of idleness, the most arrogant of all men and the most humble, cynical in much and in more naively simple, reckless in speech and loyal in spirit, a broken man and a triumphant genius, he remains the most perplexing, the most fascinating, the most wonderful personality of the Victorian era.[44]

The volume from which this extraordinary passage comes is Sharp's treatise on English painting published in 1902, *The Progress of Art in the Nineteenth Century*. It is significant in relation to his "double" vision not only because it contained numerous applications of that vision to individual artists also but because it raised the concept of artistic duality to a principle of good criticism. In evaluating Turner, Sharp observed that while his art demonstrated a passion for beauty his "external life" was "mean and even sordid." He concluded from this and similar observations about other artists that man and artist were totally separate entities. The true critic, he insisted, knows "how little a part 'conduct of life' plays in art."[45] This truth had, by 1900, been submitted to substantial proof by trial, for the figure of Fiona Macleod had been planned and executed as just such a division of Sharp's artistic self from his workaday, "bread-and-butter making" one.[46]

The Sharp-Macleod division, proffered to the literary world in 1894 but in the making since 1891, is therefore not difficult to explain as a dramatization of opposing tendencies which Sharp recognized in his own character. Its only difference from other such dramatizations is the degree of permanent hold it obtained upon him. Both in its racial duality and in its separation of the creating artist from the acting man, it is, as we have seen, a division prefigured or paralleled numerous times.

One other dynamic investing the Sharp-Macleod division, the sexual one, merits special treatment because the process of its evolution was much more subtle and inexplicit than that of the other components of the drama of the self. The sexual tension as such is not visible in Sharp's published work in the same way as are those other tensions already analyzed. No artist or writer figuring in his criticism or biography, no character in his fiction or his poetry lives a peculiarly hermaphroditic form of dual existence. We have only frequent private testimony that Sharp thought he contained such sexual tension within himself, that he felt a deep sense of identity with woman and her problems. "Rarely a day passed," writes his wife, "in which he did not try to imagine himself living the life of a woman, to see through her eyes, and feel and view life from her standpoint, and so vividly that 'sometimes I forget I am not the woman I am trying to imagine.' "[47] Similar and even less restrained testimony came from Lilian Rea, his personal secretary during the Fiona Macleod period: "In him seemed to live again the child of Hermes and Aphrodite, the twain that became one flesh—man and woman in one."[48] Considering that Sharp was not slow to find imaginative representatives for all of his other internal contrasts, we may only reason that the absence of correlatives in his writings for the sexual one—beyond, that is, the secret maintenance of the dual role as Sharp and Macleod—was the effect of cultural inhibition. This may also provide a partial explanation for the secrecy in which the role itself was held for so long. From Lilian Rea's viewpoint, at least, it did: "Personally, I should explain Mr. Sharp's unbroken reticence on this point by a certain delicacy which he felt in acknowledging his belief to the world at large that a woman's soul really lived within himself in dual unity with his distinct man's nature."[49]

Yet the inhibitions hedging the literary "staging" of the sexual drama did not altogether keep Sharp from dealing with it. Staying within the limits of the normal sex relationship, he nevertheless conveyed that drama in terms that strongly suggested the fragmentation of the individual. His technique was, in other words, the reverse of that used to delineate other oppositions. It amounted to lifting a female character to a level of partnership with the male, to the point of her actually transcending her physical role. Thus the psychological and spiritual affinities between the love-partners are emphasized in almost every instance in which Sharp dramatized the relationship between the sexes.

Quite early there had been the union of John and Lillian described in the third cycle of Sharp's early epic *The Human Inheritance*, where the hero finds the counterpart of his own sensibility in his partner and where their marriage is a union in its true and root sense, a making of one spirit where two existed before. A similar transcendence was one of the conditions for the relationships between Hew and Mona in *The Sport of Chance*, Felix and Sanpriel in *The Children of To-morrow*, Madge and Jim in "Madge o' the Pool," and numerous other minor pairs scattered throughout his poetry. The sexual drama gained in intensity of feeling, as had every other duality, from the circumstances surrounding Sharp's stay in Italy in 1890-91, deriving special benefit from the added piquancy of Sharp's encounter there with his woman-inspirer. Evidence suggests too that Reclus' linking of transvestism with the occult or prophetic personality may have played an extremely important part in assisting Sharp's sexually mixed self-image.[50] For these reasons the strategy of transcendent union was not only acted out in Sharp's pseudonym, but was borne with increasing depth and conviction into the work of Fiona Macleod, where it became that work's single most prevalent theme. There, the affinity of two people for each other is attenuated to an almost utter psychic identity, the love-partner, in other words, becoming merely an aspect of the realization of the self.

Sharp's early biography and criticism had not been without their similar tendency to idealize the sex partnership. Rossetti and Elizabeth Siddal he considered "likes," both, as he described them, possessing a heightened romantic and artistic sensibility.[51] He took an analogous view of the Browning union and went so far as to compare the two marriages in the Rossetti biography. His feelings had not changed by the time of his essay on Browning, where, ever true to the Victorian legend, he reasserted the spiritual union of Robert and Elizabeth Barrett. Shelley, of course, came in for a large share of Sharp's expatiations on the ideal sexual relationship; indeed he was probably the source of many of the terms and much of the vocabulary in which Sharp's own convictions were expressed. In his Shelley biography, Sharp underscored the pathos of Shelley's continual failure to evolve out of the materials of his own life the ideal relationship so frequently glorified in his poetry, especially in such works as "Alastor" and "Epipsychidion," in which the relationship was quite explicitly expressed as a finding of— or a search for—one's "other self." The validity of such a quest, although in life ever destined to end tragically, Sharp never called into question.

Sharp's conviction regarding the possibility of transcendent union was remarkably obstinate. Certainly both Rossetti's and Shelley's experience belied it, but so also did the tragic experience of many of Sharp's own fictional characters. In a poem like "Desolation," Sharp even countered it with an opposite conviction that the human condition was one of inexorable isolation and loneliness.[52] The presence of the contradiction is not in inself unusual. The coexistence of the two views might well be deemed a constant in Victorian literature, so often did the Victorians yearn for realization of the perfect union, so often deplore the tragic incompatibility of one human being with another. Matthew Arnold, of course, provided excellent evidence that one man could straddle such inconsistency and still survive:

> Ah, *love*, let us be true
> To one another! For the world . . .
> Hath really neither joy, nor *love* . . .[53]

Perhaps Arnold's strength lay in his conscious perception and acceptance of this paradox, to the point that it was no longer really a paradox but a distinction between cosmic love and private loyalty.

Sharp, apparently, not only failed to postulate any such resolving distinction but did not even achieve consciousness of the paradox. The cosmos that is inimical to his ideal unions is the same cosmos of which the unions, in their very ideality, seem to be a part. These unions come to their ends not through the agency of the partners themselves, in whose antagonistic egos would lie the true tragic drama of love, but through the power of unearthly forces. The conventional fidelity of Mona and Hew Armitage is blasted by a supernatural villainy, the unconventional liaison of Felix and Sanpriel is blasted by lightning, as was the poignant adolescent passion of the British merchant marine and his nut-brown maid in "Youth's Inheritance." These are not partners divided by their own will or merely by circumstances, but by the nature of matter, the nature of reality, the very nature of the universe which Sharp has devised, whose simultaneous function it is to unite and to divide. The fatal end of the Children of To-morrow is a prefiguration of almost every beautiful union later to be created by Fiona Macleod—Lora and Alistair in *Pharais*, Sorcha and Alan in *The Mountain Lovers*, Ula and Urla,

Dierdre and Naois, Eilidh and Cormac, Ethlenn and Ian, and others too numerous to mention. Death for so many of these star-crossed lovers comes, as it had for Felix and Sanpriel, precisely at the utmost height of their attempt to realize their spiritual harmony—even more, their *identity*—in the physical embrace. We are meant to recognize and to rejoice that such supernatural affinity can only be resolved beyond nature itself. The moment of fusion is the moment of transfiguration, of ascension into a harmony that is not of this world; without such transfiguration, it is implied, such fusion is not possible.

Such an awesome state of affairs in Sharp's imagination securely defines the peculiar outcome of all his efforts at reexamination of the "second self." When similar self-examination is conducted in psychotherapy, it is ordinarily intended to realize the "other self" as part of a whole—in Jung's terms, to integrate the personality. For Sharp, however, the investigation of hidden, repressed, or outlaw motivating forces seems to have proceeded on terms of secrecy from the ordinary self, the public "mask." The result was thus not integration at all, but increased polarization of all the forces constituting the personality. The only possible conclusion may be that Sharp was actually conducting a search for tension rather than for a means of relieving it. He was, of course, a man who had learned to live with the most basic and fundamental paradox: daily he confronted in his own mirror a tall figure in a state of utter physical grace and outward health, nevertheless being wasted by a diseased heart and disordered nerves. Sharp knew he could not hold out long against their erosion. Perhaps that is why "not to save the body and soothe the mind" but instead "to live a briefer while at a higher reach of the spirit and the uplifted if overwrought physical part of one"[54] was for him the only way to conduct his life. Perhaps with a body always tending to total collapse, such tense, concentrated living was the only means of creating the energy by which life in the present was to be sustained and by which art at any time was to be produced.

7

WOMAN

An Unexplored Country

The cautious devices Sharp employed both to express and disguise his second, "female" nature are a good deal less problematical than the causes for his compelling sympathy for women. One of the earliest manifestations of that sympathy was the compassionate response of the sensitive boy he was to his mother's childbearing. That this compassion developed thereafter into a tendency to homosexuality could possibly be inferred from his frequent expressions of disturbing pain at "what a woman can be made to suffer," as well as from his habit of associating the sexual relationship with violent or fatal consequences in his fiction.

Yet the use of such a term as "homosexual" ultimately tells us little and is in fact misleading, owing to the vast spectrum of latent and overt behavior it is made to cover in careless modern usage. In its narrowest sense, "homosexual" has little application to a man who, in his actual relations with men and women, did not at all deviate from the "norm." There was nothing effeminate, certainly, about his appearance or about his apparent capacity to be sexually aroused by women. Indeed, in an overanxiety to put labels on human behavior, it is possible to ignore variations in "norms" occurring from era to era. Of and by itself, an exaggerated sympathy for women was no more an aberration in Sharp than it was in many another mind of the Victorian period. Perhaps at no other time, before or since, has that sympathy been such an essential component of the English, if not the universal, sensibility. At no other time, before or since, was it deemed so necessary to indemnify women for the cultural subjection in which they had so long been held. The few major names that come immediately to mind in this connection—Mill, Meredith, Hardy—are a mere sampling of a sentiment that had extraordinarily wide and international diffusion.

To be able to trace the sources in the history of human sensibility of the social phenomenon called "woman," so distinctly the creation, so persistently the concern of European and American society in the

116

nineteenth century, would be perhaps to possess the key to romanticism itself. John Stuart Mill (who showed his persevering rationalism by referring always to "women" and never to "woman," as magniloquent feminists so commonly did), placed the movement for female emancipation squarely at the door of the larger movement toward widespread political and civil liberty initiated by the revolutionary eighteenth century.[1] Certainly there is something to this: exponents of civil and political rights for women in the United States, for example, were frequently the same people—Thomas Wentworth Higginson, for one—who had worked as abolitionists until what they saw as success left them with new frontiers to conquer.[2] They employed the same language, logic, and rhetoric in defense of female emancipation that had served them in defense of the emancipation of the slaves, drawing frequent parallels between the two causes. Meanwhile, Olive Schreiner, in her treatise on *Woman and Labor*, saw the movement almost entirely as a function of economic change, attributing its atmosphere of war to the difficulties created by an advancing industrial and technical civilization and compounded by the entry of womanpower into the labor market. From her viewpoint, "female parasitism" could no longer be tolerated in a new order of economic society that placed a premium on brain and skill rather than on sheer physical strength.[3]

Yet one can hardly avoid dissatisfaction with these two judgments, however valuable as historical or sociological insights they may otherwise be, when one considers how little they seem to illuminate the artistic—and particularly the literary—representations of women in this period. It might possibly be argued that to the degree romanticism exalted feeling over mind—earthbound associations of sentiment over metaphysics and speculation, things over ideas, intuition over reason—it was implicitly finding woman a metaphor for its outlook. In defense of this possibility is the fact that the feminism of the nineteenth century, at least in some of its varieties, tended to accept the conventional view that made such romantic qualities of feeling and temperament characteristic of woman, dividing only on the question whether or not the qualities were part of the biological make-up of women or were merely culturally ingrained. The equation was responsible for some strange propositions, including, for example, that of Henry Thomas Buckle, the eminent scholar and historian, who argued that the historical role of women had been to supply, by some strange alchemy, the faculty of intuition we find in scientific men of genius![4] Whatever the illogic it served, however, the thriving existence of the equation was itself of singular significance.

But there remain still other possibilities. The exploration of the internal self, of hidden psychological forces, of repressed, secret, or subliminal motives and feelings, all of which tended to unite romantic art with the science of the age, inevitably led to an intensified study of those components of human society least understood and least explored before. It is somewhat commonplace to recognize this motive behind the romantic fascination with children, less common but equally reasonable to see it behind the romantic fascination with women. This may be one cause of the success of Wordsworth's "Lucy" poems, where the poet stands in the face of the combined mysteries of woman and child. Evoking the mystery, rather than solving it, is the task the pre-Victorian poet set himself, and we have thus the obscurely haunting women of Shelley's and Byron's poetry, not to mention the darkly fatal figures of the so-called romantic agony in poets like Keats and Coleridge. Likewise, we have the woman-peopled gardens of art of Tennyson's early poetry—the Hesperides, the soul in the Palace of Art, the Lady of Shalott.

In fiction, women emerge in full force only slightly later than children, and in fullest force among the Victorians, perhaps because the novel began by then to permit the full social articulation of the female personality, mystery notwithstanding. In Dickens, for instance, the boundary between woman and child is often lost, what is good in the child being subsumed into the "good woman" in such figures as Esther Summerson and Little Dorrit. Considering what genuine ignorance there seems to have been (and probably still is) about female sensibility and psychology, especially sexual psychology,[5] it is no surprise that the nineteenth-century novelist found in the principal female character an extraordinary instrument for exploring one of his fundamental themes, the process by which experience is accumulated and maturity acquired. Evidence to support the case is easily rendered by Henry James's Isabel Archer, George Eliot's Dorothea Brooke, among others, and George Meredith's several heroines, Clara, Diana, and so on. Nor is it a surprise that novelists not primarily engaged in the study of the maturing process, but rather perhaps committed to exploring permanent immaturity or steadfastness in the face of change, found enthusiastic audiences for such figures as Catherine Earnshaw, Emma Bovary, Anna Karenina, or Tess Durbeyfield. The innocent woman has become a surrogate for all innocence, woman in love the surrogate for all devotion or dedication, whether wrongly or rightly inspired; and as such the novelistic heroine has retained her importance, as both metaphor and symbol, well into the more sophisticated twentieth century.

Yet perhaps even these possibilities do not exhaust speculation on the cause of the extraordinary nineteenth-century awareness of women. It may well be that one of the prerequisites for the success of the modern middle-class urbanized society is the general softening of its manners, the gradual blurring of sharp distinctions between male and female, and, from the point of view of an earlier masculine-dominated society, its increasing feminization. And just as a rising production of pornography, which represents primarily the fantasy of eternal male-mastery, may be one form of reaction to this loss of male dominion,[6] so too may be the increased sympathy for homosexuality, or at least for what the diehard male would term effeminate sensibility. The so-called novel of sensibility starts here, and it is indebted to those forays into female consciousness begun so intrepidly by Samuel Richardson, and continued through the novel's long and varied career in realism.

Whatever its roots, either in this complex of motives or in others, the feminist revolution found no lack of men in all fields and disciplines, in this respect no different from Sharp, willing to enlist themselves in its support. At their deepest, they were capable of virtually suffering the sufferings of women—flagellating themselves as they flagellated their society with recriminations against the intolerable "subjection" to which women had been submitted. More commonly they studied them, always with sympathy, often with celebration, lending themselves doggedly to the task of making women self-aware.

Journalistic and pamphlet literature, particularly in the eighties, shows how much the Victorian phase of this revolution had accomplished by way of filling the gaps in previous woman-knowledge. Every traditional view of the female role and the sexual relationship, from physical to metaphysical, was being submitted to total reexamination and reevaluation. A few titles of contemporary articles and pamphlets are amply suggestive: "Womanhood in Its Eternal Aspect," *The Position of the Mother in the Family in Its Legal and Scientific Aspects, The Physiology of Woman, Women and Marriage; or Evolution in Sex, Marriage*

119

and Parentage; or the Reproductive Element in Man as a Means to his Elevation and Happiness,[7] and so on.

Havelock Ellis, who began his long and controversial career as a sociologist of sex in the 1880's, figured largely in this enterprise of woman-consciousness. Rhys's statement in Everyman Remembers that as for Ellis, "a better foil to Fiona Macleod could not have been invented," seems odd in the light of their similarly avant-garde attitudes and ideologies. Ellis was in the eighties and nineties editor of the Contemporary Science series, another of those characteristic late-Victorian publishing ventures into popularization that in itself links him with Sharp. In his volume The New Spirit (1890), moreover, Ellis proved himself not only an art and culture critic of some dimensions but also a man in complete sympathy with many of the neo-romantic principles characterizing the artistic circles in which Sharp moved, including their antagonism to contemporary social and artistic convention, their cosmopolitanism, and, not least, their fierce championing of women. In an article in the Westminster Review (October 1887) called "The Changing Status of Women," he daringly asserted that "the destiny of the race rests with women" and stood by Walt Whitman's statement that "the sole avenue and means to a reconstructed society depended . . . on a new birth, elevation, expansion, invigoration of women."[8] Even Sharp's later associates in the Edinburgh Celtic movement, Patrick Geddes and J. Arthur Thompson, in their Evolution of Sex, admitted the sociological consequences of their biological discoveries. "The social order," they proclaimed with splendid optimism, "will clear itself, as it comes more in touch with biology." For biology had, they certified, determined beyond a shadow of doubt that women were the agents through whom "altruism, patience, affection, intuition, subtlety, feeling, and memory" found their way into society.[9] There could hardly be a better précis of the principles behind the use of the woman in many later British novels, where she often functions as the vehicle and repository of these essential creative or regenerative powers.

This was the positive side of the movement, with its spirit of comprehensive vitalism. On the other side, and perhaps equally capable of stirring extraordinary compassion in a man like Sharp, was the literature that bore witness to woman's suffering. The same edition of the National Review (March 1887) that carried one of Sharp's essays on

Rossetti contained another, signed in sibylline fashion by "A Woman," which viciously indicted society for its oppression of women throughout history and bitterly and graphically evoked the horrors of childbearing.[10] Sharp could hardly have missed this article or many another like it. One may safely guess that such pieces impressed him greatly, given his sensitivity to the physical aspect of the female role, already demonstrated in a poem like "Motherhood."

Though preoccupied with the "woman problem," Sharp was reluctant to involve himself outside of his fiction or poetry in the controversy surrounding women's demand for rights. He had stated the conviction quite early that "people won't be preached to. Truth can be inculcated far better by inference, by suggestion."[11] This rule, set up at the age of twenty, he lived by remarkably well: no controversial social question ever engaged his explicit support in any tract or article, and his outright concern with the marriage question and with the reevaluation of the sexual relationship in the terms developed by his contemporaries was limited almost entirely to his early fiction and his biography of Shelley (1887). It seems a curious restraint for him to have exercised upon his passion for protest, nevertheless, for his wife claims that he took an "active interest" in "movements of the day."[12] Moreover, in later and one would assume wiser years, he gave unqualified praise to William Morris for his sense of social responsibility, his dedication to direct social action, and his efforts to give himself the technical education necessary for remedying "the plight of the poor."[13]

From the sheer practical standpoint, perhaps, Sharp's reluctance to propagandize, at least on the issue of women's legal and political rights, need not be questionable. He was literally surrounded by women's champions actively and vociferously engaged in their cause. There was Olive Schreiner, for one, whose novel *The Story of an African Farm* (1883) was one of the earliest expressions of the new feminism to come from a woman (though interestingly published under the male pseudonym Ralph Iron). Another was the frontline feminist Mona Caird, whose "brave articles" (as Elizabeth Sharp called them) on the legal position of women were published in various periodicals in the late eighties and were eventually incorporated into the controversial book *The Morality of Marriage*.[14] Both Schreiner and Caird were subtle and ironic thinkers and writers of considerable power and craft. Even Mill's influential study of female subjection pales beside the erudition and polemical skill of such women. To their influence Sharp must have owed many of the ideas expressed in his fiction on what constituted an unhappy marriage, and even perhaps some of his opinions on how a happy union could be created without conventional sanction. An example of this thesis and antithesis, it may be recalled, appeared in *The Children of To-morrow*, where Felix Dane was unhappily married to a typical female parasite before he met his true spiritual partner. In that volume, Sharp asserted not only the stifling mutual repression of the Dane's union, but its actual immorality. Although Dane's wife Lydia, equally the victim of their error, was not treated with great sympathy, there was a flicker of pathos in her compelling need for respectability, something which Schreiner and Caird might well have assisted Sharp in understanding. His failure to enlarge upon Lydia's problem may be explained by his desire to focus in this novel upon the artist as the especial victim of conventional social values, and by his determination to reserve particular sympathy for the "other woman," Sanpriel, not only a woman but an artist in her own right. In terms of the marriage polemic, it is her legally unsanctioned relationship with Dane that represents the true morality—a morality, however, not completely defined by its challenge of marriage convention. After Lydia dies and Felix Dane is free to remarry, he does propose to Sanpriel. She rejects his proposal only on the grounds that her devotion to the cause of the Jews is incompatible with a contract of marriage to a Christian. The alternative, Dane's adoption of Judaism, is also rejected, as representing an equally damaging sacrifice of his integrity, and the two have agreed, just before the fatal lightning strikes, to live together without benefit of ceremony, despite the fact that no legal or social obstacle stands in the way of its performance.

"Madge o' the Pool" may likewise be considered a treatise opposing the commonly-accepted notion of marriage, in the sympathetic interpretation it gives to Madge's unwillingness to put a worldly seal on a love she deems too fine for the sordid place she takes the world to be. "The girl, in fact, was one of those rare creatures to whom the thing was everything, and the symbol of no moment."[15]

Of course neither of these works represents more than a restatement of the current feministic opinions regarding marriage and the spiritual richness of woman. But *The Children of To-morrow* was written and published, and "Madge o' the Pool" largely composed, though not published, before the Sharps's trip to Italy in 1890. It is only after that trip that two remarkable shifts in emphasis appear in Sharp's work. One of these, occurring in his more realistic fiction, is a resolution of the conflict posed until then between marriage on the one hand and true love on the other. This later synthetic view admits loyalty as a standard for evaluating and defending a marriage soured or gone stale. It may seem more felt, more real, than Sharp's previous stance simply, perhaps, because it is more mature—as though, "the young effects defunct," he had graduated from a purely romantic notion of love defiant. Indeed, appearing as it does in so few works, it would be of minor interest in itself were it not owing to the other shift in emphasis taking place at this same stage of his development. Simultaneously, Sharp began to express that theme upon which analyses of his psychology have so often foundered—the overwhelming compassion for women represented by the staggering number of repetitions of miscarriages and stillbirths, and of women suffering terrible agonies in labor, sometimes premature labor, and often dying as a result. At the same time he began to formulate, through the agency of the woman "friend" to whom he and his wife repeatedly stated his debt for inspiration, the female literary identity that came to be known as Fiona Macleod. It is only after 1891 that the woman's nature is described as living in "dual unity" with his own, only then that the effects of his boyhood experiences of childbirth and of his reading on the subject of woman's suffering seem to have taken total hold of his sensibility and emerged in the way that has made him so problematical a figure, so strongly transcending the compassion of the other male "feminists" who were his contemporaries.

It would seem only natural, then, to look to Sharp's activities during this period of the early nineties for the immediate causes that turned a sensitivity "normal" for his time into an extraordinary one for any time.

Many factors, some slow-working, with their roots in preceding years, some sudden, all complex, went into the making of Sharp's new strategy with regard to woman and marriage. His own marriage in 1884, though a satisfactory and even a happy one from all appearances, had nevertheless been subjected between then and 1890 to many kinds of strain. Childlessness was one. Sharp seems to have loved children; witness his editorship of the Young Folks' Paper[16] and his later creation of a book of Celtic tales for children (tenderly dedicated to Mona Caird's young daughter).[17] And he seems also to have longed for

123

children of his own, as a poem entitled "The Unborn Child" amply reveals in its poignant expression of the yearning of would-be parents for the child of their union.[18]

But equally demoralizing (and perhaps an effective cause of the Sharps's failure to have children) must have been the constantly precarious state of Sharp's health. The weakness of his rheumatic heart and the hypertensity of his nervous system, though belied by his appearance of robust good health and Viking strength, must for that same reason have offered frequent temptation to abuse. Many periods of total nervous and physical prostration are recorded in the *Memoir*, gradually becoming more lengthy in their demands for recuperative time and energy. It was partly for his health, it may be remembered, that he had been sent to Australia in 1876. He became seriously ill again in 1886 when, according to his wife, he underwent his first so-called "psychic experiences" in a debilitated and bed-ridden state.[19] Thereafter he was under dire strictures not to exhaust himself unduly. The potential threat that existed in his uncertain health and his restless urge for travel working reciprocally upon one another, and putting a terrible strain upon the Sharps's meager financial resources, must have demanded from Elizabeth a stupendous capacity for wifely endurance.

Ironically, the trip to Italy, so thoughtfully planned as a means of reviving their depressed spirits, may merely have aggravated Elizabeth's difficulties by supplying the conditions for her husband's catastrophic meeting with the "other woman." The grounds for this perilous possibility are not entirely conjectural. Sharp admitted his own frailty, observing in his journal, after conferring with Blanche Willis Howard on their projected novel, that he was near to falling in love with her and cautioning himself to "be on guard against my too susceptible self."[20] The important "other woman" in Sharp's life at the time, however, was not Miss Howard but the "friend" of such frequent mention. Who she was is not difficult to determine. In one of the essays written after Sharp's death in an attempt to explain the "Fiona Macleod mystery," Richard Le Gallienne, speaking of the circumstances that might have had causal connection with the use of the female pseudonym, cannily directed his readers to the *Memoir*. He pieced together Elizabeth's discreet revelations and paraphrased the following passage from volume II: "Though this newer phase of his work [i.e., Fiona Macleod] was at no time a result of collaboration, as certain of his critics have suggested, he was deeply conscious of his indebtedness to [the] . . . friend [who had provided] the desired incentive towards a true expression of himself, in [her] stimulus and sympathetic understanding."[21] He pointed to the further clue in Elizabeth's describing this friend as the person to whom Sharp "dedicated the first of the books published under his pseudonym."[22] This was *Pharais*, published in 1894.

For one so close a friend of the Sharps, whose name is juxtaposed with this mysterious lady's in one of Mrs. Sharp's Sunday guest-lists, Le Gallienne appears strikingly disingenuous in his pedantic efforts to trace the identity of the woman in Rome. Had it merely been a literary influence he was uncovering, one is tempted to feel he would not have been so cautious. Even a second-rate sleuth would scarcely have stopped at the "bewildering" (Le Gallienne's own adjective) initials "E.W.R." contained in the dedication to *Pharais*, for the name behind the initials is easily located in the passage from the *Memoir* dealing with Sharp's sojourn in Rome, 1890-91. There, says Elizabeth, "Mrs. [Edith] Wingate Rinder joined us for three weeks, and with her my husband greatly enjoyed long walks over the Campagna and expeditions to little neighboring hill towns."[23]

But this is all mere intrigue beside Sharp's own declaration, "in a letter of instructions, written before he went to America in 1896, concerning his wishes in the event of his death," that it was "to her," that is, Mrs. Rinder, "I owe my development as 'Fiona Macleod,'" that "without her there would have been no 'Fiona Macleod.'"[24] Evidence in the *Sospiri di Roma* indicates that "without her" neither might several of those poems have been written. *Pharais* may have been the first of the Fiona Macleod writings dedicated to Mrs. Rinder, but it was not the first of Sharp's. "A Winter Evening," which Elizabeth described as one of the first of the *Sospiri* to be composed in Italy, was explicitly dedicated to E.W.R. It is a tempestuous piece, certainly, and contains foreboding of "strange joy or strange sorrow," but beyond that is really too cryptic to supply any reason for the dedication. But there are two poems dedicated thus: "To ———." They are the Prologue and Epilogue and are openly love poems. The first speaks of "a flower of love" that sprang from the heart of a poet who loved a lady on the hills of Tusculum, the flower representing a promise of "deathless joy." The Epilogue, subtitled "Il Bosco Sacro" (The Sacred Wood), is an even more effusively sexual lyric. In it the poet relives the "passion and pain" of rapture experienced in a wooded grove somewhere in the Campagna.[25] Whether or not the "passion and pain" have any connection with the "strange joy or strange sorrow" of "A Winter Evening" is difficult to say. Either these are totally factitious love rhapsodies, in which case the mysterious dedications are gratuitous, or they are the results of an attempt on the poet's part to be both gallant and cautious about a romance he had actually experienced "on the hills of Tusculum." If it is the latter, Mrs. Rinder is the only available candidate, for no one else is mentioned in the Memoir as having accompanied him alone on his excursions through the Roman Campagna, not even Elizabeth herself.

Moreover, Mrs. Rinder is the only "other woman" with whom Sharp may be linked in any significant way thereafter. That link is provided by his two most prevalent literary concerns after his return from Italy, the impressionist drama, especially Maeterlinck and the others of the Belgian school, and the Scoto-Celtic outburst represented by the Celtic studies at the University of Edinburgh and by the publication of the Evergreen (1895-96) and the Celtic Library series. The latter included a good deal of the work of Fiona Macleod, as well as Edith Rinder's translations of Breton folktales, entitled The Shadow of Arvor (1896). Sharp's letters from this period indicate that he made several special appeals to Patrick Geddes, the financial as well as spiritual force behind the Edinburgh movement, to have the Celtic Library include such Breton translations and also translations from the Belgians. In both these areas he had Mrs. Rinder in mind as translator.[26] Beyond these good offices, he also gave her the sub-editorship of a volume in the Canterbury Poets series, Poems and Lyrics of Nature, which was appropriately dedicated "To W.S."[27]

But these facts are scarcely sufficient basis for describing with any certainty the bounds of the liaison between Sharp and Edith Rinder. Elizabeth tells us only that the "friend" of whom she cryptically spoke, with her "beauty," her "strong sense of life and of the joy of life," her "keen intuition and mental alertness," stood for him "as a symbol of the heroic women of Greek and Celtic days."[28] What Elizabeth does not touch is the nature of the exchange that made these insights possible and ultimately provided the inspiration for Fiona Macleod. It is even possible to believe her when she says that whenever Sharp wrote

126

the pronoun "we" into his letters from Scotland during the mid-nineties, he intended it to mean "himself in his dual capacity."[29] He was a sufficient illusionist to do so, and it is barely a step from this device to the letters she tells us Sharp wrote to himself "in his dual capacity." Her technique of limiting herself to explaining Sharp's motives almost strictly in terms of conscious, voluntary motives, and avoiding discussions of normal human weaknesses—trials, mistakes, discomfitures, the accidents of outside experience in general—comes near to being impenetrable.

It is quite possible, of course, that the secrecy and evasion in which Elizabeth shrouded the Sharp-Rinder relationship was motivated not by a desire to hush a scandal, but by the desire to prevent one from being inferred where none existed. If that is the case then one can only lament, with the wisdom of hindsight, that her (and probably Edith Rinder's) excruciating exercise of caution was all but completely vain. Le Gallienne's article, written after the Memoir, was clearly designed to sensationalize by innuendo. And Ernest Rhys, later on, went even further than Le Gallienne, quoting alleged conversations in which Sharp hinted of secret trysts with his woman-inspirer.[30] But where Elizabeth Sharp misjudged her readers, Rhys and Le Gallienne perhaps more seriously misjudged the man. Sharp was fully capable of sensual and even sexual rhapsodizing over a strong emotional affinity, unrealized physically. For a man of his emotional tinder, such an affinity could have supplied flame enough to make a substantial change in his life. Indeed, the very fact that Edith Rinder was unattainable might have functioned to exaggerate his passion.[31] The evidence also suggests that Mrs. Rinder was of the same stuff as Sharp, for it was her flame that seems to have ignited him, spiritually if not otherwise. At any rate, their relationship appears to have yielded nothing overt beyond Fiona Macleod and a few French translations, stuff for dull scandal indeed. The Sharps and the Rinders remained close friends, and Frank Rinder, Edith's husband, wrote a glowing tribute to Sharp when he died.[32]

The effect this relationship may have had on Elizabeth's psychology—and therefore indirectly on Sharp's—would, of course, be every bit as important as its direct effects on Sharp and Mrs. Rinder. It is very difficult to believe that, even if temporarily, Elizabeth was not in some way perturbed by it, no matter how innocent it may have been. One can hardly imagine her contemplating in utter detachment her husband's passion for another woman—even if it were an imaginative passion only—and intruding absolutely no claims of self. Yet even supposing that Edith Rinder had taken care to spare her, Elizabeth, in no more than her role as second mother to Sharp, would have been disturbed by the strain he suffered sustaining two completely separate bodies of literary production. It must be admitted here, of course, that evidence of any marital difficulty is extremely circumstantial. Although Sharp was, between flying stops to London, suffering a more than ordinary siege of wanderlust during the year following the Italian trip, Elizabeth describes his mood as "exultant" and, as usual, does not describe her own. Sharp, on his travels, wrote lengthy epistolary calendars to his friends, projecting, among other things, various plans for meeting with his wife—in Paris, in Scotland, in Sicily.[33] "Regretfully," says Elizabeth, the "wanderings" together through Scotland and to Sicily "had to be postponed. During the summer of 1892, Sharp went for a time to Loch Goil with a friend [unnamed], and I went to Bayreuth." The explanation offered for this postponement was the discovery of a "pleasant cottage" in Sussex.[34] At the summer's end Elizabeth's probable hopes for some kind of settled life were at last realized, and they established themselves in that "pleasant cottage" at Phenice Croft, Rudgwick, for two entire years, perhaps a record for Sharp's career.

The few of Sharp's letters quoted by the *Memoir* from the period preceding the Phenice Croft episode, for Sharp a time of frenzied exhilaration, are newsy and superficial; surviving letters to his wife after Phenice Croft (from 1895 on) are thoroughly warm and devoted. These display no evidence whatsoever that a strain in their affections resulted from any of the causes so far delineated. And yet one of Sharp's letters quoted by the *Memoir*, which Mrs. Sharp has dated 1898, does suggest that the Sharps had undergone some form of adjustment in their relationship, and seems to touch on some past alienation of spirit for which no previous explanation had been given:

> Yes, in essentials, we are all at one. We have both learned and unlearned so much, and we have come to see that we are wrought mysteriously by forces beyond ourselves, but in so seeing we know that there is a great and deep love that conquers even disillusion and disappointment . . .

128

The hiatus here is Elizabeth's. The letter goes on:

> Not all the wishing, not all the dreaming, not all the will and hope and prayer we can summon can alter that within us which is stronger than ourselves. This is a hard lesson to learn for all of us, and most for a woman.

Is Sharp referring perhaps to an earlier reluctance on Elizabeth's part to accept some aspect of the status quo?

> We are brought up within such an atmosphere of conventional untruth to life that most people never perceive the hopeless futility in the arbitrary ideals which are imposed upon us—and the result for the deeper endless tragic miscarriage of love peace and hope. But, fortunately, those of us who to our own suffering *do* see only too clearly, can still strike out a nobler ideal—one that does not shrink from the deepest responsibilities and yet can so widen and deepen the heart and spirit with love that what else would be irremediable pain can be transmuted into hope, into peace, and even into joy.[35]

Here, quite clearly, is evidence of the synthesizing of a new relationship on a principle of "responsibility" after the disillusioning destruction of an earlier one by some internal strife. The cause of the "suffering" of which Sharp speaks is vaguely alluded to:

> People talk much of this and that frailty or this or that circumstance as being among the commonest disintegrants of happiness. But far more fatal for many of us is that supreme disintegrant, the Tyranny of Love—the love which is forever demanding *as its due* that which is wholly independent of bonds.[36]

Meredith had already written a satisfactory marginal note upon these remarks: "We are betrayed by what is false within." Indeed this personal conversion on Sharp's part was no doubt largely responsible for his statement in 1899 that Meredith's *Modern Love* and Rossetti's *House of Life*, both dealing with the anguish of love disintegrated, were "among the finest legacies of poetic genius left to us in the latter half of the nineteenth century."[37]

As Sharp's letter to his wife continues, the autobiography implicit in its generalizations is obvious:

> We are taught such hopeless lies, and so men and women start life with ideals which seem fair, but are radically consumptive: ideals

that are not only bound to perish, but that could not survive. The man of fifty who could be the same as he was at twenty is simply a man whose mental and spiritual life stopped short when he was yet a youth. The woman of forty who could have the same outlook in life as the girl of 19 or 20 would never have been other than one ignominiously deceived or hopelessly self-sophisticated. This ought not to be—but it must be as long as young men and women are fed mentally and spiritually upon the foolish and cowardly lies of a false and corrupt conventionalism . . . Some can never learn that their unhappiness is the result, not of the falling short of others, but of the falsity of those ideals which they had so cherished—and while others learn first strength to endure the transmutations, and then power to weld these to far nobler and finer uses and ends—for both there is suffering. Yet . . . often, Sorrow is our best ally.[38]

It is a sane letter, with little hint of the remorse of a man who feels himself partly to blame for the misunderstanding. But it seems also to be a reply to a letter from Elizabeth, and it could well have been the outcome of a long period during which she had expressed sympathy for her husband's troubled sense of guilt and a willingness to understand the cause of what she had described in the Sharp of the middle and later nineties as "suffering for him and anxiety for me."[39]

However equivocal this complex series of events in the Sharps' marriage, they may explain the appearance of a theme of infidelity in Sharp's fiction between 1891 and 1894 that is very different from the infidelity treated in The Children of To-morrow. There is little reason to doubt that Sharp meant, in that novel and in "Madge," to decry the marriage bond only insofar as it put strictures upon the marriage of true minds, and enough sheer bravado in both these tales reassures the motive-hunting critic that they did not originate from tensions existing in Sharp's own marriage. Where they touched on the marriage issue they were more social diatribes à la Caird than autobiographical romans à clef. But in the epistolary novel written with Blanche Willis Howard, A Fellowe and His Wife (1892), comes the first instance of Sharp's representing the bond of matrimony as one of honor rather than slavery, and suggesting that the power of honor itself can lend to married people strength to achieve a new and higher level of harmony and compatibility.

The story concerns a newly-married young woman who has convinced

Sketches and Studies
from the unachievable
"Book of Woman"

The Comedy of Woman :
Sketches and Studies
"One of the principal occupations of men is to divine women."
Lacretelle .

"There will always remain something to be said of woman, as
long as there is one on the earth."
Bouffless .

"When one writes of Woman, he must reserve the right to
laugh at his ideas of the day before."
A. Ricard .

1 . The Hedonist . . . . (woman, conceiving making pleasure her one aim)
2 . Madge o' the Pool . . . . . . (one fine side of the Barbaric in contemp. life)
3 . The Eurasian . . . . (a kind of ambitious Zora)
4 . The Bondager . . . . (The brutal side of the Barbaric in contemp. life)
5 . The Dancer . . . . . . (girl becomes actress : goes mad on the stage : heredity)
6 . From the Loom of Love . . . . (The woman who gladly forfeits all in passion and imperils all)
7 . The Beauty of the World . . . . (The Beauty of Passion)
8 . Lydia . . . . (The woman in love with herself)
9 . Desirée . . . . (The child of the woman who believed (what had conceived) a la Tom Gordon)
10 . The Bride of God . . . . (Religious mania)
11 . The Fruit of Eden . . . . . (The beauty of maternity)
12 . Motherhood . . . . . (The Passionate . . . . craving for maternity)
13 . Spindrift . . . . . (The wreckage of honour)
14 . Aftermath . . . . . (a letter to my first born)
15 . The Outcome of it all . . . . . (The diary of Althaea Proudfoot)

A manuscript page from the Sharp collection in the National Library of
Scotland outlining what Sharp hopelessly characterizes as "the unachievable
'Book of Woman.'" "Madge o' the Pool" is the only finished and published
story recognizable by title or description. The other notes clearly reflect
Sharp's sense of women's complexity and inexhaustibility as subjects of
imaginative literature.

William Sharp, 1903

Elizabeth Sharp, 1909

William Sharp in his study, about 1900

Castello di Maniace, near Taormina, Sicily, with Mount Etna in the back-
ground, where Sharp spent the winters of 1902-1905 as the guest of the
Duke of Bronte. He died there in December 1905 and is buried beneath a
Celtic cross in a nearby grove.

her husband to allow her to go to Rome alone in order to pursue her study of sculpture, assuring him that such a liberty is only the truest expression of their equality and fraternity. While in Rome, unfortunately, she permits herself to get entangled in an extramarital affair. At the crucial moment, however, she discovers her lover's betrayal of another woman, calls off their elopement, and breaks completely with him. Overcome with guilt and self-recrimination at her violation of her husband's trust, she attempts to forestall his wrath by nobly offering to separate from him. Equally noble, he forgives her completely and draws her tenderly back to his embrace. Though the infidelity is the woman's, it is to be noted that the man in this collaborative enterprise wrote the woman's part—in this case, in other words, Sharp was not the "fellowe" but the wife.

Frau von Teuffel's contribution to this novel and to its marriage problem ought not, of course, to be neglected. She may well have been the model for the wife with artistic propensities, and her husband, Julius von Teuffel, the original for the understanding husband, for von Teuffel has been elsewhere described as encouraging his wife in her literary career.[40] But from there on one can be fairly assured Sharp's invention took over. The "wife" of his conception is virtually obsessed with duality and role-playing. She confesses in her letters to a vague but irresistible sense of slipping in and out of personalities, and all her doubts surrounding her marriage rest ultimately on the notion that her mercurial artistic nature can be satisfied by her husband in only one of its aspects, leaving the remainder restless and unfulfilled. Clearly at work is the "man-artist" dichotomy so frequently seen in Sharp's biographies, but here it is offered as an explanation of instability in marriage and the craving of other partners.[41] This change in application might easily have emerged from Sharp's recent discovery about himself.

A Fellowe and His Wife was written in 1891. Between 1892 and 1894, Sharp wrote many of a large group of stories published several years later under two titles, The Gipsy Christ and Other Tales (1895), and Ecce Puella and Other Prose Imaginings (1896). Two of the stories, "The Lady in Hosea" from the first volume and "The Birth, Death, and Resurrection of a Tear" from the second, are especially appropriate here. Both concern marital infidelity, in one case actual and in the other a truancy of spirit, and both are resolved by the reconciliation of the marriage partners in a manner similar to that of

131

A Fellowe and His Wife. The plot of "The Lady in Hosea" follows the novel's outline very closely—wifely infidelity, disillusion with the lover, and return to the husband's bosom. The triteness of its episodes, as so frequently with Sharp, is in sad contrast with its often bold and sensitive revelations of character, particularly in the case of the lover, who cuts a rather pathetic and not wholly villainous figure as the conscience-salving roué. The woman scorned by this lover, suggestive in her beguiled romanticism of Madame Bovary, has her pathos too, but also a capacity for wisdom that is truer perhaps to Sharp's sense of female dignity than to nature. This careful delineation of mixed motives, offering a range of alternative courses of action to the characters, is new to Sharp's fiction in this period.

More interesting, however, both in concept and treatment, is the relationship described in "The Birth, Death, and Resurrection of a Tear." Its essential situation somewhat parallels that of Felix Dane and his wife in *The Children of To-morrow,* but its resolution is significantly different. The husband, through whose stream-of-consciousness the story is told, has been alienated from his wife by her coldness. At the critical moment when he is prepared to reject her, he discovers that her coldness has merely been a device for self-protection and that it disguises a love she could not express. That critical moment for him is a moment of weakness for her. A tear she allows to fall is the simple revelation he needs that beneath her glacial reserve is imprisoned the warm, ideal woman he had sought, and of whom he had had, during the wanderings of his fancy, a fleeting vision. It is quite conceivable that Sharp found in his own wife the source of this gallant inspiration, and in their own process of "birth, death, and resurrection" the inspiration for the process outlined in the title.

Although these stories are not followed by other works concentrating on marriage, the bulk of Sharp's writings after 1891 evince a prevailing concern that may reflect in another very important way the circumstances surrounding his experiences with women. The concern was to find some means of sympathetically expressing, more often than not from the viewpoint of a woman, the nature of women's sufferings and humiliations. There is a possibility that Sharp's anguished preoccupation with suffering in childbirth may have had its direct and immediate source in some miscarried attempts of his wife to have children. Even if this is not so, however, the births of both Mona Caird's and Edith

Rinder's daughters in the early nineties would have provided sufficient substitute. At any rate, Sharp linked the three together when, in a letter to his wife during the composition of Fiona Macleod's "Rune of the Sorrow of Women" in 1896, he confessed that "you, Mona, Edith, and others swam into my brain."[42]

The cause or causes of the dramatic increase in the force and passion of Sharp's concern with the suffering of women may only be conjectured. But dramatic the increase certainly was. His early poem "Motherhood" (1882) had been a relatively impersonal study of childbirth as it revealed evolutionary development. Mona in *The Sport of Chance* (1887) delivers her child prematurely, but there is no hint of any difficulties in labor—so standard in Sharp's later fiction—and the child Lora survives remarkably well. "Madge o' the Pool" provides the first instance of stillbirth, and even there the story's delayed publication may well indicate a later hand in the introduction of that event.

The earliest authentic portent of Sharp's darker vision of womanhood comes in 1889, in "Fragments from the Lost Journals of Piero di Cosimo." Piero reflects ominously upon a woman he is painting: "She was with child, and oft looked suddenly at naught, in a wild trouble, as I have seen a white hart do at the falling echo of a far-off baying hound." And he cries out, "Ah! this terrible brutality of motherhood. It is a device of nature to humiliate the soul, of which she is jealous unto death. She has conveyed it in a rainbow, as a Borgia might convey a debilitating slow-killing poison in an exquisite rose."[43] By 1891 Sharp was capable of developing this hint of the "brutality of motherhood" into the copious and explicit detail of "The Birth of a Soul," one of the "psychic dramas" later included in *Vistas* (1894). The entire action of this drama takes place in a woman's bedchamber during the convulsive agonies of her labor. Dying as her child is born, the mother utters this pitiful exclamation: "O God, may the child that is within me not be a woman-child, so that she may never know the bitterness of shame and all the heritage of woman's woe."[44] From there on the theme is taken over by Fiona Macleod, and her roster of suffering women is painfully long. Perhaps it is significant that *Green Fire*, published in 1896 as Fiona Macleod's third novel, contains the only instance of a wife's losing her first child but having her second survive. Was this a fresh expression of hope on Sharp's part that was unfortunately not to see fulfillment?

But *Green Fire* provides more than an unusual instance of the theme of compassionate identification with woman, for in it Sharp gives a strikingly clear illustration of the theme of divided loyalties in love, exploring that theme as had William Sharp's realistic fiction and resolving it with a reconciliation in marriage. *Green Fire*, perhaps more than any other single work, suggests the complex, reciprocal interplay of Sharp's strangely contrary impulses to truancy and compassion. Like the "wife" of *A Fellow and His Wife*, the hero of *Green Fire* is compelled by opposing forces in his personality to seek fulfillment in more than one partner. In a letter written in 1896, Sharp spoke of the two women entangled thus in Alan's fortunes, Ynys, his betrothed, and Annaik, his "woman": "Annaik *is* the real human magnet. Ynys is an idealised type, what I mean by Ideala or Esclarmoundo, but she did not take hold of me like Annaik . . . Annaik has for me a strange and deep attraction: and I am sure the abiding personal interest is in her."[45] The characterizations of both Alan and the earlier "wife" are reminiscent of Shelley's "Epipsychidion."[46] The *Memoir* also notes that Sharp was reading Restif de la Bretonne's autobiography during this period of reappraisal of "the sexual morale." If so, he may have been culling some of his material from Restif's account of his own multiplied affections, based on a theory of shared ideality or "transfusion of souls," which supplies a striking analogy for Alan's divided loyalties.

But Sharp had his own divided loyalties too. By the time of *Green Fire* in 1896, Sharp was already deeply in literary debt to Edith Rinder—and perhaps deeply in love with her too; it seems unlikely, at least, that his "susceptible self" impassively acknowledged the "beauty," "strong sense of life and the joy of life," and "mental alertness" of which Mrs. Sharp later spoke. But it is equally unlikely that his love for Edith could entirely obscure the debt for inspiration he owed to the woman who had received his first love poems and waited nine long years to marry him. In fact, Elizabeth's strength and capacity for sacrifice were formidable. The delights of travel could scarcely have been full compensation for a married life consisting of the rigors of Victorian tourism when she accompanied her husband, the solitude of home life when she did not, and the strain of nursing and breadwinning when Sharp was ill and unable to work. She herself gave only the barest hint of how she felt. "To me," she recalls in the *Memoir*, "he came for sympathy in his work and difficulties and to others he went for gaiety and diversion."[47]

Some of the mystery of Sharp's split literary personality is entangled in this complicated web of divided feelings. Loving two women, but like Alan of *Green Fire* sure of his loyalty to the woman he had loved first, Sharp may well have sought to adjust to his emotional fracture by dividing the allegiances of his imagination, giving them separate representation in the public images of William Sharp and Fiona Macleod. For Edith Rinder, Fiona Macleod, because Edith Rinder embodied all the fullness of his new creative life and had awakened in him a Celtic enthusiasm he had not known himself capable of feeling. It was she who had seen him as the re-maker of Scottish legend, she who had inspired him and perhaps collaborated in the conception, if not the execution, of his Celtic work. But William Sharp, nursed by "Lill" through a career of potboiling to a modest, if dandyish artistic success, in a real sense belonged to her and could not also belong to someone else. Sharp seems to have made his conciliation through pseudonym, a device comfortingly familiar, since the *Pagan Review*, for reconciling the dilemmas of opposing forces within himself. Edith Rinder, for her part, appears to have contented herself, like the Thea of Ibsen's *Hedda Gabler*, with a form of spiritual wifehood.[48]

Sharp's choice of a female pseudonym, however, requires some further analysis, and may hinge upon another aspect of his emotional life. He had long been aware of possessing unusual insight into the psychology of women and was increasingly conscious, as he moved into his new and freer imaginative life, of the extraordinary character of his identification with them. Edith Rinder's inspiration at this critical moment was an explosive reagent. Experiencing that special mystic affinity with her that he was inclined to attribute to truly kindred souls in his work, Sharp may well have thought at times that he shared one personality with her. The theory then in vogue among some men and women of his artistic generation that the prophetic artist was hermaphroditic by nature would have sealed his determination to become Fiona Macleod, had he required anything more to seal it.

But such ideal resolutions never entirely make over reality, and the reality of Elizabeth's suffering and of his desire to sustain their marriage may still have existed. This might explain the depression, the anxiety, the guilt that expressed themselves in a hypersensivity to the plight of woman, primarily in the mother-role, and particularly in the work of Fiona Macleod, where woman is symbol of patience and forbearance, type of the sufferer, suffering in the getting of love, suffering in the losing of it, suffering in childbirth—yet devoted, helping, inspiring. Moreover, Fiona Macleod's work in this vein represented a mere fraction of all Sharp had hoped to write. Among his notes were plans for a novel, *The Woman of Thirty*, a collection of short stories, *The Comedy of Woman* (planned to be sent forth, significantly, under the name of H. P. Siwaärmill), and a dramatic version of *Anna Karenina*.[49]

The testimony of some of the people to whom Sharp spoke of the "mystery" of Fiona Macleod would lead one to conclude that Sharp grew to believe—or to think he believed—a woman's nature really dwelt within him, whether by possession or some other means he never clearly specified. His reading in contemporary anthropology and folklore confirming the sexual duality of the seer; his strong sympathy with the literature of extraordinarily heightened sensibility (a French literary tradition since Rousseau, and exemplified by Maeterlinck, Loti, Coppée, Bourget, and others), characterized by an extreme poignancy, and affecting the entire early Celtic movement; his identification with the arguments and feelings of the strong-minded and sensitive women around him—all of these must have led him to exaggerate his claims to a special understanding of women.

He was, moreover, given in life as well as in fiction to attributing fixed ideas of any sort to fatal or occult motives. What he failed to see, perhaps, was that to take away the principle of unearthly mystery from the cause did not necessarily impinge upon the pathos and humanity of the effect. Suffering need not be preordained to be suffering, nor joy cut down by fate to evoke the sense of loss. Like many people, he possessed a tender and vulnerable inner life which had, because of his childhood and later accidents of experience, become associated with womanhood. What he needed more than others usually do, perhaps, was to impose upon that inner life a secrecy that could give him both the joy of possessing a personal, inviolable domain and the terror of its being under constant threat of exposure. It was more important to the quality of his inner life, however, that in childhood it had been victimized—perhaps even terrorized—and in manhood it had accreted to itself all forms of victimization.

This identification with the victimized was the source of his pleasure in the work of Pierre Loti, just as it was assuredly his reason for admiring Maeterlinck. They expressed what Sharp called "the distinguishing feature of our [modern] literature":

> the piteousness of the blind and baffled struggles of the human soul . . . Pity—Pity for the baffled, the weary, the poor, the maimed, the unfortunate of all kinds and in all ways, but most of all pity for the weak . . . Pity for the weak, the deep, understanding, inalienable pity for the weak, is the highest the human soul has reached to . . . A hundred writers speak of the piteous evils of life around us: of the outcast of the street, of the woman wedded to the drunkard or madman, of the child worn out at puberty by the life of the factory, of the bitter toil of the extreme poor, of the diurnal sordid life of tens of thousands, of the brutal misuse of animals, of the horrible torturing of innocent and helpless brutes.

But there is nothing in contemporary literature apart from the work of Maeterlinck "which so poignantly conveys the sense of overwhelming pity for the tragic and inevitable mischance of the weak, of those who live and go to disaster and death blind and baffled, the sport apparently of terrible and august powers."[50] It was just such pity, such desire to appeal for the victimized, that inspired Sharp's own essay on the exiles of nocturnal London, those whose only home is "The Hotel of the Beautiful Star." It was out of this pity that he exalted this "dull monotony of wreckage"[51] to the level of special creatures perversely blessed by nature and the night to know, as no one else in demoniacal London could know, how much in the deep quiet of night the city could possess "a beauty as of the remote country, a spaciousness as of the desert, a silence as of ocean in calm."[52] And it was, of course, just such pity that inspired his own peculiar view of the condition of woman.

Fiona Macleod was indeed the creation of a mind or heart divided, but there was no need for the theory Sharp hinted at, and which others occasionally advanced, that the lifelong maintenance of this special pose was evidence of a dual or split personality; the theory indeed is usually employed without real knowledge of what it means.[53] The tension borne of suppression of what was most weak and tender in him he had always required and would have found some way of sustaining, even had the accident of Edith Rinder never occurred to give it its special feminine direction.

137

But there is another essential reason that Fiona Macleod endured where H. P. Siwaärmill and W. H. Brooks did not, for a pose that achieves popular success is thereby provided with its own principle of survival. The Fiona Macleod myth that "E.W.R." had helped to create was quickly to become the rock on which were built several hectically productive, if shortlived, publishing enterprises. In the course of a few years, the myth was to develop into a sacred premise for an entire movement, an article of faith for a whole generation of neo-romantics. When the combined strictures of poor health and depleted finances seemed to require in 1902 that Sharp appeal to the Home Secretary to be placed on the Civil Pension List, he refused to do so because it would have entailed revealing his secret authorship. In a letter written at the time to Alec Hood, he confessed that, in addition to his deep need for the "aloofness and spiritual isolation of Fiona Macleod," he also felt that "a great responsibility to others has come to me, through the winning of so already large and deepening a circle of those of like ideals or at least like sympathies in our own country and in America."[54] He was well aware that had Fiona Macleod been revealed as a man the entire architecture built upon her would have collapsed.

Sharp in his practical moods was as susceptible to the female charms that made Fiona Macleod successful as he was to those that made her a convenient and secure means of expression. It may be a curious paradox, but it is true nonetheless, that in this period of transition for women's rights, when women were crying oppression and lack of dignity, among those "of like sympathies" to Sharp's it was very fashionable to be female. At a time when both men and women were awakening to potentialities in woman no previous era had even thought of realizing, the possibilities of exploring, through her, infinite new realms of human experience must have seemed exhilarating. This second, smaller English renaissance has perhaps not been given the place it deserves in literary history, though its reverberations are enormous and obvious. Hitting upon Fiona Macleod was like striking the rich vein of woman-receptiveness in Sharp's generation. A romantic infinity of possibilities in women must have seemed to lie beneath the magical surface of Fiona Macleod's strange, evocative prose. She herself was a conception exotic and outrée. And where the very nature of convention with regard to women was being disputed, one could risk the unconventional and dare the wavering tribunal to bring its charges.

Certainly it must have appeared so to Sharp, who, in his characteristic metaphor of place, spoke of woman as "an unexplored country,"[55] and again later as "the Dark Continent of Man."[56] Woman was for him, in these characteristic terms, another imaginative Eden of desire. "We are all seeking," he said in "Ecce Puella," "the Fountain of Youth, the Golden Isles, Avalon, Woman,"[57] and he quoted as a companion to his own metaphor that of the Flemish novelist Georges Eekhoud: "Ma contrée de déliction n'existe pour aucun touriste, et jamais guide ou médicin ne la racommandera."[58] Certainly, too, Sharp could tell as a woman the story of his debt to them and his sympathy for them in a way that could cause no raising of prejudiced eyebrows, either among women doubtful of his sincerity or among men doubtful of his manhood.[59]

For Fiona Macleod's first three novels, at least, that is precisely the story that he told. In *Pharais* (1894)—Gaelic for Paradise—the wife of a Highlander doomed to be lost to her by the gradual "clouding of his mind," and therefore in a sense by his transmigration into a wholly new and isolated personality, determines that they shall die together rather than suffer this alteration in the conditions of their love. They attempt this union by binding themselves together with seaweed in the dark belly of a cavern, dry at ebb, but filled by the ocean at high tide. Their "sea-change" does not quite succeed as planned, for the tide not only unbinds them but casts both of them up alive and separated, neither aware that the other still lives. The wife gives birth prematurely to the child she had wanted to die with them, but mother and child are weak and ill, and they die just as the husband reappears. He has suffered the sea-change, however, and dimly conscious of his wife's sacrifice as the "cloud" slowly engulfs his mind, he goes forth to his new, transfigured life with her strength having somehow passed into him. Similarly, in *The Mountain Lovers* (1895), a beloved wife, dying in childbirth, leaves to her surviving husband a new revelation in the human capacity for suffering and sacrifice. The blissful dream of their young, pastoral love, shattered by the agony of her labor and her death, is supplanted by a new, more compassionate ideal, a transformation which the child symbolizes and to which the husband rededicates himself.[60]

Finally, in *Green Fire* (1896), a novel already partially treated for its suggestions of autobiography, the hero Alan is torn between his

139

attraction to two sisters, Ynys and Annaik, both of whom love him. Ynys is dark, earthy, stable; Annaik is fair, gay, a spirit of natural joy and pagan freedom. Though betrothed to Ynys, Alan yields to a night of passion with her sister. The child of this illicit union dies, and Annaik, the pagan spirit, returns whence she symbolically came, joining the forest-dwellers and disappearing into the woods with them. Alan's marriage with Ynys is eventually sanctified by the birth of a child, though a first child had died, and in this birth Alan sees through woman the realization of his own desire for immortality. In the course of a long reflective passage in the novel, Alan analyzes the nature of his divided affections and resolves the quest they had represented by asserting that it was through Ynys that he first conceived an understanding of woman and of motherhood, but through his mysterious relationship with Annaik that he realized a newer and "deeper conception of womanhood."

The significance of this "deeper conception" to Alan is emblematic of its significance to all the work of Fiona Macleod. It involved a belief that woman would be the medium of a universal redemption, for in woman are summed up all the powers of continuum, all the beneficence of Nature, in fact all the love respondent to the pathos of mankind both individually and as a race. Must there not inevitably be, Alan envisions, "a woman saviour, who would come near to all of us, because in her heart would be the blind tears of the child, and the bitter tears of the man, and the patient tears of the woman; who would be the Compassionate One, with no doctrine to teach, no way to show, but only deep, wonderful, beautiful, inalienable, unquenchable compassion?"

"For in truth," he continues, "there is the divine, eternal feminine counterpart to the divine eternal male, and both are needed to explain the mystery of the dual spirit within us—the mystery of the Two in One."[61] It is not surprising that Sharp should recall as late as 1895, in an essay on Christina Rossetti, her eminent brother's dictum, irritating to Christina, that the worship of Mary was "the lasting grit of the Romish faith" and an "idealization of humanity, through the mother idea."[62] This same idea was one of the pervasive, near-religious doctrines of the Fiona Macleod "faith," with its heavy emphasis upon St. Bridget, "St. Bride of the Isles," "The Second Mother of Christ," as the center of Celtic folklore, and with its promise of a "second coming," a reincarnation of the deity in the form of a woman, as the salvation of the world.[63]

Paradoxically, this messianic view of woman may explain Sharp's aloofness from the practical, activist branch of the feminist movement, and ally him with the artistic generation that followed him. The feminism that was largely the product of positivist attitudes toward social reform in the later nineteenth century had as its major goals the social and economic emancipation of women. It involved the leveling of sexual distinctions and, as far as possible, the equalization of the sexes. In Sharp's view, however, the sexes are neither alike nor equal in their virtues or capacities. They are instead complementary, with woman figuring in her traditional role as matrix of future generations. Sharp shared the outlook of radical feminists to the extent that he desired greater acknowledgment and appreciation of women's contributions to the progress of the race. But the distinction of his outlook from theirs—and, though slight, it is a distinction—is that while they viewed woman as agent of social and cultural change, he viewed her as instrument or catalyst of such change. To be such, in the Sharp scheme, she must retain rather than alter her traditional functions, and conserve the values—feeling, sympathy, intuition—through which men must work.

It is not too gross to suggest, then, that compared with some of his contemporaries Sharp was something of a reactionary. This may explain why Lafcadio Hearn should once again prove himself Sharp's Oriental counterpart. Hearn's adoption of Eastern culture was sufficiently thoroughgoing to entail his acceptance of its traditional social subjection of women. Yet, like Sharp, he possessed an extraordinary interest in women's role as a crucial and defining factor in developing and perfecting general human culture, from both its Eastern and its Western sides. He regarded Baudelaire's conception of "the woman thou shalt never know" as the best expression of Western man's aspirations toward the impossible and unattainable. His Japanese woman, no less than Sharp's Celtic woman, symbolized "all the possibilities of the race for goodness."[64]

At the height of the feminist movement of the nineties, this oblique, conservative aspect of feminism was not recognized as a challenge to its social and political goals. Indeed, some radical feminist arguments, like those of Olive Schreiner, for example, depended for some of their force upon such symbolic interpretations of female nature. Thus, while the figure of Fiona Macleod herself, along with the female characters Sharp created through her, epitomized and embodied a kind of feminist counter-revolution, the subversive element in them went unperceived. It was not until after the turn of the century that literary artists, often in partisan opposition to the "new woman" of the age, began to make full use of the "symbolic" woman as the advance guard of a counter-force. Thus Fiona Macleod has something in common with Molly Bloom of *Ulysses* and with the peasant women who appear in the luminous background of James Joyce's *Portrait of the Artist as a Young Man*. Her image can perhaps lay claim to archetypal value: she might be the end result of a process by which intellectual and denatured woman is de-intellectualized and re-natured, a process undergone by many of D. H. Lawrence's heroines. In a sense she is the same woman, hands outstretched in final supplication and benediction, who closes Conrad's *Heart of Darkness*, or the same who, as Lena Grove in William Faulkner's *Light in August*, bears the burden of regeneration forfeited by the missionizing American "new woman." She is linked to the mother whose incanted name, "Esmiss Esmoor," is heard over the gulf between East and West in Forster's *A Passage to India*. She represents the creative spirit of our culture, as twentieth-century literature has defined it, supplying an explicit rebuke to radical feminism, and perhaps testimony of its failure.[65] Though Fiona Macleod expressed no vocal antagonism to the social and political goals of the feminist movement, she was conceived in a spirit that cut deeply across them. She stands as Sharp's canny resolution of a Victorian dilemma regarding women. The success of Fiona Macleod is thus a phenomenon of genuine importance to literary history and no mere eccentricity of a strayed imagination.

Yet it must be said that in the sense demanded by the canons of twentieth-century taste, Sharp did not realize the full potential of his creation. Through her, his private reconciliations were made, dramatized in his literary life, and transmuted into a principle of belief. Fiona Macleod and her people were intended to dwell in a world of prophecy, where ordinary woman, ordinary marriage, ordinary human trials had no place. Sharp appears to have decided from the very beginning that the Macleod vein would be evocative, poeticized prose and that nearly all the relationships expressed in it would be conceived in idealized form. Essentially this meant that, whatever vicissitudes are suffered by the lovers Fiona Macleod depicts, they are never more than temporary exiles from Eden and always gravitate back to the ideal state of innocence, which experience may "transmute" but can never wholly alter. As in the adventures of Eilidh and Isla in *The Sin-Eater* (1895) and of Ula and Urla in *The Washer of the Ford* (1895), the direction of movement is merely from one ideal plane to another. Love divided inevitably becomes love reunited in another more permanent world that is like the immobilized reflection of the real one in some dark mountain tarn. The change by water is appropriate, for it is often by way of water that such metamorphoses take place; sexual unions between men and seals are, for example, a repeated motif in the stories of *The Washer of The Ford*.

Only in rare moments did the real touch of human feeling break through Fiona Macleod's attempts to evoke the spiritual and emotional scope of womanhood. One of these occurs in "The Rune of the Passion of Women," with its plaintive refrain echoing the sounds of life lived close to the earth—

> Far upon the lonely hills I have heard the crying,
> The lamentable crying of the ewes—

with its pity for the "sorrow of lonely women," the desolation of lives lived for others—

> the lonely silence,
> The void bed, the hearthside void,
> The void heart, and only the grave not void—

and with its perception of the painful passing of sensual joy—

> To see the fairness of the body passing,
> To see the beauty wither, the sweet colour
> Fade, the coming of the wintry lines
> Upon pale faces chilled with idle loving . . .
> To grope blindly for the warm hand, for the swift touch . . .[66]

Fiona Macleod dealt with the love of this world only as unresolved, lost, or misplaced. Such love represented a spiritual condition in itself and in one of her stories was symbolized, with a typical Sharp metaphor of place, as "The Distant Country."[67] Yet Sharp's concern with this theme was not to be bound by the strictures of dual and secret authorship. His last major work of fiction as William Sharp, *Silence Farm,* was an attempt to bring the distant country into realistic focus, to trace the "sorrow of women" in the unlovely history of Margaret Gray, a rural girl struggling with the poor bargain of womanhood's inheritance. Margaret is an illegitimate and unwanted child, grinding out her life in the poverty of a dying countryside, a menial in her father's household, where she ought to be honored as a daughter. Her sorrow is unwittingly to waste her devotion upon her worthless brother, and be deserted by him. Sharp at this point in the narrative provides a vivid and grotesque dramatization of Margaret's experience of dead love:

At first she could neither see nor hear. The howl and rush of the wind, the soaking whirl of the tempest, the drowning blackness overwhelmed her. She gave a gasp of physical relief when the rain drenched through to the skin. It was like a cool hand upon her breast. She felt her hair matting with the damp, but the flame in her had cooled.

It was not till she shivered with chill that she stirred. Then, with a weary gesture, she turned, muttering something about the "coo," in the coarse, farmyard Lallam tongue.

"It's all I'm fit for" . . .

With stumbling feet she made her way to the byre. The sow grunted heavily as she passed the ready-made sty at the angle of the ramshackle building. A hot, fetid smell filled the byre, which was warm and close despite the draughts which whistled through the chinks, and the monotonous moaning hiss of the wind-eddies among the torn rafters and loose thatch. When the sow rose, snorting and grunting, her litter scurried round her, squealing. Their trampling hoofs set free the odours of garbage and filth. Margaret stood by the sty for a minute.

"She's in his arms now," she muttered, "warm and sweet."

The stench sickened her. She felt herself grow white in the darkness. Turning to a ledge on the wall, she fumbled for a lantern, lit the tallow dip within it, and holding it above her head, stared about her.

The black sow leered up at her with bloodshot little eyes, the slobbering snout wrinkled at the fangs as though she were ready to fasten these in this nocturnal intruder.

There was a broom-handle lying against the sty. Margaret took it and hit the grunting brute on the flank.

"Lie quiet," she said with sullen anger, "or they'll hear ye, the two lovers. D'ye think she can hear him whisper *Kirsten, Kirsten, Kirsten,* wi' you gruntin' awa' like that, you an' your dirty litter, ye hideous black brute?"[68]

Later, when Margaret's father dies, she addresses the corpse with a frantic and pitiful abandon that is a moment of stinging insight into the potential tragedy of womanhood:

Ah, perhaps you've met *her* now, the woman you wronged, the mother of Margaret Gray: your wanton, old man—you who a little ago put the shameful word on me! What is she saying to you? Is God listening? Ah, He's a man, too; He won't hear *her*, He won't hear *me*: we are women.[69]

Margaret is "Madge o' the Pool" set in a totally different atmosphere, but like her trapped between the fragrant incense of a spiritualized love-ideal and the stink of material decay. The theme was obviously suited to Sharp's gifts; there might have been more to hope for from him had he not chosen with such singleness of purpose to avoid the road of Hardy and Gissing and take his way instead through Fiona Macleod's myths and allegories.[70] Perhaps too long preoccupied with these, as well as too exhausted by his own consuming restlessness, he could not sustain a conception like Margaret Gray, even through the rest of *Silence Farm.* In this novel, Sharp came as close as he was capable to a Hardy-like success and revealed in technique, and in the urgency with which he seems to have written it, that Hardy was the novelist with whom he was in most basic sympathy, and that *Jude the Obscure,* that immense epic of cancered ideals of love and loveless marriages, was the Hardy novel after *Tess* which most impressed him.[71]

But after *Silence Farm* the creative voice of William Sharp grew fairly silent, and the tone of Fiona Macleod was allowed to prevail. Sharp's pity for the Madges and Margarets of this world was only powerful enough to evoke briefly their lonely and desolate images— images of the essential woman, abandoned if not destroyed by the swift, ruthless pace of "progress." That pity was not powerful enough to create a mediating vision, a theory of redemption more palpable than his "woman-redeemer," that might fully unite his grief for the disintegrated Edens of this world with his passion for the Edens of desire.

145

8

THE NEW COSMOPOLITANISM

The Celtic Never-Never Land

The surge of female sympathy that would seem to have overwhelmed Sharp during the early and middle nineties in reality engaged only part of his extremely variegated literary identity. More than the sexual dynamic in him was seeking resolution in the personality of Fiona Macleod.

Sharp's temporary desertion of the London literary world in 1890 was symbolic of his rejection of the city and the limits that life there put upon his creative work. But even more than that, it was a rejection of what the city had come to stand for—the stolid, Philistine, Grundy-istic English mind, which he described to his wife as "this atmosphere of deadening, crushing, paralyzing, death-in-life respectability."[1] There was genuine alarm in his feeling that, if tendencies remained unchecked, the world would someday be "reduced to the sway of the plumber and builder, the artificial gardener and Bumbledom."[2] Walking out on this world was a private effort to forestall that day and was merely one form of a general protest against Anglo-Saxonism, aroused by his early travels in Europe and by the Celtic associations he had made in London in the mid-eighties.

But the fire those associations had started, sending Sharp back to the literature and landscape of Scotland for inspiration, was by 1890 burning itself out and stood very much in need of refueling. This refueling Edith Wingate Rinder provided with her Celtic enthusiasm. Her interest in Scottish Celtism was not, however, exclusive. It was combined with broader interests in other literatures, and this combination was in itself, perhaps, the fullest source of the effectiveness of her inspiration. When E.W.R. encountered Sharp in Rome, he was, it is true, more ready than ever to reflect on the quality of his literary predilections and the direction his literary career would take. But he had, it must be recalled, great incipient leanings toward a cosmopolitan-ism which, if allowed to run its course without her, might never have yielded the particular results it did—that is, might never have so intensively represented itself in what, for all purposes, was the highly nativistic vein of Fiona Macleod. The vague hope he may have had of combining with his cosmopolitan commitment the strong nostalgia he felt for Celtism became, through her, a conviction he would pursue with passionate devotion thereafter. His effort to absorb and translate this paradox into a logical critical and artistic philosophy provides a good part of the drama of his later years.

Mrs. Rinder exercised the not-very-eminent talents she possessed largely as translator of French literature, and like most translators she looked to the moderns for fresh material. She had, therefore, an interest in contemporary literature written in French which she must have conveyed to Sharp, who was at the time, though learned on the subject of French art, probably still more widely than deeply read in its literature. Under her influence this situation immediately changed. Sharp began reading her apparent favorites, Maeterlinck and the Belgian school of impressionistic dramatists, in 1891. By 1892 he was sufficiently informed to write a review of a new volume of Maeterlinck translations to which Hall Caine had decided to lend his support.

There seemed to be no area in which Caine was not prepared to make himself Sharp's rival: he had in the 1880's published volumes competing with two of Sharp's major entries into the popular market, the Rossetti biography and an anthology of sonnets. But it is obvious that Sharp was not going to permit him to blunder into this new field unchallenged. He attacked Caine's introduction to the Maeterlinck volume, charging him with "an evident unfamiliarity with much that M. Maeterlinck has done, and what, perhaps wrongly, I take to be his obliviousness of the contemporary Franco-Flemish movement," in which Maeterlinck, he said, was "but one among several."[3] After complaining further that Caine misunderstood Maeterlinck largely because of the "playwright fallacy"—criticizing, in other words, for poor stagecraft what was not intended for the stage—Sharp moved to defend Maeterlinck on another much more vital score, that of his alleged failure to give support to the national Belgian cause. Maeterlinck, Sharp asserted, insisted on being Flemish only until "he found that a Belgian wrote and spoke a universal tongue, and a Fleming what from a broad standpoint can be called only a provincial dialect."[4] The polemic of these words can be explained by more than professional rivalry, for the critical atmosphere in which they were written was unfavorable to Maeterlinck, and can be defined by Richard Burton's attitude in a slightly later article in the *Atlantic Monthly*. Burton there classified the Belgian dramatist with the "decadents" and declared him to be French rather than Belgian—the French "of the boulevards of Paris," with its connotations of the unwholesome and foppish. As far as Burton was concerned, Maeterlinck had "deserted" the Belgian national movement.[5]

This must indeed have been a sore point for Sharp, who, with the addition of E.W.R.'s mixture of enthusiasms, had seen in the so-called Belgian Renascence a perfect analogy to the condition of the British Celts, particularly the Scots. Intrinsic to the Belgian school was a dilemma similar to that of the Celts created by the desire for a national form of expression and the availability of two languages in which that expression could be couched. The question was, would the wish to avoid complete submission to the domination of the culture to which they had been annexed best be realized by going to war with that culture or by submitting to it partially and utilizing some of its resources for nationalistic ends? An argument for the second, more pragmatic alternative was the incontrovertible fact of the wider diffusion, and the effective adoption by the Belgians, of the French language, an argument which Sharp (as Fiona Macleod) was later to use to defend his opposition to the Celts' use of Gaelic.

In the meantime, however, not yet a Celt in the popular mind, Sharp limited himself to expressing his opinions vis-à-vis the Belgians in terms that would only later prove to have equally forcible application to the Celtic movement. By 1893, he was more adamantly than ever a spokesman for the Belgian movement as represented by Maeterlinck and was growing increasingly firm in his conviction of the compatibility of a native movement with what appeared to be a non-native language. In an article called "La Jeune Belgique," he asserted that the school of which Maeterlinck and Eekhoud, among others, were members was "always in passionate accord with the racial and national Belgic sentiment." It was a movement, he protested, "to bring about a reaction against literary ignorance, disorder, and general backbonelessness." In defense of their use of French, he claimed that the Belgians "have maintained steadfastly the demands of the fundamental laws of French poetry without hurt to, or transformation of, those particular aspects and methods of thought and sentiment characteristic of every patriotic

Belgian—the legacy of his race, of his Northern climate, and of that political condition which has given his country an intermediate situation between the most powerful, as well as the most occidental of the Latin peoples, and the most potent of the Germanic races."[6] Quite a tight-rope to have walked successfully! But the Belgians had so done, says Sharp, and had realized "a radical distinction between Belgic and French literature." For him there was no doubt that "the whole energy" of the Belgian movement was, "consciously or unconsciously, concentrated in the effort to withstand Paris."[7] For "the Belgian movement" read "the Celtic movement," and for "the effort to withstand Paris," "the effort to withstand London," and the result resembles very closely Sharp's thinking on the nature of the Celtic "renascence" at the time.[8]

By 1895 Sharp had not only a firmer grasp of the debate and a cooler view of its issues, especially with regard to the nationalist claims of Belgian enthusiasts, but a more intimate recognition of the application of these to the movement in which he was by then deeply involved:

> Obviously, the primary and almost overwhelming handicap [to the Belgian nationalists] lay in the fact that the official and literary language of this small country—this vague *congeries* called the Belgic Netherlands . . . was that of its most powerful neighbour, a neighbour upon whose amity its very existence depended. The young Belgian had, like the young Celt of Western Ireland or the Scottish Highlander, no alternative. He had either to use the dominant official and literary language, or to be content to have no audience, no reader.

"Fifty years ago and less," he recalls somewhat wryly, "Celtic Irish and Celtic Scots obscured rather than obtruded their Celtism, partly out of persecution or active annoyance, partly out of weakness and folly, but mainly because of a perverse utilitarian instinct." A similar spirit had pervaded mid-century Belgium, he goes on, and by the time the tide of popular sentiment had turned it was too late to save what the Belgians themselves had destroyed: "Critics, students, general readers, and poets and novelists themselves, saw that Flemish was a steadily narrowing and inevitably doomed language . . . By this time . . . the clearest-eyed . . . realized that it would be madness to attempt the cult of what is necessarily transient."[9] Also by this time, a more "clear-eyed" Sharp had divided what he considered the transient from the permanent in the literature of the Belgian school, a process of isolating characteristics of a racial and cultural nature from those strictly political or linguistic. He describes Eekhoud, for example, as "a Fleming of the Flemings": "and though he no longer writes in Flemish, his stories are charged with Flemish sentiment, idioms, enthusiasms, and prejudices. In his work, as in that of some of his abler confrères, there is a remarkable strain of brutality, a peculiarly characteristic Flemish coarseness."[10] And further on, he points to another characteristic distinguishing the Fleming from the French, a "more distinctly Teutonic side of this Belgian literary development, the mystic, the symbolic."[11] It was a vein of literature toward which, by virtue of his natural disaffection with political nationalism, he was growing more sympathetic.

To trace Sharp thus through the three years of study of the relationship between Belgian literature and Belgian nationalism is to record in capsule form the evolution of his highly complex—often apparently contradictory—role within the Celtic movement. It is to see him devise a stance as spokesman of a national movement while remaining at the same time fiercely critical of nationalism in its strict political sense. But he did not develop this role entirely by himself. Behind him and E.W.R. were his Edinburgh colleagues of the *Evergreen* group, who shared his conviction that a broad nonpolitical base must be given to the various national movements burgeoning around them, and who seem to have been totally reluctant to make their own Celtic "renascence" either an entirely Gaelic movement or a nationalistic one, as some of their brothers in Ireland were dead set upon doing.

One of the most distinct characteristics of this "band of Edinburgh reformers," led to a great extent by Patrick Geddes of the University of Edinburgh, was the internationalism of its tendencies. Geddes had said that "our little scholastic colony in the heart of Edinburgh symbolises a movement which while national to the core, is really cosmopolitan in its intellectual reach."[12] Israel Zangwill, whose own cosmopolitanism was intense, records in one of his many peripatetic articles his meeting with Geddes, "the Emperor of Edinburgh," and speaks of Geddes' plans for restoring Edinburgh as a "European capital": "While the men of 'The Evergreen' 'would renew local feeling and local colour,' they 'would also express the larger view of Edinburgh . . .' an aspiration with which all intelligent men must sympathise." For Zangwill, "the quest at once of local colour and cosmopolitanism is not at all self-contradictory." "The truest cosmopolitanism goes with the intensest local colour, for otherwise you contribute nothing to the human treasury and make mankind a featureless monotony. Harmonious diversity is the true cosmopolitan concept."[13] "Our sentiments precisely," Geddes might have said, for he acted upon them. The Edinburgh group, though most attractive to the French and Belgians, formed a magnetic center toward which many writers of very diverse backgrounds gravitated.

Critics commenting on the *Evergreen*, for two years (1895-1896) the major organ of this group, did not let this distinguishing quality go unnoticed. Victor Branford, himself a member, underscored its "international note" in a review of the *Evergreen* for the *Bookman*, recalling that one of the "local and national" traditions of patriotic Scotsmen had always in fact been "the old continental sympathies of Scotland (more particularly the 'ancient league with France')": "The *Evergreen* . . . [gives] some evidence that the continental connection is still a living and fruitful one. The Franco-Scottish Society now being organized in Paris and Edinburgh is a formal academic recognition of the lately revived custom of interchange between French and Scottish students."[14]

"The ancient league with France" had, of course, been cemented, from the standpoint of literature, by the Ossian rage of the later eighteenth century, and it therefore had a strong basis in literary history alone. But the Scottish Celts could afford to be more international in spirit than their Irish counterparts on other grounds besides the very genuine ones of sympathy and affinity with the European literary community, and these were purely, almost embarrassingly practical. There is convincing testimony that none of the Scots (not even Sharp) was very able in Gaelic[15] or had any special passion for it that might guarantee their working toward its survival. Besides, the equally ancient Scottish league with England had practically precluded a linguistic rebirth of that kind, and the Scots, in contrast to the Irish, had been unable to rouse any serious protest against political and cultural subjection.

But the clearest practical reason for the generous breadth of vision among this handful of Scots was the uncertain power of their own combination of gifts. The leaders of the group, Patrick Geddes and J. Arthur Thompson, though broadly cultured men, were themselves

151

not artists or belle-lettrists but biologists by training. Though a fair translator, Edith Rinder, one of the principal Edinburgh contributors to the *Evergreen* and the Celtic Library, was not a literary artist in the usual sense. Moreover, apart from her immeasurable gift to William Sharp's creative life, she was able to give legitimate sustenance to the movement only as an expert on Celtic Brittany. Elizabeth Sharp, who also helped to swell the ranks of the band, possessed literary talents that were mainly journalistic and editorial. That left in the credits given on the flyleaves of the Celtic Library only two other names of significance, and they were actually only one—William Sharp and Fiona Macleod. The reputation of the group as spokesmen of a literary movement of any distinction rested almost entirely, therefore, upon the Fiona Macleod myth. Of this Elizabeth Sharp, at least, seemed to be aware—perhaps all too painfully aware. "No conspicuous modern [Scottish] Celtic work had hitherto been written in the English tongue," she wrote in the *Memoir*, "until the appearance of the writings of Fiona Macleod, and later of Mr. Neil Munro."[16]

This was an enormous obligation with which to charge one man— or supposed woman—and was more than valid cause for the absolute necessity of maintaining the image of Fiona Macleod in the public eye. Yet regardless of being almost the unique claim to regard possessed by the Edinburgh group—or perhaps because of it—Sharp, under both names, engaged himself in widening rather than narrowing its international tendencies. The name for the Celtic Library to which he strongly leaned was the "Cosmopolitan" series. He urged the publication in it "of occasional volumes by foreign authors of marked power and distinction," and there was an enormous range to those he proposed: Jonas Lie, Ola Hansson, Gabriele D'Annunzio, Antonio Fogazzaro, Matilda Serao, José Echegaray, Hermann Sudermann, Anatole France, J. H. Rosny, Georges Eekhoud, Camille Lemonnier, Hamlin Garland.[17]

The study of Celtic folklore, combined with his own breadth of outlook, gave Sharp a capacity to appreciate indigenous efforts to revive native cultures that was unusual even for his broadminded era. In the case of D'Annunzio, whom few critics knew outside of his notorious novels, Sharp's deeper knowledge coincided with his interest in the impressionistic drama, and he made himself an expert on D'Annunzio's even now little-known dramas of Abruzzi life.[18] He had also read Giovanni Verga, an Italian whose struggle for recognition against the alien popular taste of his own Italy was herculean, and he recognized, long before Verga became generally fashionable, the power and universality of his depictions of Sicilian peasant life.[19]

Sharp's astute perceptions regarding Belgian, Italian, and other little-read literatures were in advance of their time, and for them he deserves the full measure of personal credit. Yet there is room to wonder whether or not the widening of literary horizons that made them possible reflected no more than his own generous vision, his own cosmopolitan experiences, his own anti-British reaction, or his own simply practical needs. If he shared a very practically-based cosmopolitanism with his Edinburgh colleagues, he also shared a less practically-based cosmopolitanism with many others who might have disagreed with him on specific issues. Though they were his rivals when it came to interpreting the relationship between literature and nationalism, even men like Caine and Burton were at one with him in devoting their critical energies to studying examples of that relationship in foreign literatures. In fact, cosmopolitanism gave every evidence of being a strong trend in criticism by the mid-nineties, a consensus among many writers seeking to give new breadth to the English literary outlook, and shared by nearly every avant-garde journal of any significance. The roots of this mood lay deep in the ability of these men of Sharp's generation to respond in the same way to similar influences.

Cosmopolitan opinion certainly did not lack support from the philosophy and science rooted in ubiquitous nineteenth-century evolutionary theory. W. K. Clifford, in his highly influential analysis of *Cosmic Emotion* in 1888, on the hypothesis that matter had a natural tendency to become increasingly organic, envisioned man's moral evolution toward increased unity and "cooperation."[20] The growing solidarity of the entire human race, he thought, would be the result of "much patient practice of comradeship"[21] and might eventually yield the union of man with macrocosm of which romantic poets had had a prevision. Clifford's attempt to devise a scientifically tenable bridge between man's delighted contemplation of self and his awe and veneration of the world not-himself, his "cosmic emotion," perhaps lay behind the concept of "cosmic consciousness" prevalent among the Theosophists and among many students of occultism and exponents of racial or organic memory in the later century, including, of course, Yeats, A.E., and others, as well as Sharp. Such a concept was elaborated by Lafcadio Hearn, who argued that "the flesh-and-blood man is only the visible end of an invisible column of force reaching out of the infinite past into the momentary present." Hearn illustrated the chain linking organic memory first to an esthetic philosophy of universal sympathy—"pity" or "humanity"—and then to a fundamental cosmopolitanism of thought. He envisioned a world literature, initiated by a spirit of "unselfish sympathy" and revitalizing every national tradition by mutual influence and inspiration, "a search," he called it, "for the oneness of life in the exuberant flowerings of the geniuses of many world races." Like humanity, world literature would be "one" without sacrificing its variety.[22]

Meanwhile, the philosophy of universality was systematized during the nineties by Edward Carpenter, who himself had close connections with the London circle in which Sharp moved. For Carpenter, flashes of insight that brought men into a sense of union with the macrocosm were hints of the underlying oneness of all creation. "All these beings and personalities" of the universe, he wrote in *The Art of Creation* (1904), "must root down in one ultimate Life and Intelligence; all of them in the end must have a common purpose and object of existence."[23]

This form of idealism had many proponents, of course, and was rooted in romanticism. But it was taking on a new significance in the broader world vision of the later nineteenth century. Many practical and political strategies were growing within the semimystical concepts of universal union and solidarity that were part of the period's intellectual and spiritual ambient. Socialism and unionism based themselves on the ideal of human community within any given national area or within the labor force; communism went even further with its concept of international brotherhood. And some thinkers were beginning to restore Dante's mystical thirteenth-century vision in new terms, as a concept of nonmonarchical world government.

Whether these philosophies were the result or the cause of breakdowns in English nationalism and chauvinistic sympathies would probably be impossible to determine. A narrow Marxist might adduce as the source of their intensity a disaffection with the idea of English supremacy caused by the economic conditions that prevailed from 1873 to 1896, the years of the Great Depression. As one historian has pointed out, the growing tendency during those years simply was "to depreciate things English and exalt things foreign."[24]

At any rate, both cosmic thought and cosmopolitanism flourished simultaneously, and the writings of cosmopolitans took on more or less philosophical reverberation according to the depth of their acknowledgement of such cosmic philosophies. Certainly Sharp's own cosmopolitanism, implicitly at first, later explicitly, acknowledged them. To this extent his romanticism had gone beyond mere comradeship toward what Irving Babbitt calls a "superrational perception," and, as will be seen, it was to achieve the character of a genuine ethic.

The question of susceptibility to foreign influence in the later part of the century has wide and sometimes conflicting ramifications. For one thing, it was no sudden explosion: throughout the century foreign culture had played a large if unsystematic social and artistic role in England, a natural result of both a growing technology of communication and the experimental, sympathetic temper of the romantics. Even colonial imperialism, appearing to exert its pressure from another moral side entirely, stirred in the most jingoistic of writers, like Rudyard Kipling, warm sensations of universal sympathy and fellow feeling.

Without pretending to reduce the complexity of the causes of the cosmopolitan movement, one might well conjecture that its quality as a movement—systematic, coherent, and genuinely philosophic—came about in reaction to the false cosmopolitanism of the British imperialist. The glorification of the foreign and exotic, insofar as it in turn brought glory to the British Empire and sanctified the pride of Englishmen, has to be distinguished from the glorification inspired by a feeling antagonistic to English hegemony and superiority. In both cases a mystical idea of union may have been at work. But whereas the imperialistic cosmopolitan, if such he may be called, venerated that union as a function of the British Empire, and tended to derogate the race or nation that could not or would not be embraced by it, the true cosmopolitan saw union as worldwide and gratuitous; he was provoked to outrage at the claims of any one nation or race to superiority over another. In this sense Sharp's cosmopolitanism, being of the latter kind, represented a new phase of an old tradition. The egalitarian spirit that had had its first exercise within the boundaries of single nations was now being given universal scope.

The genesis of Victorian literary cosmopolitanism can be studied separately only if it is clearly seen as part of this larger cultural—even political—context, since as a movement it is marked by its conscious awareness of that context. Matthew Arnold's role as first standard-bearer in the cause of an expanded European literary conscience makes him a good starting point, for the range of concerns, interests, and attitudes Arnold opened in the sixties touched those of the next generation at several points. Sharp expressed his direct debt to him by subscribing to Andrew Lang's characterization of Arnold's mentor, Ernest Renan, as the Moses and Arnold himself as the Aaron of the Celtic movement. And Arnold's deep interest in Sainte-Beuve and his study of Heine during the earlier part of his career as critic appear almost to have been handed down to Sharp as a bequest. In general, the kind of wider literary perception demonstrated by Sharp and his group in the nineties was precisely what Arnold had called for in his first collection of *Essays in Criticism*, published in 1865, and in his lectures on the Celtic spirit in literature in 1866.

If the effectiveness with which Arnold performed his standard-bearing role in the movement for literary cosmopolitanism remains in dispute among modern scholars, it is because he anticipated in a still more pertinent way the spirit behind the movement. Arnold was fully conscious that, as far as his English audience was concerned, the application of critical "disinterestedness" to the literary community of Europe as a whole had an outlaw taint upon it. For this reason, it has been suggested, he later backed away from his own early stand against British snobbism and insularity.[25] What critics of his alleged failure of nerve have not recognized is that Arnold's early remarks had already received their sympathetic and enthusiastic hearing among the young men and women of Sharp's generation, and had stirred something in them that no amount of subsequent equivocation or recantation on Arnold's part could quell, and that their own experience could do nothing but confirm.

Arnold's voice had been by no means isolated, however. In many ways, direct and indirect, British vanity had been attacked throughout the high Victorian period. The Brownings had exerted a strong cosmopolitan influence by making foreign culture present and vivid to English readers and by insisting that the cause of Italian nationalism was their vital concern. Ruskin's graphic reevocations of the artistic, architectural, and sociological experience of the well-traveled Englishman had given impetus to the spirit of foreign appreciation. Walter Pater had influenced it with his interest in French symbolism, and Swinburne by underwriting Baudelaire, Rimbaud, and Verlaine, and by his passion for Mazzini. Rossetti had encouraged it with his recollections of François Villon, and by reenfranchising the Italian "dolce stil nuovo." George Eliot and George Henry Lewes had contributed to it with their importation of German and French philosophy and higher criticism. And George Meredith, already in his early work representing the first swell of the new and stronger wave to come, was beginning to prick the swollen egos of the English bourgeoisie with sharp satire.

Nevertheless, the committed, near-religious elite of Edinburgh needed their special prophet. They found him not among the great literary names in England and Scotland, but on the outer edge of their own circle. He was the Frenchman Joseph Texte, whose interesting, unpretentious book *Jean-Jacques Rousseau and the Cosmopolitan Spirit in Literature* (1895) must have given the cosmopolitans of Sharp's Edinburgh circle the joy of a private scripture and just the broad literary and historical basis they needed for a consolidation of views.

It is not precisely clear when Sharp discovered this volume. Though he refers to it in a late work, *Literary Geography* (1903-1904), a case may well be made for his having encountered it a good deal earlier, partly because of his liaison with French literary circles, and partly because the sentiments expressed in it are so akin to his own during the nineties that it is difficult to believe it did not either directly influence the framing of his ideas or confirm opinions he already held and give them a cogent vocabulary and an historical validity. As such, it merits special consideration here.

As a historian of French literature, Texte was of course concerned with cosmopolitanism as an essential part of the modern French tradition. Yet the conditions which he saw as causal in the development of this tradition were strikingly reproduced in the England of the late nineteenth century, and this Sharp and his *Evergreen* circle would not have failed to see. Texte borrowed for an axiom of his thesis the same vocabulary that Matthew Arnold had used in "The Function of Criticism" to define the relationship between national and cultural movements. Texte stated that the history of nations "in their moral no less than their political life" could be divided into periods of concentration and expansion.[26] But his definitions of these terms are curiously the reverse of Arnold's. The period of "expansion" for Texte coincided with strong nationalism, even imperialism, and was characterized by a tendency to chauvinism in literary and artistic taste. Conversely, "concentration" implied a reappraisal of traditional values, reflected in internal political and intellectual strife and a tendency to national self-criticism. (Arnold had considered the period of nationalism a period of reaction, and thus an "epoch of concentration," and had defined an "epoch of expansion" as a time characterized by the tendency to explore outside the intellectual boundaries of a single nation.)

From this point on Texte moved independently. As he saw it, neither concentration nor expansion was ever totally comprehensive as a national movement of mind. Residual national vanity, like residual internal criticism, was present even when the national mind appeared wholly taken up with the principle peculiar to the current phase of its development. An obvious distinction, it is yet an important one, providing a rationale for the apparently contradictory presence of the two mentalities at any given period—a presence especially notable in later Victorian England.

To illustrate this aspect of his theory, Texte provided a studious analysis of Voltaire's opposition to the prevailing current of cosmopolitanism in the late eighteenth century. That period in France was, in his view, just such a period of concentration as has been described. At that time, he says, apart from Voltaire, the major luminaries of French literature, whose efforts coincided with, and were in some cases identical with, the romantic movement, were only partially French. Rousseau, Mme. de Staël, Benjamin Constant, Chateaubriand, all took their signal from their outstation in Geneva, and often expressly considered themselves racially mixed. National allegiance among French intellectuals was, as a result, diffused, patriotism weak. The outcome, says Texte, was the raising of a protest "in the name of foreign and modern literatures, against the influence of the classical spirit."[27]

This clear division between the classical spirit as nativist and the modern and romantic spirit as cosmopolitan did not obtain in England in the nineteenth century. Yet any imaginative Victorian would have seen in much of the literature of the later part of the century a reasonable parallel. Alongside a romantic tendency for experimentation in life as well as in art, there seems to have run a diffused if not completely disoriented patriotism and a distinct readiness to criticize the pious values of mid-Victorianism, values that often smacked distinctly of national pride. Sharp was hardly the inventor of the attitude which, as early as the Heine biography in 1888, revealed itself in a vitriolic assault upon the smugness of the British reception of Heine's apostasy. "Those upholders of the opium trade," he snarled, "the despoilers of the weak, the land-grabbers *par excellence*" were hardly in a moral position to be critical of the supposed hypocrisy of a member of another race.[28] It may partially have been this arrogant Anglo-Saxon posture that provoked his ad hoc popagandizing for Judaism in *The Children of To-morrow*; in his instinct for protest, certainly, Sharp could as readily be ruled by a negative passion as a positive one. By 1892, this same passion had reached a height in the outspoken iconoclasm of the *Pagan Review*, which could be identified by its irreverent motto and by its appeal to the Gallic Gautier to establish the review's general tone.

Any reader of the periodical literature of the nineties is aware how widespread was such sentiment. There is strength in the argument that much of the Gallicizing that represented itself as sophisticated art and criticism was deeply rooted in anti-nationalism, and that men like John Addington Symonds and Arthur Symons were not unaware of the shock value inherent in their exhibition of such widely European sensibility as they demonstrated in their major works. But if anti-nationalism were the sole motive of cosmopolitanism, it would have limited, sensational value alone, and the argument for allying the spirit of foreign appreciation with decadence would be strong. This, as previously shown, was not the case at all. True cosmopolitanism was grounded deep in cosmic, near-mystical ideology, and this was as true of men who prided themselves on their scientific minds as of others. Havelock Ellis, expressing hope for ever-increasing "social organization," or "communalization," and foreseeing an amalgamation of races as a partial result of colonialism, was capable of striking a note of great ironic disdain for British imperial methods. "On the whole," he says, in his introduction to The New Spirit, "we stamp [the "lower races"] out as mercifully as may be, supplying our victims liberally with missionaries and blankets." Yet in typical cosmopolitan spirit, while he envisioned England eventually succumbing to its own principle of greatness, "dispersion," he also saw it realizing that same greatness in its survival as a symbol, a "Holy-Land" for the English-speaking race.[29]

Texte's view of the modern cosmopolitan imagination is reflected in the greater as well as the lesser literary men of the period. One might hazard a broad generalization, in fact, and say that the prevailing theme of later Victorian fiction (and in modern times fiction has been the most important literary proving ground for the current social dynamic) can be reduced to the simple proposition that growth, maturity, and wisdom are in direct proportion to cosmopolitan experience—that an expanded conscience is, in other words, the outcome of an expanded horizon. Just how absolute this relationship is can be seen in the novels of Henry James and Joseph Conrad, where morality itself becomes increasingly a function of mobility; and whatever James and Conrad left out of the expression of this philosophy remained only to be filled in by Forster, Lawrence, and Hemingway. Thus modern fiction, growing out of and beyond travel literature, allies itself with cosmopolitanism's underlying ethos, the breaking down of personal and national prejudices, the realization of the fullest humanity of the individual and the fullest potential of the community through enlarged, cosmic sympathy.

To the extent that cosmopolitanism provided the writer himself with a special ethic for action, it made him a student of world culture. The primitivism that is so variously expressed a motif in the literature of this period, marking so abundantly, for example, the work of William Morris, and providing through works like The Golden Bough a seminal education for the next literary generation, was, from the point of view of literary history, cosmopolitanism's most significant product. Thus Sharp's connection in the mid-nineties with the scholarly racial studies of Warner's Library[30] was the most natural and inevitable result of his outlook, and no more than his private contribution to a movement. The many ethnological pieces in Warner's represented a mere fraction of the scholarship and pseudo-scholarship in comparative studies during this period. It might well be concluded that the vast variety of investigations of this kind shared the single factor of anti-English reaction, and that the Irish movement was not alone to be accounted for in these terms. The extraordinarily wide diffusion of efforts on all levels to resuscitate each and every "racial spirit" in itself belied pure scientific disinterestedness, a facade which could easily disguise real discontent with the national or racial bond to which the "scientists" were ostensibly attached. If Matthew Arnold illustrates the spirit in which the first stimulus to broad racial theorizing in England was conceived, then it may be said that popular ethnology among the English originated, however weakly, as a challenge to Anglo-Saxonism. But it was Texte again who undoubtedly provided the most comprehensive statement of the "philosophy" behind Sharp's cosmopolitanism and that of hordes of other students of Celtic, Teutonic, Slavic, Icelandic, and Semitic cultures, to mention but a few— behind, in fact, the whole movement of comparative studies of which Sharp made himself a distinct part.[31] "To be a citizen 'of every nation,'" said Texte, "not to belong to one's 'native country'—this was the dream of French writers in the eighteenth century . . . Is it not a mark of the 'philosopher' to possess just this absolute detachment from the national bond which may very well be one of the most absurd prejudices handed down from early ages?"[32]

Texte's thesis is applicable to certain later Victorian literary phenomena in another way. It suggests links by which movements not obviously definable as cosmopolitan may be proven to have connections with that attitude—connections which were embodied in Sharp's work. If, as has been pointed out, the cosmopolitanism of the period cannot so readily be defined as a revolt against classical literature as can the French romantic movement, nonetheless it may still be advanced as a revolt against a form of classicism. The "Greek spirit" as conceived by the later Victorians continued to be more romantic then classical in the traditional senses of these terms. Among them, "pagan joy" was promoted as the Greeks' most apparent and laudable characteristic. And this "joy" was posed, in typical antithesis, against the Greeks' brooding, highly "romantic" melancholy, their tragic sense, their spirit of protest in the face even of the inexorable. Appropriately, Euripides was Sharp's favorite among the Greek tragedians, if not among all classical writers. Indeed Sharp was possessed with the notion of writing drama that would ultimately mold out of the blend of Maeterlinckian "psychic" drama, Celtic myth, and the principles of Greek tragedy a new and formidable modern tragedy that would rid itself of what he called the "stifling" bonds of Ibsen's "realistic" stage.[33] When he was not fashioning this new Celtic buskin, he was rhapsodizing over the Greeks themselves. Greek themes haunted him, and the attractions of Sicily were immeasurably augmented by the drumbeats of vestigial Greek cults he found still pulsing in the bloodstreams of the Sicilians.[34] He spoke of Renan's "Prayer on the Acropolis" as something he too could live by.[35] It was not surprising, of course, that he should link himself with this most prominent and controversial ethnologist, the Celtic scholar to whom Arnold traced his roots. Renan was another national relativist whose racial passion for the Greeks was conceived out of the same cosmopolitan logic Sharp used: Greek culture claimed permanence in having, in effect, died its national death, but risen again, phoenix-like, as a standard borne by all western nations, capable of uniting them in their diversity.

More, however, than the restoration of Greek antiquity made up the countercurrent to the imperialistic spirit that had characterized Tennyson's generation and grown into a form of national hysteria after it. The Italian Renaissance was another favorite source of sustenance for the cosmopolitans. The chaotic individualism of the period of the *condottieri* that, via Browning and Jakob Burckhardt, had become so tantalizing to students of Italian history and culture among the later Victorians was an implicit reflection upon the leveling demands of an austerely ordered and unified Britannia. While a part of British liberal opinion was expressing satisfaction with Italy's unification, literary men were simultaneously expressing a nostalgia for a spirit that was not only the opposite of the spirit of political unification but that, historically, most worked toward making that unification a near impossibility. Pater's *Studies in the Renaissance* and Symonds' *History* are cases in point. It was not the "Italianism" that expressed national self-consciousness and singleness of political purpose, but Italy's quality of picturesque disorder, of variety designed to tantalize and reawaken the jaded taste, that usually supplied its inevitable "magic."

Sharp's own passion for Italian "variety" has already been documented, though with his inclinations toward the Etruscans, the

Campagna, and Sicily, he demonstrated that his passion was for a primitivism at still one further remove from the civilization of the Renaissance. Probably Browning best exemplified the liberal's confusion with regard to Italy—free it, he seemed to say, but don't make it less interesting—perhaps one reason that he let his wife handle the propaganda. To the extent that Browning's uses of the south were a rebuke to the northern values with which he had been reared, he was an expatriate ahead of his time, and this may partially account for the endurance of his reputation beyond the Victorian period.

In one other area the cosmopolitanism of the last part of the nineteenth century revealed itself as a protest against the spirit of English "expansion," and that is in its attitude toward the Protestant orthodoxy. Again on this score Texte expressed what might easily be considered the typical cosmopolitan view, and Sharp drew upon it. The romanticism of late eighteenth-century France had, of course, been characterized by a strong pro-Protestantism, since its main affinity was for the literature of the northern Protestant countries. Mme. de Staël, and Charles Bonstetten after her, had seen what they construed as an essential relationship between the "free" northern spirit and the preeminence of Protestantism in northern cultures. This view, combined with a natural tendency for those discontented with what they have to praise what they do not have, served to advance the French romantic's alienation—and therefore, says Texte, the future alienation of all French literary men—from the Catholic tradition and to make French romanticism a movement protestant in the generic sense, that is, almost totally secularist in its tendencies.

In France, of course, where the Catholic orthodoxy was a powerful suppressive force, this may have been a justifiable alienation. In England, however, such a situation did not exist, or if anything, it existed in reverse. Although the Protestant establishment gave undeniably greater latitude for freedom of thought and expression in England, even a sympathetic Frenchman like Texte could see that the establishment of a Protestant orthodoxy did not yield all the advantages it might seem to promise for individual free-thinking. The bitter cries going up in mid-Victorian England in the name of religious power could have given him ample evidence that, although "the Reformation had infused the English mind with a calm and dignified gravity, with intense and imperious conviction," it had given it "at the same time narrowness and false pride."[36]

This "narrowness and false pride," conceived as an ineradicable part of the English spirit in all its Grundyist aspects, may well have been responsible for the strange occurrence of the obverse of the French experience, the quiet recrudescence of a sympathy for Catholicism that partially characterizes the art and literature of the later Victorians. The early cosmopolitan Bonstetten, who had to a great extent brought more levelheadedness to Mme. de Staël's views on the relationship of religion to art, had long before Texte observed that a predominance of imagination and sense appreciation went inevitably with a religion of dogma and ceremony. The Latin countries, therefore, satisfied with the appeals of their religious forms to their most primitive devotional needs, were giving evidence of their preponderantly imaginative and sensual racial tendencies. Bonstetten's view was, though perhaps not intended as such, a blow to the northern Protestant insofar as it gave to the Latin a preeminence in those faculties—feeling and imagination—most important to art, even as it may have taken away the Latin's claims to intellectual superiority.

But for Sharp's artistic brethren of the circle around Edinburgh, as for the Pre-Raphaelites before them and the Dubliners at their side, there was small need of more reason and intellect. The "rationalism" of English Protestantism, if such indeed it was, had only served to demonstrate the limits of reason when applied to faith; and if reason had been the mainstay of the English opposition to Catholicism, that mainstay may very well have been lost to the new and shining encampment of science. In the war between science and belief English orthodoxy was to become the strange fellow-traveler of a religion it had considered its mortal enemy since the sixteenth century. But the ecumenical recognition that all religions find their common foe in secularism, though so brilliantly foreseen by Newman, was then a long way off. In the jungle stage of the evolution that ultimately produced that ecumenicism, English orthodoxy, like any other orthodoxy in the same position, thought only to save itself by fastidious reentrenchment. As a result of this stance, many sophisticated Victorians undertook a healthy reevaluation of a previous posture toward all religions, including Catholicism, that had long been taken for granted. Thus the popular, if somewhat mistaken, identification of Catholicism with art and ceremony, with gorgeous display and the submersion of the intellect in emotional and devotional glamor, curiously worked in its favor with all of those whose varying commitments to the dictum of "art for art's sake" had given them a concern for, and appreciation of, emotion and imagination as the supreme creative faculties. When Yeats and Havelock Ellis, among others, said that the arts had become religious, the religion they intended involved the broadest possible latitude, and, in the root sense, catholicity. Yet it was a catholicity that sustained no embarrassment at its connotations—that included rather than excluded the spirit of Roman Catholicism. Notwithstanding the generous tolerance extended Catholicism by the greatest Victorians, Arnold, Ruskin, and Pater (not to mention Newman, of course), this was still, in the context of the English Protestant tradition, something of a new and reverse Bloodless Revolution.

This religious phase of cosmopolitanism is readily visible in Sharp's work. That first horrified shrinking from the vivid dramatizations of devotional themes like the crucifixion in Italian Catholicism was gradually transformed into a profound sympathy, and, when devising a *vita* for Fiona Macleod, Sharp expressly identified her as a Roman Catholic.[37] Through her he came to equate the Italian Catholic emotional bath with the Italian mystical tradition, and with this new vision he looked favorably upon the same things from which the William Sharp of previous years had recoiled—among them Assisi and the dark devotions of southern Italians. The veneration of Mary, which some spokesmen for the rational Protestant mind termed Mariolatry and censured as a degradation of man's spiritual instincts, began to appear to Sharp as the means by which man expressed his persistent craving for a maternal spirit in which to submerge himself, a craving that reformed religions were wrong to deny. Surely too it was a reduction of the usual prejudice against "Latin degradation," if not a prejudice in its favor, that led Sharp to announce so victoriously the alliance between the Latin and Celtic races, and to allege that their coalition was the one thing capable of preventing Anglo-Saxon dominance of America's new racial "reorganization."[38]

A similar cosmopolitan bias informs Sharp's report of his visit to North Africa in 1893, in which he daringly put the work of Catholic missioners there above that of Protestants. The success of that work, he asserted, sprang from precisely that quality of sympathetic identification he had so often pronounced the first prerequisite for the artist, "that particular quality of imagination, or sympathy, call it what you will, which enables some missioners literally to be all things to all men." These words are supposedly quoted from a Protestant missioner's appraisal of the Catholic success, but the style and the concept were Sharp's own. "We are, broadly speaking, always ourselves," the missioner went on, "always English, or Scottish, or American; always conscious of our Protestant calling, our Protestant arrogance, our Protestant aloofness." But the French Catholic "White Fathers" had instead, he continued, made less of the divergence between Christian and Arab, more of their cooperation toward the same end. By avoiding theological controversy and by simplifying doctrine, they had also avoided the intellectual confusion that seemed to be the harvest of the Protestant approach to conversion.[39]

The tendency to favor an emotional or moral Catholicism, if not a doctrinal one, grew as Sharp, becoming more engrossed with the Celtic labors of Fiona Macleod, obtained firsthand experience of modern Celtdom on various excursions through the Scottish Isles. He found occasion to observe in the introductions and forewords to Macleod works that it was in the outlying regions of Scotland or in the isles, where Presbyterianism had failed to gain a foothold, that the people had been able to maintain the remnants of the beautiful old cults. In its tolerance of old ways and adaptability to them, Catholicism did not seem to ravage the Celtic traditions so much as Protestantism. To the Protestant's retort that the two superstitions went hand in hand, Fiona Macleod indignantly replied: "How common the foolish utterance of narrow lives, that all those old ways of thought are superstitions."[40] These so-called superstitions were for Fiona Macleod the remains, fragmentary but persistent, of the Celt's true sense of union with the other world of which nature, in mystical terms, was but the garment.

Sharp's tolerance of Catholicism was thus a practical as well as a spiritual matter. In the process of collecting materials useful to his work as Fiona Macleod, he was finding himself frustrated by the dying of Gaelic tradition and legendry. Among the social and historical causes he found for this decline, the growth of towns was a peculiar source of bitterness. But sharing a nearly equal position of dishonor was what

Sharp called "the sterilizing effect of Calvinism." A story in the Mac-leod collection entitled *The Sunset of Old Tales*—the title itself a metaphor for the slow passing of folklore—is a fictionalized damnation of the Calvinist spirit, seen as crushing the natural charity and benevolence of the unspoiled Celt. In that story, "The Wayfarer," a Calvinist preacher castigates a young woman for having a child out of wedlock. In innocent, Christ-like indignation, a passing wayfarer, representing the Celt's better and truer self, prays the townspeople to heed his own message of love, and they in their natural compassion move to his voice and receive the girl again into their fold.[41]

An article called "The Gael and His Heritage" contained more direct criticism of Calvinism: "I do not think any one who has not lived intimately in the Highlands can realize the extent to which the blight of Calvinism has fallen upon the people."[42] It was only in the Catholic rituals, Fiona Macleod continued here, that the amalgam of pagan and Christian symbolism had survived. For this reason the larger number of Sharp's Celtic stories, where they were not legendary in basis, were set among the Catholic islanders and islemen. "The Children of the Dark Star," a series of tales recounting the vicissitudes of an island family, tells of a son entering the priesthood.[43] "Fara-Ghaol" (false love) deals with an island woman who, though she is a Christian, suffers nonetheless from the anguished belief that her own child has been replaced by a changeling.[44] "Cuilidh Moire" documents the persistence of pagan water rites among the Catholic islemen, who call the sea, with no sense of inconsistency, "the treasury of Mary." And the Latin-Celtic alliance, so closely related to Sharp's Catholic sympathies, was even pressed so far in one tale as to suggest a link between the Scottish McRoban family and the Italian Robani.[45]

It has already been suggested that Sharp's affinity for the Catholic tradition may be interpreted as another bond between the Celtism of Fiona Macleod and other so-called "decadent" movements conceived in a spirit antagonistic to English insularity. But his Catholic tendencies also contained elements inherently antagonistic to the Protestant Scots, whose nationalism Fiona Macleod seemed otherwise designed to flatter. Sharp was, in other words, taking a particular religious stance before his own people that could meet with only little general favor. This division of allegiances was of one piece with the conviction (founded in his natural cosmopolitanism, fostered by his training in

Belgian nationalism, and never betrayed thereafter) that he could not support Celtic nationalism in any political sense.

The anti-nationalism of Sharp's Celtism was utterly comprehensive. It extended to the Irishman as well as the Scot, and it was formalized from the very beginning of his Celtic phase in the dogma that the Celt belonged to a "passing race."[46] In 1896, collaborating as William Sharp on an anthology of Celtic poetry, *Lyra Celtica*, he sustained his view, though now in the tone of one under attack: "No, it is no 'disastrous end': whether the Celtic peoples be slowly perishing or are spreading innumerable fibres of life towards a richer and fuller, if less national and distinctive existence."[47] His comments on Yeats in this volume predicted the thrust of Yeats's future work. Yeats, he said, in language that bore in its echoes of Arnold the discomfort of a man walking a fine line, "is too wise, too clear-sighted, too poetic in fact, to aim at being Irish at the expense of being English in the high and best sense of the word. This, fortunately, is consistent with being paramountly national in all else. In the world of literature there is no geography save that of the mind."[48]

But Sharp's distinction between literature and "all else" seemed to Celtic enthusiasts an evasion of political conscience. This position was interpreted by Celtic supporters, as it had been earlier by Belgian supporters, as a cowardly reluctance to stand behind the political exponents of the national movement and as a sell-out to Anglo-Saxon domination. It drew him into hot controversy, but that very controversy was the means by which he developed a mature and realistic ideal, respecting the bond with Anglo-Saxonism, while rejecting subservience to it. An essay called "Iona" and an article called "Celtic," both published as Fiona Macleod's in 1899, sought to isolate in the Celtic genius—as Sharp's earlier articles had sought to isolate in the Belgian— those factors most contributory to its survival as a literary and cultural "spirit" rather than as a national entity. He referred in "Iona" to his phrase, familiar by now to Fiona Macleod readers, anent "the doomed and passing" Celt. "I have been taken to task for these words. [Yet, as] the Celt fades . . . his spirit rises in the heart and mind of the Anglo-Celtic peoples, with whom are the destinies of the generation to come."[49] He insisted that the Celts' spiritual and artistic genius for mythmaking, rather than any imagined ability to unify and to exert power as a distinct race, was what alone would foster their survival. In

"Celtic" he especially urged that it must be the duty of those honoring this peculiar genius to avoid expressions of political nationalism and to attempt to realize the "ideal of art . . . to represent beautiful life." He pressed for a Celtic movement "that is not partisan, but content to participate in the English tradition, and to give it in English what itself possesses that is distinctive . . . the vision of 'The Land of Heart's Desire,' the regret of lost beauty—the dwelling among noble memories and immortal desires."[50]

Some critics gradually conceded Fiona Macleod's wisdom, but others continued to attack her as pro-English, a point on which Sharp might still be easily inclined to sensitivity. He continued to retaliate, and in Fiona Macleod's essay "Prelude" he again prophesied a kind of rebirth of the Celtic spirit, though not one that contented diehard Celtic enthusiasts. His self-defense, now very much in the Arnold tradition of disinterestedness, demonstrated how deeply his literary cosmopolitanism had by this time worked out his rancor against Anglo-Saxon "Bumbledom":

> I have no ill-will to those who, no doubt in part through a hurried habit of mind, sought by somewhat intemperate means to discredit [my] plea. I believe—I would say I know, so sure am I—these had at heart the thought of Ireland, that passion which is indeed the foremost lamp of the Gael, the passion of nationality; and having this thought and this passion, considered little or for the time ignored the "sweet reasonableness," the courtesy cherished by minds less sick with hope deferred, less desperate with defeated dreams.[51]

Having made this gallant bow, however, the author rose to his full height:

> I am not English, and have not the English mind or the English temper, and in many things do not share the English ideals; and to possess these would mean to relinquish my own heritage. But why should I be irreconcilably hostile to that mind and that temper and those ideals? Why should I not do my utmost to understand, sympathise, fall into line with them so far as may be, since we all have a common bond and a common destiny? To that mind and that temper and those ideals do we not owe some of the noblest achievements of the human race, some of the lordliest conquests over the instincts and forces of barbarism, some of the loveliest and most deathless things of the spirit and the imagination?[52]

169

Sharp's ultimate statement on the subject came in 1904, undoubtedly in a more friendly atmosphere. Still writing as Fiona Macleod, he published a two-part essay entitled "The Irish Muse," using as his point of departure Yeats's *Book of Irish Verse*. There he expressed firmly and simply his new ideal: "A national genius should seek rather for the beauty that can stand apart from time and country, than for that which must bear the impress of the time in the accent of the country."[53] Crediting Yeats with the achievement of this difficult aim, Sharp maintained that "a country lives truly only when it realizes that its sole aim is not to live"—not to live, that is, in the ordinary political sense, but in a spiritual one; and in the case of the Celt this meant to live for the present within the English tradition, and by doing so to guarantee survival even beyond it. The intent of the essay was wholly summarized by an earlier statement in "Prelude": "Another and greater independence is within our reach, is ours, to preserve and ennoble."[54]

Sharp was, of course, wisely and prophetically right: the Yeats whose later sense of literary purpose eschewed pure partisanship and realized the survival of the Celtic "mythopoeic" faculty in a world to which that faculty was becoming more and more alien was the Yeats of genuine literary permanence. It is to Sharp's credit that never in the heat of argument did he yield his conviction that only by giving symbolic meaning to any particular national identity could an artist assure its universality, and therefore its endurance.

Amid all this controversy, however, Sharp had not neglected to seek an actual landscape that, in his typical way, he might imaginatively utilize as a metaphor for his philosophical stance. This he found in the isle of Iona, whose "spiritual history" he composed side by side with his most forceful battle cries, "Celtic" and "Prelude." The long essay "Iona" was an impressionistic rendering of what its author, Fiona Macleod, called "the spirit of the isle." But that "spirit" had little of the actual about it. Iona served as a geographical means of dramatizing nearly every aspect of transcendent Celtism until then perceived by Fiona Macleod's fiction and criticism. Calling Iona "the mecca of the Gael," Sharp observed in the spiritual life of the island the same "blending of paganism and romance and spiritual beauty" that had formed the keynote of Fiona Macleod's technique of recasting Celtic folklore. In the legends of St. Columba with which the isle's history was invested he saw the survival of precious druid lore in the midst of the Catholic tradition. He found too, among the isle's legends, the same prophecy of the "woman-redeemer" that had been the singular apocalyptic vision of his own work. Iona, in short, was the very earth in which the Celtic spirit had been stored—"the microcosm of the Gaelic world"—and the soil from which Fiona Macleod saw the Celtic spirit, newly conceived, rise again as a "lamp unto the world." The symbolism of this prophecy was clear: "That greater change may yet be, may well have already come."[55]

Fiona Macleod's pleas for the remission of partisanship and the acceptance of "spiritual rebirth" had their sympathetic hearing. In a review of *The Winged Destiny*—under which title were collected in 1904 most of Fiona Macleod's essays on the transcendent nationalism of the true Celtic spirit—the Irish author Ethel Goddard praised the "art and philosophy" of Fiona Macleod for its refusal to accept "any bondage to tradition or national feeling."[56] Miss Goddard left no doubt that she shared the cosmopolitan outlook that characterized many of Sharp's generation. She chose as Fiona Macleod's central theme this passage from "Celtic": "It is well that the people in the isles should love the isles above all else . . . But it is not well that because of the whistling of the wind in the heather one should imagine that nowhere else does the wind suddenly stir the reeds and the grasses in its incalculable hour." Calling up echoes from the entire course of Sharp's past literary life—echoes all the more startling because it was impossible for her to have known their full significance as part of Sharp's spiritual biography—the reviewer described Fiona Macleod's vision of the future of Celtism as giving it "a destiny akin to that of a fallen Greece and a dispersed Israel . . . Our most desired country is not the real Ireland, the real Scotland, the real Brittany, but . . . the shadowy land of heart's desire."[57]

If the wisdom of transcendent nationalism proved for Sharp to be incapable of translation, beyond the "spiritual history" of Iona, into a lucid and self-sustaining artistic product, it may be because, unlike the Yeats he so much admired, he implacably refused to dramatize the Celt caught halfway between an ancient world and a modern one. "The growth of towns," which he deplored in statement, was nonetheless an irreversible fact which he chose to ignore in Fiona Macleod's art. He restricted her efforts to retelling legendary tales of Celtic pre-history and of the initial invasion of the native druidic spirit by Christianity.

Where he did permit Fiona Macleod to write about "The World That Is,"[58] as he called it, he limited his settings to places where the ancient traditions had survived fragmentarily and as though in a vacuum. His resentment of urban encroachment remained insistent, but it did not reveal itself as an internal theme of his Celtic fiction. He spoke of the life of the Celt, from the very start of his career as Fiona Macleod, as "alien in all ways from the life of cities."[59] Even in the essay "Iona," into which he had so generously blended every aspect of his vision of the future of Celtdom, he had waived its inevitable present condition and held that "in the maelstrom of the cities the old race perishes, drowns."[60] If this was indeed true, how was the Celtic spirit to survive and undergo its spiritual rebirth?

But Sharp's turning away in this sense from the modernity he had earlier championed may not necessarily have been the only cause of the spurious character of some of his Macleod work. The deep truth of what he did say about the nonpartisanship of art might still have been translated into artistic success but for the relentless inhibitions of time and circumstance. The key to the problem defined here lay once again in the typical geographical metaphor into which his imagination transposed his insight. No matter how geographically real Iona might be, it effectively remained for Sharp another correlative for an "illimitable" land of dreams, "the land of heart's desire," the Eden of our universal quest. Elsewhere the metaphor remained substantially the same— "The Hills of Dream," "Sundown Shores," "The Dominion of Dreams." These, collectively, were but one figure that expressed his longing to exceed the partisan limits of the existing places of his world. But as a luminous and prescient symbol for a new human community that could yet be of this world, it was a failure. It remained instead a fantasy overwhelmed with longing and nostalgia—a fantasy to which the "doomed" Celt has long lent his vocabulary, and which Sharp could only describe as a far-off land of beauty "with the light of home upon it."[61] Certainly for him, the "light of home" was not really upon any other than a far-off, inaccessible land. He was a man without a real country, either native or adopted, at a time when to have lost the partisan spirit of one's own country did not yet mean to have gained the whole world.

9

THE GEOGRAPHY OF THE MIND

Toward the Illimitable

Although the symbolism of Fiona Macleod's "land of heart's desire" was artistically precarious, it was nonetheless morally and intellectually sound. It represented Sharp's effort to reconcile the conflict between his desire to express himself in national or racial terms and his equally compelling desire to perceive widely the value of all racial and national literatures. His reconciliation through symbolism was one instance of an advance over Texte, who had appeared to make nationality in art and cosmopolitanism in criticism the aims of two entirely separate activities. However necessary for criticism Texte found "absolute detachment from the national bond," it was precisely to the intensification of nationality that he credited the production of the best creative work: "That which differentiates races, is, strictly, literature or art, that is to say, the expression of their manners and inherent genius, what unites them, on the other hand, is the philosophic or scientific spirit. Art is infinitely various, philosophy is one. The relativity of the former is opposed to the universality of the latter.'" This dogmatic utterance plants an enormous gulf between critic and creator—a gulf that possibly no single man can span though he may choose to exercise both faculties. Sharp's literary duality seems to make him a paragon of such schizophrenia. Superficially, in fact, his work might convey the ready impression that he actually sought to enact the Texte proposition, with the art of Fiona Macleod realizing the national spirit to which Sharp was allied, and William Sharp realizing the national disinterestedness allegedly demanded of criticism. Had Sharp not urged the transcendent nature of Fiona Macleod's Celtic nationalism—a subtle concept anyway—readers could easily have mistaken it (and did mistake it) for a nationalism like any other nationalism. Texte's thesis, in fact, would have tended only to make such a critical misapprehension of Sharp's intention more likely, and Sharp's pursuit of anything but Texte's course more difficult. As long as educated opinion supported Texte's view that "by eliminating this essential notion of race, we surrender . . . all possibility of accounting for anything beyond the individual,"[2] then Sharp's mind, no less than the popular mind, would have to struggle with the conflicting literary values that were corollary. Here was a Texte, a persuasive and sympathetic literary student, condemning Voltaire because he "always obstinately refused to admit that the object of literary criticism is to make us admire what is most national in the genius of each people,"[3] and alleging that, "to a large extent, the differences between literatures are bound up with the profound differences between peoples."[4] As a writer groping for principles of artistic conduct to which such distinctions were crucial, Sharp must have felt the full force of such ideas and been compelled by the need to work out a viable challenge to them if he could not accept them.

It was an unfortunate distinction to make, that of art and nationality on the one side and cosmopolitanism and science on the other, a distinction in this case unlike the others Texte made in being applicable to the French eighteenth century but daily losing its appropriateness to the nineteenth. But Sharp's critical instincts were good. In spite of his apparently conscious aim to apply such views at first, he proved himself capable of going beyond them, and in his later years as critic he demonstrated an increasing awareness that symbolism was his new and saving artistic dispensation. As he allowed Fiona Macleod to say, "There is no racial road to beauty"; and beauty alone was the land "with the light of home upon it."

The combination of Texte's principles with his own was perhaps most apparent in a volume of art criticism on which he worked through 1899 and 1900. *The Progress of Art in the Nineteenth Century* was an explicit realization of Texte's statement that "the object of . . . criticism is to make us admire what is most national in the genius of each people." The book's structure was based on a division of art into national groups, and its statements were designed to express the qualities peculiar to each of the nationalities studied. Yet the book was prefaced by an "Author's Note" that seemed to belie that very design: "Art," he says, "does not grow this way in England or America, or that way in France or Germany or Holland, but is continually and inevitably interrelated."[5] Sharp was not, of course, asserting the identity of artistic production in all countries. But he was referring to the fact of "influence," a fact in itself disturbing to the strict theory of separate and

174

distinct national cultures. *The Progress of Art* was largely based on the premise of "influence," and cohered by way of the supposition that "all that is great in contemporary art" derived originally from John Constable.[6]

In so saying, Sharp was indeed handing the laurel of artistic preeminence in the nineteenth century to the English, but that was obviously not his only intention. The volume does not open with a study of Constable per se, but with an analysis of Nature as the one concept that unites all the varieties of artistic experience, and on which Constable might merely be credited with throwing new light.

As a concept for analyzing the vicissitudes of artistic development on the basis of a single constant, "Nature" is anything but new and anything but applicable to the nineteenth century alone. Yet it is important to see what value Sharp placed upon it and why Constable was therefore such an important starting point. "Nature," Sharp says early in the volume, "is a profound symbol, a symbolic word of many interpretations."[7] Constable, he continues, "recognized the paramount value of atmosphere," emphasized "the play of light and shadow," in short, validated the subjective exploitation of natural phenomena for the purpose of revealing internal truth. This conclusion becomes clearer when Sharp adds that "others are so preoccupied with being faithful that they lose all synthetic vision."[8] Even Constable's predecessor Thomas Gainsborough had assisted this development by teaching that "how you saw it," the "impression" and not "an arbitrary pictorialism," was the desired end of art.[9]

One implication in this form of criticism, that the capacity to have such insights belonged to a special English susceptibility to nature, might well have been provoked by Texte's statement that "certain races, prepared by certain climates or certain conditions of social life, can more easily sustain that abrupt disturbance of the moral equilibrium which must precede the love of physical nature."[10] Yet Sharp, no matter how much moved in his later years by the peacemaking spirit, could never be conceived of as a mere apologist for the English race and character. If moved at all by the conviction of English supremacy in this area, he was probably moved much more by the deep certainty that, whatever this "race" of artists who understood nature, he himself was of it.

Sharp's bias in favor of certain methods of handling landscape points up his deviation from the tenets of Texte's cosmopolitan esthetic. He devised a distinction of some value between what he termed the "idyllist" view of nature and the "pastoralist" or "naturist" view, which he preferred—a distinction that bore no especial parallel to national differences. "Both approach nature as a poetic and beautiful reality that has to be interpreted through the poetic and beautiful medium of the imagination . . . But the pastoralists are content with less poignancy, with less emotion, with less human interest," in short, less sentimentality. "Their art, therefore, is generally more serene, more broad and virile. Moreover, even where they paint subjects of direct human interest they subordinate this to the sense of something greater beyond, either solemn and austere beauty of unchanging nature, or the tragically indifferent operation of mysterious laws." Sharp's choice of Millet's *Angelus* as an example clearly involves a distinction between pathos and sentimentality. In this work, he says,

> what we are aware of is the deep implicit pathos of those hardship-worn lives, that seem as absolutely of the soil as the brown fallows or the seeding grain or the trampled grass and yet have their dreams of a nature beyond this nature, a life beyond this life . . . There is the melancholy, too, that all great modern art has. If the melancholy is not obvious in the poetic and plastic art of Greece, it is because in these later ages the soul . . . has looked inward, and so has had a new vision and known a new ache.[11]

We see in ourselves, he goes on, impermanence, and we seek in nature the truth embodied in "the vast unchanging scope of natural laws."[12] Thus, through the "naturist" approach, nature in art receives a new dimension: "More and more, we may be sure, the world of nature and the world of man will be interpreted as indissolubly wedded companions."[13]

The dimension Sharp speaks of is not so new, of course, if conceived as the ancient theory of correspondence and symbol merely reinterpreted for modern art. Yet it serves as a reminder that symbolism as a phenomenon of the later nineteenth century begins with the seemingly innocuous love for nature and for landscape that characterizes much of its art. The sense of "new dimension" had also derived support from the cosmic philosophies of which Sharp's cosmopolitanism was itself so redolent. These had emphasized man's intuitive capacity to vibrate in sympathy with the macrocosm. Edward Carpenter was, in effect, summarizing such views, prevalent throughout the later part of the century, when he wrote in 1904:

> Nature is a great vehicle, an innumerable network and channel of intelligence and emotion; and this whole domain of the universe the theatre of an immense interchange of conscious life. Countless hosts of living beings, of every grade of organization and consciousness, are giving utterance to themselves, expressing and unfolding that which is within them—even as every child of man from birth to death is constantly endeavouring to express and unfold and give utterance to what lies within him.[14]

Such "anthropomorphism," said Carpenter, was "wisdom"—"the primitive recognition of the single really tenable view of matter as a supply of intelligences, beings, 'selves' relating to our own."[15] Simply as a generalized philosophic statement, Carpenter's throws another light entirely upon the supposedly "peculiar," "uncanny," and "protean" capacity Sharp possessed for reflecting his surroundings, and to which he had been giving vent from his earliest years. Rather than following what critics of romanticism like Irving Babbitt were to consider the traditional romantic drift toward increased eccentricity, he was aiming more and more at a fixed and permanent center amid the flux of experience.

Sharp's fully conscious perception of the symbolic uses of nature affected his literary as well as his art criticism. Well-known by the turn of the century as a traveler and nature-lover, as well as a broadly appreciative reader of modern literatures, he was commissioned by *Pall Mall Magazine* to write a series of essays on "place" in literature for its 1903 to 1904 numbers. These twelve essays, later bound and published by *Pall Mall* under the title *Literary Geography*, were generally anecdotal, geared in their tone to the superficially eclectic popular taste. But there was also apparent in them Sharp's developed tendency to see the use of particular place in fiction as symbolic, and not as a submission to the call for the picturesque. For him, the writer best seized nature when he appropriated it to his imaginative conception, when he made it, in other words, the servant of his theme and subject and placed it under the control of his imagination. Thus Sharp could avoid lumping together all fiction that was in any way scenic. He could logically separate what was mere vicarious expedition into the foreign and exotic from what made place the inevitable concomitant of human action. His distinction was elaborated early in the volume, in a discussion of Meredithian "geography":

> The secret of the vivid and abiding charm of Mr. Meredith's backgrounds to the tragi-comedy of his outstanding men and women is just in their aloofness from anything "kaleidoscopic," with its implications of the arbitrary and accidental. He does not go to Venice or to Limburg to write about these places, or to note the bloom of local colour for artistic decoration; nor does he diverge by the Adriatic or by the winding ways of Lahn, so as to introduce this gondola-view of the sea-set city or that forest-vision which for English folk has given a touch of beauty to Nassau which before it hardly owned in literary remembrance. His men and women are there, for a time, or passingly; and so the beauty that is in the background closes round upon them, or is flashed out for a moment, through the magic of the same power which gave themselves the breath of life.[16]

In a later essay Sharp laments that Thackeray did not have, like his two great contemporaries, Dickens and Charlotte Brontë, that sense for the "imaginative value of background," "that larger vision and deeper intellectual and artistic sentiment which has since been so distinguishing a feature of every great achievement in contemporary imaginative fiction." In Thackeray's work we remain unaware, he continues, as we are so distinctly aware in Dickens, in Brontë, and also in Robert Louis Stevenson, of the "indescribable presence and secret influence" of nature.[17]

But Sharp did not always limit himself to the "indescribable" and "secret." He was aware in the Brontës' work of the precise character of the "places" and of what they contribute to and elicit from the drama of the lives of the characters themselves. He recognized the "stern aloofness," the almost "arrogant independence," that the moors leave as their heritage to the moorlanders and the solitude, the "wildness," of those "great spaces," where the breath is free, and yet the spirit depressed.[18] "The reader," he explained in still another essay, this one on *Aylwin*, "knows the difference between what is merely depicted, however beautiful, and what is *thought in*." In the East Anglian scenery drawn by Theodore Watts-Dunton, the reader recognizes ("naturistically," as it were) "the sense of something tragical in nature . . . The spirit is . . . uplifted to those unpassing things of which

great solitary places and still lonelinesses, and all the sombre phantasmagoria of land and sky are symbolic."[19] "It all," he said, "strikes the
note of correspondence."[20]

Sharp's use of natural symbolism in his own fiction was, as one might
expect, much more deliberate and pervasive in his later work than in
any written during the eighties. Though he gave by far the greater
share to his work as Fiona Macleod, he did admit one opportunity
during the Macleod period for William Sharp to exploit this sensibility.
Silence Farm, his last novel and his last significant imaginative work
as William Sharp was—as its title suggests—designed to convey symbolic force through natural place. Silence Farm is no mere background;
nor is it simply an "environment" that must be there to supply the
physical needs of those who dwell in it.[21] It is, rather, a spiritual force
in itself, personal and inexorable, exercising its gloomy and unhealthy
influence upon all its inhabitants: "It is there we are to live; it is there
we are to grow old in weariness and the dull round of unchanging
days."[22] When the heroine, Margaret Gray, at last returns to work as
a hand on the farm that her father had once owned, it is as though
she were a part of the very earth of the farm itself, as though her return
symbolized a resignation to the inevitability of her union with the soil.
In a manner suggestive of Hardy, Sharp ends the novel with a picture
of the girl standing barefoot in the furrows, sensible of the clods of
earth under her feet and of the wind blowing through her hair.

Sharp's sensitivity to the correspondent uses of nature, implicit in
this novel and expressed in *Literary Geography*, had, of course, gone
through many years of evolution. Such exploitation of atmosphere had
always played a considerable part in his use of place. But as a principle
of critical perception to be applied to the work of others and to be
deliberately and consciously exploited in his own, it seemed to crystal-
lize, like so much of his thought, when he encountered the Belgian
dramatists. His comments on Auguste Jenart's *Le Barbare* in 1893 were
instinct with the pleasure of discovery that he himself was but one
member of a race of "naturists":

Perhaps the most notable thing in *Le Barbare* from the point of
view of the literary student is the poetic and singularly impressive
way in which the animate and inanimate environment of the per-
sonages of the drama play their part in the general scheme of psychic
effect. The wind, the snow, the tempest, the water of the lake that

clucks and gurgles . . . the old tapestries, the firelight, the deep gloom of chill rooms, the ominous silence, the leaping or crawling of shadows—all are wrought into the same tragic weft.[23]

The perception had then proceeded with increasing sureness via the "natural magic" of Fiona Macleod's fiction. In *Green Fire* (1896) he had theorized that the Celts were perishing as a visionary clan because of the "slow waning of our joy, of our passionate delight in the Beauty of the World."

> We have been unable to look out upon the shining of our star, for the vision overcomes us; and we have used veils which we call "scenery," "picturesqueness," and the like—poor, barren words that are so voiceless and remote before the rustle of leaves and the lap of water; before the ancient music of the wind, and all the sovran eloquence of the tides of light. But a day may come—nay, shall surely come—when indeed the poor and humble shall inherit the earth.[24]

Other early Macleod works sought to partake of this inheritance. A series of brief pieces collectively entitled "Tragic Landscapes," from *The Sin-Eater and Other Tales* (1895), succeeded in evoking through several of the moods of nature some of the more obvious moods of the human spirit, the character of which is suggested by their subtitles: "The Tempest," "Mist," and "Summer Sleep."[25] These, and the sketches included in *The Silence of Amor* (1896), have much in common with the sensitive visualizations of "Earth's Voices" and "Transcripts from Nature" that had formed a principal part of Sharp's second volume of verse, far back in 1884. But there is a significant difference. The earlier sketches were in verse and were united by the attempt to find a lyric equivalent for natural images; the later sketches were instead written in prose. Sharp was moving obviously within the impressionistic sphere opened by the French in calling these "prose-poetry" and considering them a distinct form responding to the need "under the stress of emotion" for "an inevitable reversion to the impulse of chant."[26] The use of the word "chant," with its overtones of poetic vision and prophecy and its associations with the "mythopoeic faculty," was Sharp's way of emphasizing that these prose-poems were no mere evocations of natural scene, but that they used images clearly symbolic or of symbolic suggestiveness, and carried the burden of a message which might be termed philosophic or metaphysical. One such prose-poem in *The Silence of Amor*, called simply "Nocturne," posits a universal order through images representing a formula for harmony, somewhat in the manner of Japanese haiku. Another, "The White Merle," employs a bird symbol that sharply recalls Hopkins' "Windhover," and suggests the indwelling of deity and the repetition of the mystery of sacrifice.

> Long, long ago, a white merle flew out of Eden. Its song has been in the world ever since, but few there are who have seen the flash of its white wings through the green-gloom of the living wood—the sun-splashed, rain-drenched, mist-girt, storm-beat wood of human life.

> But to-day, as I came through the wood, under an arch of tempest, and led by lightnings, I passed into a green sun-splashed place. There, there, I heard the singing of a rapt song of joy! there, ah, there I saw the flash of white wings!

Still another, "The Reed-Player," stirs up a vague but accessible sense of the artist as symbolically both priest and victim with its portrait of a rustic "myth-maker":

> I saw one put a hollow reed to his lips. It was a forlorn, sweet air that he played, an ancient forgotten strain learned of a shepherding woman upon the hills. The Song of Songs it was that he played: and the beating of hearts was heard, and I heard sighs, and a voice like a distant bird-song rose and fell.

> "Play me a song of Death," I said. Then he who had the hollow reed at his lips smiled, and he played again the Song of Songs.

And the passionate God that set the stars in ecstatic motion in Van Gogh's *Starry Night* seems to be the same that created the vision of "Whirled Stars" that is another among these often extraordinary pieces.[27]

The use of "chant" is itself intimately connected with the pervasive tendency of the Celts, as Sharp often described them, to see "the thing beyond the thing," to view surface phenomena as signs and symbols, a tendency which was quite legitimately extended to language. The passion for the study of language, especially poetic language, as symbol was primitively demonstrated in a Fiona Macleod work called "The Lynn of Dreams" (1902). Here a young writer seeks the "secret" of words, first in all language, then in his own work, and at last in the "other world." He is given, through the agency of Dalua, the Celtic personification of the power of illusion, a glimpse into the immortal shape and color of words—into a kind of sphere of Platonic ideas. The experience is at first deceptively revivifying. But as the writer attempts to re-evolve the shapes of his vision in his own writing, he fails miserably:

> It was all gone: the master touch, the secret art, the craft. He became an obscure stammerer. At the last he was dumb. And then his heart broke, and he died.

> But had not the Master of Illusions shown him his heart's desire and made it his?[28]

The last lines of this equivocal story can, in one way, be used as an epigraph to all the later imaginative work of Fiona Macleod, which is so much marked by a condition of futility. They suggest that the power of the "seer" is also a threat, and well they might. Sharp's own efforts to re-evoke, consciously and deliberately, the ecstatic inspiration that had produced Fiona Macleod's first and best novels and short stories in the mid-nineties had yielded nothing but frustration. Unable, however, to sacrifice the pseudonym, he continued to exercise the symbolic vision, but in work that more and more blurred the line between artist and philosopher-critic.[29]

Fiona Macleod's first forays into literary criticism, in the late nineties, were symptomatic of this shift. They indicate Sharp's awareness from the vantage point of his whole imaginative vision that even if he could only look in retrospect upon his best imaginative work, he could still articulate the principles behind it and encourage their application by others. "The arts have become religious," Fiona Macleod, in "Celtic," quoted Yeats as saying (though the idea was nothing if not widespread among the contemporary avant-garde). They must, Fiona Macleod continued, "as religious thought has always done, utter themselves through legends; and the Gaelic legends have so much of a new beauty that they may well give the opening century its most memorable symbols."[30]

Sharp's later efforts under his pseudonym seem to have been designed as a way of making Fiona Macleod continue as handmaiden to the movement she had earlier led. They form a compendium of all the legendry, Gaelic mainly but not exclusively, that could convey the religiosity of symbol and assist or explicate the work of others. "Iona," "By Sundown Shores," "The Sunset of Old Tales," and similar pieces were the residue of Fiona Macleod's Gaelic memory and imagination. But universality was the keynote of a series of evocative essays called *Where the Forest Murmurs* (1904-1905). Their title, which might make them immediately suspect as sentimental descriptions of nature in the vein Sharp himself had described as "idyllist," was completely deceptive. The essays actually displayed an intimate firsthand knowledge of natural phenomena that was as tough-minded as scientific disquisition—with this difference, that into them Fiona Macleod also deftly spun the mythology of nature and the folklores of innumerable countries. Through them Sharp bore witness to his belief in the unity underlying all primitive perceptions that nature is the veil of another kind of wisdom.

Notable among these essays is one called "The Mountain Charm," in which the author analyzes in psychological terms the influence mountains seem to exert, "the overwhelming sense of their imagined eternity," and in which he perceives the shift in sensibility that caused the nineteenth century to make mountains a special medium for conveying the experience of the romantic. The sea, and water in general, receives its share of scrutiny in several other essays. With a detachment and straightforward power unmatched by much of his fictional writing as Fiona Macleod, Sharp studies the tendency to see in the ebb and flow of water "the secret of life," and in its continuum "the secret of eternity." "The Sea Spell" pursues the "influence" of water, analyzing its relation to womanhood, as "Still Waters" analyzes various other kinds of anthropomorphic life-parallels evoked by pools, tarns, and quiet waters in forest places. Sharp ranges through the year, casually and with a pleasant sureness in his knowledge. He succeeds in expressing the vitality of nature even in winter, giving a form of symbolic life to the phenomena of ice, wind, clouds, stars, birds. Whether symbols of joy or symbols of sorrow or evil, or complex, reverberating symbols of both, they call us, he says with suggestive power, to "the wastes of the imagination."[31] This image has a rich, double-edged significance that, in its relevance to modern literature, might give one cause to wonder whether the "wasteland" is not wrongly construed as a metaphor for desolation.

Regardless of its debt to Frazer and other collectors of and commentators upon folklore, a debt that clearly was great, *Where the Forest Murmurs* is a worthy transposition of anthropology into another key and on another instrument. The essays are prophetic in their recognition of the scope of natural symbols—particularly of the way natural symbols have of accreting meaning and suggestiveness.

> For nothing is more strange than the life of natural symbols. We may discern in them a new illusion, a new meaning: the thought we slip into them may be shaped to a new desire and coloured with some new fantasy of dreams or of the unspoken and nameless longing in the heart: but the symbol has seen a multitude of desires come and go like shadows, has been troubled with many longings and baffled wings of the veiled passions of the soul.[32]

This passage is from the essay "Rosa Mystica," which disengages from the rest and explores, with a steady control of very eclectic materials, the one "eternal and unchanging symbol" that has seemed to possess a peculiar fascination for modern writers and scholars.

This catalogue of Sharp's views of nature in literature and art represents his underlying religious respect for the imagination of the artist. It is the imagination that not only responds to the data provided by the senses but stores up and recasts past experiences, associations, and feelings, and that recognizes them as a part—perhaps the more important part—of the present. Moreover, it has a visionary power: "with the second sight of the imagination we can often see more clearly in the perspectives of the past than in the maze of the present"—we can see what lies "below the accidents of time and circumstance."[33]

But a still more remarkable power of the imagination is its freedom to range internally as well as externally. The enterprise of the artist is, in other words, not only to return nature and natural phenomena to their imaginative correlatives but to create shapes and embodiments for strictly imaginative concepts. This was the intent of Fiona Macleod's "The Divine Adventure" (1899), a drama of inner division and reconciliation, a journey through psychic space of the three faculties of Body, Will, and Soul.

In an apologia for this piece, Fiona Macleod curiously asserted that its author, as symbolist, was "supremely a realist." He claimed to abhor the "vague" and to be incapable of disregarding "the actual reality as it seems."[34] These were strange claims indeed to make of a tale where the only verisimilitude lay in the truth of the existence of an inner life. Beyond that it was an allegory in the traditional sense. But there is a persistence in Sharp's application of the terms "realist" and "reality" that, however strange, characterizes all of his remarks on the uses of the imagination and that must be reckoned with. Commenting, in the context of his discussion of "The Divine Adventure," upon an earlier story, "The Book of the Opal," he called it "a sketch true in essentials, but having at its close an arbitrary interpolation of external symbolism which I now regard as superfluous. I have since realized that the only living and convincing symbol is that which is conceived of the spirit, and not imagined by the mind."[35] Perhaps Sharp considered the spirit "realist" in its technique because it stored up experience for symbolic re-use. In this case, the distinction between "spirit" and "mind" might well be construed as a premise derived in reverse fashion from a conclusion—that is, that there are symbols more "living and convincing," more "real" in short, than others. The problem of defining his meaning is compounded by one of application—of the appropriateness of a given symbol in a given place. The four symbols of stone, sword, spear, and cup, for the four cultures of North, East, South, and West, were those he had rejected as "superfluous" in "The Book of the Opal." Yet he employed them again, to his own apparent satisfaction, in a Fiona Macleod poem called "The Dirge of the Four Cities."[36]

Sharp's increasing efforts to work Fiona Macleod as literary critic gave him, however, further opportunities to analyze the distinction between the true and the false symbol. This distinction was elaborated in an essay, "The Later Work of Mr. Yeats" (1902), where Fiona Macleod spoke of Yeats as a "priest" of the symbolic, as one of those poets who "see and dream in a reality so vivid that it is called imagination . . . With him the imagination is in truth the second-sight of the mind. Thus it is that he lives with symbols, as unimaginative natures live with facts." Then he proceeded to the crucial issue:

> The symbolist stands in some danger here. The obvious peril is a confusion of the spiritual beauty behind the symbol with the arbitrary expression of that spiritual beauty through that particular symbol . . . Perhaps a truer wisdom is that which would see the symbols in the facts, and the facts translated from their material body to their spiritual significance.

"One may speak with the tongue of angels," he added, "but the accent must be human and familiar."[37]

In the case of the Celtic writer, symbolism could thus be very much a two-way street. Accepted and traditional symbols of accreted significance, so long as that significance was not too esoteric (as Fiona Macleod claimed many of Yeats's were), could be used to "realize" human experience of a spiritual or an emotional nature. But conversely, one might start with the imaginative emotional or spiritual experience and translate it by way of a new synthesis of commonplace "fact," thereby making that "fact" symbolic.

In explaining such a technique of imaginative translation, Sharp is perhaps no clearer than anyone has ever been. Yet whatever his meaning, he evidently believed that psychic figments possessed a reality so virtual that they could be dramatized into what he called the "psychic" or symbolic drama. Here his comments on Yeats are again appropriate, for one of the "later" works he was studying in this essay was "The Shadowy Waters." This was not, he said, a drama in the usual sense, but "lyrical thought become continuous, because it is the symbolic reflection of what is in the poet's mind, rather than the architectonic revelation of what his imagination has definitely shaped. It is not, strictly, a poetical drama, even structurally, for action and speech are subservient to the writer's entranced vision of the symbolism of the action and of the speeches." At this point, Fiona Macleod pointed allusively to Sharp's own earlier work in the impressionistic drama:

> It is one of those new and strange utterances, so perplexing to many minds, wherewith conventional methods are used for novel, perturbing, sometimes bewildering, at times bewildered, thought: one of those dramas of the mind best seen against imagined tapestries, which reveal so much more to us than do the common or familiar tapestries, the dramas of the obvious, of merely spectacular life.[08]

Sharp's Vistas (1984) had been like attempts to give "reality" to the "dramas of the mind." They strongly resembled the dramas of the Belgian school he championed so firmly, although his earliest efforts in this vein antedated his acquaintance with the work of Maeterlinck. For modern readers these would no longer be "new and strange utterances." Their manner, if not their matter, is extremely familiar, for Sharp's later prophecy that the theater would reject mere social history and attempt more and more the dramatization of psychological experience has to a great extent been realized. Modern dramatists have crossed the line between fantasy and what is normally considered reality, to give their stage conceptions the associative and imaginative value of dreams and to exploit rather than ignore the stage's basis in illusion. Sharp's work differed from theirs only in having less breadth or complexity of plot, as well, perhaps, as less assistance from advances in stagecraft. He had, it may be remembered, defended the inferior stage effects of his favored Belgians on the grounds that their dramas were not intended for production, and he was probably uncertain of the playability of works like his own.

Though the only two completed dramas of Fiona Macleod, *The House of Usna* and *The Immortal Hour*, differ from *Vistas* in having their plot basis in Celtic myth, they are actually "psychic" dramas in the same sense as *Vistas*, and in the sense in which Sharp defined Yeats's "Shadowy Waters." In *The House of Usna* the essential action related to the myth, the death of Deirdre, has already taken place before the play opens. It only remains for the author to lyricize on her death and to use "the fall of the House" as part of an elegiac theme, repeated in various moods and tempos.[39] *The Immortal Hour* is similarly evasive in plot, although more of the essential action takes place within the drama itself. The latter play bears special resemblance to the D'Annunzian drama, by which both must also have been influenced, in which sonorous, oracular, almost somnambulistic speeches are uttered by abstracted figures.[40]

It is extremely difficult to judge this type of drama by ordinary theatrical standards. The plays are not especially moving when read, though strictly as literature they evince a certain compelling quality in their atmosphere of doom—something compelling even in the obscurity of their verse. Dorothy Hoare, in her study of the uses and abuses of myth in modern literature, may have been justified in dismissing these works as vague and pretentious.[41] Critics of D'Annunzio have done the same. Yet the experience of one "captive" spectator of D'Annunzian drama, Carlo Levi, testifies to the power of this drama as played by a traveling Sicilian family that performed throughout southern Italy in simple peasant settings not unlike those in which the dramas were conceived.[42] One wonders, thinking of Fiona Macleod's plays, if such a native and deeply-felt performance might not also evoke from them what the distant and detached critic cannot conceive by himself.

Even, however, if one grants that the Celtic mythology did not prove a fruitful field for drama, the reader attempting to judge the validity of Sharp's theories must still reckon with the substantial modern success of the dramatic retelling of Greek legend. This might suggest that the weakness of the Celtic drama resulted from the limited diffusion and comprehension of the myths themselves and that Sharp was basically justified in his intentions insofar as he saw the modern dramatist's rejuvenation in a new kind of symbolic tragedy that might, if it chose, exploit the permanence and universality of ancient myth. "In tragic drama," he asserted, "it is authenticity of emotion and not authenticity of episode that matters."[43] What all heroic mythologies have in common, in other words, is emotional correspondence. "The tradition of accursed families is not the fantasy of one dramatist or of one country or of one time."[44] It is rather a basic theme of the potency and fatality of blood in which "the names stand for the elemental passions,"[45] and which numerous playwrights, in numerous civilizations, in numerous eras, have successfully transposed. What the modern "psychic" dramatist will attempt, Sharp forecasts, is to reproduce the validity of the emotions attendant on such stories as the Oresteia. This "Psychic Drama shall not be less nervous," less energetic, than the theater of the intellect, "but the emotional energy shall be along the nerves of the spirit, which sees beneath, above, and beyond, rather than merely along the nerves of material life, which sees only that which is in the line of sight."[46] This drama has but one limitation he yet hopes may eventually be overcome: "The poet, the dramatist, is not able—is not yet able—to express in beauty and convey in symbol the visible energy of these emotions without resort to the artifice of men and women set in array, with harmonious and arbitrary speech given to them, and a background of illusion made unreal by being made emphatic."[47] Someday, he says, the spectator's imagination may not require these props, and the dramatist will be permitted the "naked" expression of elemental passions.

Exactly how this was to be accomplished Sharp did not fully explain. Though he was to some extent anticipating the actual experience of twentieth-century theater, his language is still too radical to have perfect application to it. Perhaps once again he had in mind something like the cosmic consciousness of Edward Carpenter, whose elementary premise in The Art of Creation was that artistic creation was "the embodying forth of feeling" through matter. Carpenter posed such a hypothetical question as that implied by Fiona Macleod's "naked" expression of elemental passions:

> "But ought not [the artist], if your theory be correct, to be able to throw those mental images *direct* into the outer world so as to become visible and tangible to others, at once, without intermediate operations?" To which I answer, *Don't be in too great a hurry.* I believe man *has* the germ of such power, and will have it in greater degree. But because he can travel so far along the route at present it does not follow that with his yet undeveloped powers he can at once reach the point of being able to project his thoughts instantly into the world around him.[48]

Although this prophecy, which would seem so consistent with Sharp's otherwise cryptic words, still strains credibility, there was, nevertheless, soundness to Sharp's estimate of the direction modern theater would take. For him, a new theater was coming; the theater of the intellect (which he, like many of his contemporaries, equated with Ibsen) was "outworn." "The inherent tendency to demonstrate intellectually from a series of incontrovertible facts is not adequate for those who would see in the drama the means to demonstrate symbolically from a sequence of intuitive perceptions."[49] Quoting Chateaubriand's mysterious statement "To recover the desert, I took refuge in the theater," Sharp alleges that "the whole effort of a civilization become anaemic and disillusioned must be 'to recover the desert.'" Chateaubriand knew "that in the *théâtre de l'âme* lay the subtlest and most searching means for the imagination to compel reality to dreams, to compel actuality to vision, to compel the symbolic congregation of words to the bewildered throng of wandering and illusive thoughts and ideas."[50] Like most of Sharp's geographic metaphors, this one, though borrowed, has a singular appropriateness for his mind. Reminiscent of his reference, in *Where the Forest Murmurs*, to "the wastes of the imagination," the image reminds us that though the desert is a "wasteland" it is also akin to the "vast spaces" Sharp had professed to love many years before, and which he now seemed to see as "that wilderness, that actual or symbolic solitude, to which the creative imagination goes as the curlew to the wastes or as the mew to foam and wind."[51] These would be the spaces that liberate the modern soul from forms accreted and alien to it, the flatlands on which everything might be built anew.

The conviction on which Sharp's vision of the new drama was based, that in both its literary and pictorial forms art is the expression of the "reality" of inner and imaginative life, informs almost every critical essay Sharp wrote under either name from about 1898 until his death. Modern criticism uses Hopkins' word "inscape," one that it is no surprise was formulated in Sharp's era; Sharp would have been peculiarly grateful for it had it been available to him then. When Stephen Phillips, in an article in the *Dome* for February 1899, claimed to have discovered the inner life as a subject for poetry, Fiona Macleod "sharply" responded that Celtic literature had always recognized "a compelling sense of the paramount reality of the life of the spirit" and that modern poets like Yeats and A.E. had long worked from that recognition.[52]

It was an indication of how alien still was the general critical atmosphere in which he spoke that Sharp felt it necessary at the same time to express the fear that the poetry "of the spirit" so-called would be mistaken for a poetry of spiritualism: "I would rather see poetry sink to become the province of the skilled artificer than that the singer, the maker, the seer, should relinquish it to the mental drunkard, the spiritual epileptic."[53] Yet this important qualification served only as a moderately efficient warning to some of Fiona Macleod's would-be admirers. Even as late as 1919, one such admirer used a spiritualist theory of "possession" to explain the extraordinary compassion for women expressed by Sharp under his pseudonym.[54] That his purpose should be so mistaken was probably in part the fault of a vocabulary that is now familiar to literary criticism, but which spiritualists had for a time preempted. Like William Blake and like many late Victorian neo-romantics, for whom Blake was a prophet in every sense, Sharp laid emphasis, in Fiona Macleod's *Dome* article and elsewhere, on the poet as "seer" and on poetry as prophecy and revelation. His Fiona Macleod writings were filled with characterizations of prophetic, often mad poets, capable of extraordinary psychic experiences, not the least of which was second sight. These same poets were given the character, if not the name, of the Celtic type of the poet-madman, the "Amadan." Moreover, a series of semi-autobiographical tales in one Fiona Macleod volume, *The Sin-Eater* (1895), was dedicated to the phenomenon of the "sight" and those who possessed it. The passion for endowing the poet with special tools of wisdom and vision was a means for expressing Sharp's own view of his duty as an artist to see—as he put it, "with the second sight of the imagination"—the truth revealed in natural phenomena. Nevertheless, it so served to encourage the spiritualist view of his work that Yeats, himself an early devotee of the occult, thought he was doing Sharp no harm when he said of him after his death that he was "the most extraordinary psychic he had ever encountered."[55]

Sharp qua Sharp, of course, steered clear of the dangerous spiritualist vocabulary. Even had it offered no latitude for misinterpretation, his effort to avoid any confounding of his two literary personalities would have kept that vocabulary from the "bread-and-butter-making" side of his work. But he placed no restraint on his effort to promote the symbolic view of art. This course is evident in essays on Edward Burne-Jones and Puvis de Chavannes in 1898, both of them demigods of the prevailing esthetic avant-garde. Burne-Jones he considered preeminently a painter of "otherworldliness," a man for whom "the reality of dreams was much more . . . than outward actuality."[56] Though he hesitated to commit himself totally on an estimate of Burne-Jones's future fame, it would have been unlike Sharp not to suggest, in accord with his sentiments on the direction of modern art, that Burne-Jones had "bequeathed a great heritage" to the future and had already exerted an influence that, whether or not as part of his personal reputation, would continue to be felt. There is an echo of Fiona Macleod's testimony as to the new symbolic dispensation in some of Sharp's further comments. "From the outset," he says, Burne-Jones "saw life symbolically." He is "in the truest sense a profound realist—only his realism is not that aggregating observation of the detective intelligence, but the perceiving and unifying vision of the imagination."[57] "To us," he continues, "his work is ideal; to himself, real, verily existent," filled with a "new, almost hieratic vision."[58]

In connection with Burne-Jones, Sharp makes an observation that is of continuing significance to the modern reader seeking to unify the varying artistic products of the nineteenth century. Quoting in curious juxtaposition both the transcendentalist's phrase that the world is "the garment of God" and Pater's statement that "all the acts and accidents of daily life borrow a sacred color and significance,"[59] Sharp asserts that what is called the esthetic or romantic movement is no more than a simultaneous accord among many artists that the commonplace is itself symbolical. He perceived, in other words, that an equal fundamental concern with the commonplace was the point where the so-called esthete and the realist or naturalist met. As Sharp observed, they shared the common effort to evoke the "deep and poignant sense of the tragic piteousness of life," though only one of the schools felt the need to sublimate and purify it—"the imperative need to interpret through beauty its spiritual correspondences."[60]

The view of Burne-Jones that gave rise to these insights is to a large extent reiterated in Sharp's study of Puvis de Chavannes: "He worked through and towards an ideal vision . . . [But] though so dreamlike in many of his creations, Puvis de Chavannes was a realist in the truest sense. Everything he did was studied from nature, and his imagination was always based on actuality." Confronted with the complaint that Chavannes "traduced life by overmuch beauty," Sharp recalls Chavannes' own reply: "There is ample room between Hogarth and Lionardo,"[61] implying that truth to life is not the exclusive province of the realist and that it embraces an extraordinarily wide range of vision and expression.

"Ample room" was a necessity for the William Sharp of life as of literature. If "the wastes of the imagination," yielding so many possibilities of expression of truth, had as yet found no corroboration or counterpart in common experience, they had found their counterpart in his. Sharp's vision, which had always been focused on the outside world, had also always been in search of a landscape that could express the limitlessly complex geography of the inner man—indeed that could express the uncertain, often perilous geography of the soul of modern man. For this reason one comes very close to Sharp's interpretation of the needs of that man by reading the scattered travel articles that, along with *Literary Geography,* were the main preoccupation of Sharp's last years. These articles illustrate his characteristic ability to translate nature into symbol, to reconstruct out of the earth around him a vivid reflection of the breadth and range of his own imaginative vision.

Intermittently ill from 1896 on, and requiring the resuscitating agency of frequent trips to the warm south, Sharp finally found his preferred place of rest in Sicily. Many years of experience with a travel-hungry British public had made him something of an opportunist, and despite his illness he could not resist luring them with descriptions of this fascinating island, still barely touched by tourism. The resulting articles tell why Sicily held such an attraction for him. Here the primitive element was strong; here he could find, as he had found in the Tuscan

192

and Umbrian hills, the remains of an ancient, Dionysiac, ritualistic civilization, with closer and surer ties to his beloved Greeks than even the Etruscans could boast; here was a civilization steeped in "mystery cults," fatalism, and earth symbolism.[62]

Sharp's imagination was especially stirred by the ruined shrine of Venus at Erice. If Iona had been the island mecca of the Gael, this was the island mecca of all of western civilization, host through millennia of changing cultures to worshippers of the Goddess of Love and Death, Aphrodite, Astarte, Venus, and finally the Madonna herself.[63] But this variety of worship was only a single illustration of what all of Sicily seemed uniquely to symbolize for Sharp, the simultaneous existence and interplay of all religious, historical, and racial truth. It was in what he called the Sicilian Highlands that he felt the thrill of encountering "abrupt racial contrasts."[64] It was here in Sicily that the poles of civilization crossed, here that the Norman and Saracen met. Here, ever present, was the sense of "the things of the spirit that do not fade, the remembrance of great names, great deeds, terrible events, monumental heroisms, monumental sorrows."[65] Here every fragment of the symbology of the "elemental passions" had been stored and preserved. For Sharp Sicily was as near as man could come to the geography of the universal mind.

During the first years of the twentieth century, the last years of his life, Sharp spent the greater part of his time in and around Taormina, particularly at the Castello di Maniace, near Etna, as a guest in the villa of Alexander Nelson Hood, the Duke of Bronte. The Sharps no doubt had good practical reasons for finding the place especially convenient, for, apart from the sheer physical allure of the land, the villa offered the comforts only a wealthy Englishman could maintain and proximity to one of the few Sicilian resorts then developed to any extent.

But Sharp's last essay reveals that it was not Taormina's convenience and charm that held the secret of its hold upon his imagination. Written just before his death, that essay, "The Garden of the Sun," shows the inevitable effects of Sharp's physical decline. Its uneven surface poignantly conveys the struggle between his consciousness of the ephemeral and pedestrian nature of travel writing and his yearning to transcribe into words a vision he may never find a means of expressing again. To the reader who understands Sharp, it is no guide-book exercise, but a

193

cry of discovery. Taormina, in the shelter of "Mother Etna," "the soul of Sicily, the soul of Italy, the soul of Greece," had become not merely a place but "a spirit, a presence, a Past that is the Present, a Present that is the Past." It was

> the same unchanging, most lovely coign where Pythagoras himself once taught, where the dark searching eyes of St. Paul wandered for some sign of the Unknown God, where the Greek adventurers of old landed and founded a city and raised a great fane to Apollo, and where, in the dim, impenetrable past, a mysterious race worshipped a mysterious goddess of the sea whose very name has passed from the memory of man.[66]

In short, Taormina was a place where the mind and spirit, in search of the freedom to range in all the dimensions of experience, in both time and space, could be liberated for their excursions.

> Long ago the unknown town built on the scarps of Taurus merged into Tauremenion, and Tauremenion has known the Sikel, the Greek, the Carthaginian, the Roman, the Saracen, the Moor, the Spaniard, the Neapolitan, the Italian of the North.

Within that history was variety, yet within that variety, permanence: "These races, these dynasties, these triumphs and disasters, pass away like the dust of storms. Taormina remains."[67]

Before he died on December 5, 1905, Sharp selected for his epitaph two inscriptions he himself had composed. One of these had been a favorite among some of the more oracular and cryptic phrases of Fiona Macleod: "Love is greater than we conceive, and Death is the keeper of unknown redemptions." The other was subscribed "W.S." and read:

> Farewell to the known and exhausted,
> Welcome the unknown and illimitable.[68]

Both of these, but particularly the last, were profoundly wise and self-knowing for one whose search for the "illimitable" had been consuming. But in another sense, the inscription of "W.S." was no more than a sonorous footnote to his last experiment in locating a correspondent natural counterpart for his frenetic need of space, even if the place he found was after all but partially fulfilling, and once seen, already "known and exhausted." His coming to rest at last on a hillside near Etna was remarkably fitting. The resolution of his last years, the appropriation of Taormina as the supreme representative of the variety of his own identity, was the only resolution available to a man whose temperament and time forced him into the lonely role of precursor rather than participator in a movement. Taormina was a refuge of moral as well as of physical health. Taormina was a symbolic consummation of all that he felt was potential in himself.

Sharp died probably unaware how much the lure of the "unknown and illimitable" was already beginning to be felt by others. The art and literature of the near future was yet to prove Death not the only keeper of redemptions for those imaginations seeking freedom from the limits of their place, their time, their plot, however "blessed" it might be.

CONCLUSION

Apart from Time and Country

It is impossible to pass final judgment on William Sharp's exploitation of his sense of place and to put it into historical perspective without first observing that a sympathetic response to the natural world is in some degree available as creative material to all artists. The power we all know in childhood of anthropomorphizing the external world and of seeing that world as an extension of what we only later and gradually come to know as our separate selves is, as one psychologist has pointed out, merely sustained longer by artists than by other men.[1]

Yet all artistic sensibility to nature is not the same. If it were, there would be absolutely no validity to distinctions among various artistic eras, distinctions which, contrary to the antihistorical view of the psychologist, are the commonplaces of literary and artistic historiography. Every artist in every era may reverberate to his natural surroundings, but the shape and application he gives to that response define his philosophic fraternity with men of his time. "Windsor Forest" is a long way, philosophically as well as geographically, from the romantic Alps.

A distance less large, but a distance nonetheless, divides the nature sensibility of Wordsworth and of D. H. Lawrence. This is apparent. But what was the process by which this subtler distinction evolved? What did the Victorians contribute to the shape and application of the artistic response to nature that significantly altered it? As a Victorian in whose work and character was compressed every aspect of the nature sensibility and sense of place among his contemporaries, William Sharp may assist in determining and defining that evolutionary link.

Sharp's sense of place was in great part a legacy he owed to romanticism, a legacy of which not he alone but his entire generation were beneficiaries. Much more than those generic artists of whom the psychologist speaks, romantics seemed to receive more freely and to reverberate more liberally to the suggestions offered by the natural world. If the psychological premise devised to explain all such responses is correct, then the romantic distinguished himself by exceeding ordinary men—or indeed ordinary artists—in resisting the categorizing demanded

196

by the adoption of a securely defined self. Perhaps his "agony" was the result of an unusually distasteful array of available roles in his society, none presenting him with an authentic and acceptable reflection of his own desires. Certainly the history coinciding with what we know in western culture as romanticism offers analogues for infinite dissatisfaction. Disruptions in religious, ethical, social, and political systems wrought their effect by making any thorough commitment to such systems less and less possible for the instinctively recalcitrant artist.

But such disruptions did not—could not—destroy the need for some such commitment, some such identification. The continuing need and the continuing search for identity characterize the romantic phase as much as does the generously sympathetic response to the outside world. The romantic could not disavow his instinctive psychological obligation to seek in some aspect of the reality around him a satisfactory reflection of himself. So demanding is this need that somewhere even the typical romantic conceded, if only partially or temporarily, and permitted a personal boundary to be drawn around him. The boundary was, more often than not, coterminous with the landscape on which he focused. Though Wordsworth's scenery may seem generically natural and his sensibility to nature broadly responsive, even he struck a limit. Partly it was a negative limit, antisocial in the simplest sense—a rejection of the city and its supposed obstacles to communion and self-reflection. But after the brief cosmopolitan excursions of his youth, Wordsworth drew an affirmative boundary too, which by and large described a particular half-gloomy, half-joyful English kind of landscape—watery, yet at its best not too sentimentally damp, variably cloudy, with a chance of sun, a chance of rain.

For a poet like Byron, the terrain might have been broader, but the climatic conditions were even more limited. Apart from the sunny divagations of his Don Juan, Byron's landscape was almost invariably cloudy and overcast, his moral horizon dark and befogged. And Shelley, though he renounced limits, in his very renunciation acknowledged their presence. He sought his volatile image in the wind, in a bird that was not a bird, in a man-god who was neither man nor god. Perhaps for this reason appreciation of Shelley is a touchstone of the romantic temperament. It is not surprising that Sharp preferred him to the other romantic poets: in the nearly quixotic attempt to push back limits he was thoroughly Shelley's successor. Wordsworth may, by contrast with

Shelley, demonstrate the wisdom of taking a line of less resistance. In making his concession to a peculiarly English landscape of fact and feeling, he was implicitly conveying the knowledge that there is no total escape from identity, and the man who seeks it pays an enormous price, no matter how magniloquently his art may record the search.

In short, the romantic quest for freedom from traditionally imposed social roles was inevitably circumscribed. It became, in effect, a test of limits, regardless of how "illimitable" the seeker might try to make his vision. The Victorian period changed these conditions in only one significant respect, and that was but one of degree. To the concept of nation that had been formed a good deal earlier it gave a new and nearly overpowering emphasis as a boundary of man's cultural and emotional identity. The expansion that most characterized the epoch politically found its most sympathetic correspondence in the popular mind, but it was a source of "self" for many literary minds as well. It effected a cultural movement toward national identity that sustained itself practically unbroken until after the turn of the century.[2] The subcurrent of reaction that steadily developed strength toward the end of the century did not fully establish itself until the First World War.

Sharp's life thoroughly described the locus of this cultural movement. He sought his personal identity in external nature by virtue of his romantic sympathy with it, but he also could not avoid the pressure to make such a search for personal identity a search for a correspondent configuration of race or nationality at a time when the external world itself was becoming increasingly categorized by nation and race. Modern history and political reality have, to a great extent, demanded the same of all men. For some, perhaps most, it is a demand that does not engage them in any visible conflicts. They accept their identity with their own familiar national society, as most Victorians did, without challenge or difficulty. But Sharp was one of those others whose dispositions respond to currents less obvious. He was a man made by nature extraordinarily sympathetic, and by history a striking exemplar of the continuing sense of displacement among modern artists, a displacement for which the exile has become the literary symbol, and for which nationalism may have been a necessary but nonetheless only temporary therapy. Urged by the circumstances of his early life, he uprooted himself from the natural and ordinary attachment to his own native place, his "home," an attachment that even at best could only have been half of an isotonic allegiance to Scottish culture and the English culture which had embraced it.

With an advancing technology of transportation conveniently assisting him in his flight, Sharp temporarily abandoned himself to a rebellious nomadism that negated his roots, and eventually made it impossible for him ever to restore a completely natural and comfortable identification with the home that ought to have been his. The society he encountered in London was itself artificial and rootless. It reflected an urbanization that was in great measure composed of the alienated poor, those who had deserted their identity with the soil to form a dispossessed class,[3] and the alienated artists, those who had deserted their identity with English convention to form a bohemian coterie. Impelled by his own needs to espouse the city's muddled cosmopolitanism, Sharp was at the same time emotionally convulsed by the city's shapeless failure to provide a living community to which he could belong.

Given his own unsettled nature and the mistrust with which he regarded the settlements open to him, Sharp could find no satisfactory definition of himself. His quest thus remained a quest, episodic, filled with possibilities of pause, but no possibility of rest. The contrasts and oppositions of his experience provided a legitimate range within which to indulge the contrary impulses of his literary personality. His frustrated quest for limits ultimately represented itself as a quest for the illimitable; nothing less than that, or indeed more coherent than that, had revealed itself as an opportunity.

Sharp's sense of cultural exile was the expression, then, of a recalcitrant romanticism unwilling to commit itself to an English identity. But it was no isolated phenomenon. Some of the greatest writers of the period were spiritually or physically expatriated. Divided or uncertain loyalties informed their writing long before the crisis of the First World War liberated expatriates from their own diffusion and provided them with a rationale for fostering a community among themselves. Before exile was fashionable Victorians found means of revealing and disguising it at the same time.

Some of these emotional wanderers, like Samuel Butler, William Morris, and H. G. Wells, dreamed of utopias to satisfy their need for identity with place. Others, like Thomas Hardy and George Eliot, less optimistically visionary than the utopians, contracted their artistic sights and tended a small plot of earth where their belief in the basic interdependence of men could be dramatized on a microcosmic scale. Theirs was no mere regionalism or quest for local color, no simple social historian's concern with the curiosities of specific time and specific place. Rather they looked to these as reference points for all humanity. For them, as George Eliot put it, the "nightly heavens" of one's homestead were a means to "astronomy."[4] Yeats was at one with her when he wrote that "all poetry should have a local habitation when at all possible," that "we should make poems on the familiar landscape we love," for he shared Eliot's sense of the ultimate purpose of that focus. "To the greatest poets," he said, "everything they see has its relation to the national life, and through that to the universal and divine life; nothing is an isolated artistic moment; everything fulfills a purpose that is not its own."[5] The artist's object was to seize the particular and to transcend it by turning it into symbol.

Sharp's literary efforts combined both these impulses; he sought utopia and microcosm, and in combining these quests he demonstrated their intimate psychological unity. But often, too, his work found another, simpler metaphor for spiritual exile, in the dislocated wanderings of his characters. Through this metaphor he recorded a continuing emotional and psychological process of search, in which any focus upon a specific place was no more than an interpolated pause. This process is also to be found in the work of his greater contemporaries, who took up where Childe Harold and Don Juan had left off long before. The wanderings of Henry James's characters were the physical counterpart of their tortured spiritual explorations, and their search for identity was inextricably linked with concepts of national character. The same is true of the people in Conrad's novels. The English tongue may have adopted him, as he put it, but the English spirit did not. Proof lies in the very fragility of the sense of self possessed by his imperializing Englishmen—the inadequacy of their English character and rectitude to sustain an actual confrontation with man's interior jungle.[6]

All of these writers shared with one another, as they shared with Sharp, a feeling that paradoxically yet inevitably grew side by side with Victorian nationalism, a sense of the deep interrelatedness of human experience. They shared what Conrad termed "the latent feeling of fellowship with all creation—the subtle but invincible conviction of solidarity . . . which binds men to each other and all mankind to the visible world."[7]

Later Victorian fiction in general exhibits a strong tendency to express consciousness in terms of place and to endorse through that means a philosophy of cosmic solidarity and an ethic of cosmic sympathy. Such a development began early though tentatively in the Victorian novel and continued with increasing momentum over the course of the second half of the century. One may see this process of evolution by examining the novels of Dickens, for example, where the use of travel is not essentially grounded in cosmopolitanism and where travel may even tend to secure the national self-love of the English characters—as, for instance, the experience of Italy seems to do for Little Dorrit. Meredith represents a considerable step beyond this mode; even in so early a novel as *The Ordeal of Richard Feverel*, Richard is found undergoing his great epiphany in the Rhine country. Further, George Eliot, despite the essentially microcosmic impulse behind her use of place, writes a novel like *Daniel Deronda* with a wide European base, and elsewhere—everywhere—composes with a consciousness of place and movement. A similar balance prevails in Hardy, whose itineraries are usually circumspect in the extreme, but in whose work, indeed because he starts from such minuscule compass points, another village is virtually equivalent to another planet. There can be no doubt, at least, that divagation plays a considerable part in the moral experience of his characters; Angel Clare's voyage may be wide and Tess's wanderings narrow, but they are equally educative; and however much a treadmill may be the gypsy life of Jude and Sue in *Jude the Obscure*, it is still symbolic of the emotional locus of their lives.

These novelists thus go far to confirming Mary McCarthy's judgment that since the novel is rooted in the journalism of its epoch, the novelist shares the journalist's strong bias, in this period a bias toward tourism. As a corollary to this truth, one might observe that the cosmopolitan imagination is to some extent dependent upon the mobility of the writer himself. Characteristically well-traveled in life and literature are lesser fiction writers like Morris, Butler, Gissing, George Borrow, Kipling, Wells, and Stevenson, and larger ones like James and

Conrad, in whom travel comes near to becoming what it distinctly *is* for Forster and Lawrence, the single most functional metaphor for consciousness.

But, to elucidate Sharp's position in this development, another point must be made. Conrad's "invincible conviction of solidarity" was a vision he reproduced through the exploitation of a stage both real and fabricated. It was real in the sense that the exotic and primitive world he used was actually there, and quite actually upon it were being played the dramas of national cupidity. Yet it was also a fantasy in the sense that it was so distant, so unfamiliar to the ordinary man who would read his novels, that it was quite fabricable, quite responsive to sensitive shaping to an artist's ends. "The problem was," he wrote in his preface to *Within the Tides*, "to make unfamiliar things credible."[8] In doing so, he created an altar on which the Moloch of human division could himself be divided and sacrificed.

James did likewise. The drama of innocent America confronting a dissolute, if civil ancestry and attempting to resolve the discrepancy in its own moral identity was a drama that had not yet really happened —indeed may be said not yet to have happened—but it could be believed because it was so much hoped. So much hoped, in fact, that it is no surprise Sharp himself should have thought of America as an Eden where a new and believable community of men could be designed out of the materials that had seemed to decay in the old world.

If Sharp was like these men in seeking a foothold, a stage, upon which such symbolic dramas might be played, his failure to achieve like results is attributable to a less incisive sense of what gives literature its power. It is the result of his effort to fabricate a stage completely. The Celtic world—the only world he incorporated into his art to any significant extent—was, as he depicted it, virtually nonexistent. The drama of Druid against Christian might be capable of dimly reflecting more immediate cultural confrontations, but a dim reflection is after all nothing better than a dim reflection. Unlike his esthetic colleague William Morris, whose heroic fantasy *The Wood Beyond the World* made the proximity of real and ideal geography a source of profound tension and artistic excitement, Sharp shunned any effects that might have turned his own fantasies into more vivid reflections of real life. In the process he rejected one of the principal opportunities lying open to the artist of his time. Shaping itself out of the chaos of conflict between country and city was a new kind of stage on which the old Celt of dreams and visions, the mythmaker of the past, was encountering "the plumber and the artificial gardener," the industrialist, the citymaker of the present, and attempting, though not always realizing, an adjustment to a new and irreversible truth.

In rejecting this encounter, Sharp flinched from a wonderful if perilous challenge, one which even his Celtic contemporary Yeats eventually faced and made vital. Hardy's ability to confront the same challenge helped to give his last novel, *Jude the Obscure*, its strange and staggering power, and made it an immensely courageous foray into a modern jungle few of his own epoch and experience had even the courage to visualize.

There is no way to avoid seeing this failure in Sharp as a failure of artistic vision, though there is a way of pardoning him for it. It is clear that before the deep crises that shook the world after the turn of the century, few artists were able to mount a valid protest against man's trend toward mechanized loneliness and isolation amid the turbulent, self-engrossed "national life at its center," and to brave the conventions and prejudices constraining the reproduction of their mood of defiance in art. Certainly, even though his own protest did not come to artistic life, Sharp must be credited with never faltering before the engagement with national pride. Whenever he had the opportunity and the strength, he continued to eschew the limitations with which he had to temporize and to search for a community ever more expressive of his deep and abiding universal sympathies, and of the variety and upheaval that characterized the shape of the inner man. In this experimental penetration of the facades of superficial allegiances and identities—and even of superficial cosmopolitanism itself—he helped to foster what were in his own day, for the most part, unconventional and unpopular truths.

Artists who survived Sharp to live through the First World War shuddered from its shocks to national allegiances, but they endured them, for they had been in a true sense prepared by the cosmopolitan sympathies of Sharp's generation. They found, as Sharp had not found, a genuine community of distempered idealism among their fellow writers and a growing community of misgiving among their audiences. Sharp is divided from these men by the quality and temper of the convictions he fundamentally shares with them, his groping and diffident, theirs strong and certain. Thus, where Sharp chafes quietly at the barriers to international communion, Joyce rages furiously at the slovenly compromises men make in the name of national dignity. Sharp's thin dream of a new and transcendent Celtic spirit is separated by thrust as well as genius from Joyce's promised forging of the "uncreated conscience" of his race. The same principle of energetic conviction divides the outcast night-wanderers of Sharp's London from the clanless tribesmen of Joyce's Dublin, the homelessness of Sharp's "Children of To-morrow" from the sense of exile, and the formless and ever-forming allegiances of the Jew Leopold Bloom. The psychic drama Sharp hoped for and tried to shape and the doggedness of his research into "the geography of the mind" are the seedling versions of Joyce's expert and intrepid psychological scrutiny of the inner man. The articulated consciousnesses of Joyce's characters are full of symbols Sharp would have enthusiastically ratified, because they unite men rather than divide them.

The exploration of the geography of the mind and imagination that characterizes Joyce has much in common with T. S. Eliot's exploration of the "wasteland." An expatriate himself, Eliot exemplifies in his early work the dilemma imposed by shattered bonds and toppled mechanistic, mercantilistic, and militaristic supports for the human identity. One source of the aridity in "Gerontion," and a key to the riddle of international perversion in "The Wasteland," is the defeated hope of cultural intercommunion that Eliot felt as a young poet. To pursue Eliot through his later development is of course to trace a resurrection out of that despair and to discover a resolution that was hidden in the wasteland, waiting to be realized. Out of the broad catholicity of Eliot's cultural sympathies, the "fragments" from widely differing cultures which he "shored against his ruin," came the gradual fabrication of a new, transcendent community based upon a reconstituted Christian tradition.

Eliot's poetry is a body of work essentially dramatic, and it suggests the realization of Sharp's prophecy that modern literature would find its rejuvenation in a new kind of poetic drama. More than anything else, Sharp wanted the new drama to impose no obstacles to its universal reception, to be a stage from which a common idiom and vocabulary of truth might be spoken. That hopefully envisioned new stage was merely another symbolic expression of his desire for a place that could transcend all limits. Eliot's dramas do not entirely realize this hope, for they have a Christian boundary. But many of his poems are broadly and universally conceived peregrinations—with frequent use of geographical metaphor—through the geography of the soul.

Eliot's combination of the spirit of place with a sense of exile, and therefore with the compelling desire for a transcendent community, is only an extension of the combination that wholly characterized Sharp and partially characterized many writers of his generation, different as their work may otherwise be. That same combination provides a principle of unity among important later writers of extremely diverse philosophy and vision. D. H. Lawrence, whose own odyssey perhaps more closely than any other writer's resembles that of William Sharp, entitled the first chapter of his *Studies in Classic American Literature* "The Spirit of Place." Lawrence would have found Sharp incorrigibly "blue-eyed" and dream-minded, for Lawrence thought he could see through the clouds that enveloped the American "place" on which he chose to focus, and he debunked the myths with which Americans then surrounded and still surround themselves. Yet his vision shared a good deal with that of his less brilliant forerunner, and a few excerpts from Lawrence's book suggest the similarity of their intents. One can sense in Lawrence's tone that he had had and pushed away the same illusion that had moved Sharp, at least temporarily, to view America as a "fortunate Eden." Those who came to America, said Lawrence, "came largely to get away—that most simple of motives. To get way. Away from what? In the long run, away from themselves. Away from everything. That's why most people have come to America, and still do come. To get away from everything they are or have been. 'Henceforth be masterless.'" Had Sharp been more self-conscious a student of his own motives, these might have been his own words.

From the vantage point of a man who has had the true revelation, Lawrence spoke with authority of the same sense of place-identity that had obsessed Sharp:

> Every continent has its own great spirit of place. Every people is polarized in some particular locality, which is home, the homeland. Different places on the face of the earth have different vital effluence, different vibration, different chemical exhalation, different polarity with different stars: call it what you like. But the spirit of place is a great reality. The Nile Valley produced not only the corn, but the

205

terrific religions of Egypt. China produces the Chinese, and will go on doing so. The Chinese in San Francisco will in time cease to be Chinese, for America is a great melting pot.

Lawrence's historical experience, which Sharp lacked, enabled him to build upon this view. With his infallible technique for making a new paragraph seem like a new chapter of Ecclesiastes, he turned his idea upon itself:

> There was a tremendous polarity in Italy. And this seems to have died. For even places die. The Island of Great Britain had a wonderful terrestrial magnetism or polarity of its own, which made the British people. For the moment, this polarity seems to be breaking. Can England die? And what if England dies?

Lawrence's final statement needed this prologue, just as the "men" he envisioned in it had needed the prologue of William Sharp, perhaps countless William Sharps:

> Men are free when they are in a living homeland, not when they are straying and breaking away. Men are free when they are obeying some deep, inward voice of religious belief. Obeying from within. Men are free when they belong to a living, organic, *believing* community, active in fulfilling some unfulfilled, perhaps unrealized purpose . . . Men are free when they are most unconscious of freedom.[9]

Though in other respects it is the antithesis of Lawrence's, the work of another novelist, E. M. Forster, shows how much the search for a new sense of "homeland" and a new "community of belief" invaded twentieth-century literature and how inevitably it accompanied the sense of place. Forster's *A Passage to India* suggests how the writer after the First World War could give the spirit of place a broader field of play than that to which novelists like George Eliot and Thomas Hardy were limited. He demonstrates that for the later writer such comprehensiveness was acceptable, a ground sufficiently responsive to general feeling to provide a legitimate artistic foothold and to require no exercise of caution. Forster treats with familiarity, in other words, the kind of place that for Conrad's first audiences would still have been distant, strange, and exotic. He can thus confront the topography of India with an aplomb belying any claims that land might have to being exotic and faraway. If it is exotic in Forster's vision, it is so mainly by virtue of the grotesque contrasts it expresses within itself—only secondarily by virtue of the diehard associations of mystery that the word "India" trails with it still, part of the legacy that created innumerable Sharps lumping camelback through the wildernesses of distant places to bring their half-manufactured excitement to color- and travel-hungry Victorians.

Echoes of Sharp's technique in making symbolic use of place can readily be found in Forster's. That technique is thoroughly illustrated by the Marabar Caves, but its scope is no better demonstrated than in what for all purposes is the philosophical center of this symmetrical novel, Fielding's pause in Italy on his return trip to England. Forster describes Fielding's realization of this movement in these terms: "The Mediterranean is the human norm. When men leave that exquisite lake, through the Bosphorus or the Pillars of Hercules, they approach the monstrous and extraordinary."[10] The philosophizing that accompanies Forster's place descriptions is as naturally their result as any conclusion drawn from inductive reasoning or speculation, for its basis is symbolic.

Forster's earlier novel, *Howards End*, contains very explicit contact with the cosmopolitanism of Sharp's generation, though that point of contact was one of reaction rather than support. Forster seems to have feared a movement that, at the turn of the century, even disturbed some cosmopolitans—what Ethel Goddard, in discussing Fiona Macleod's anti-nationalism in 1904, described as "that vulgar indolence of cosmopolitanism which excuses its ignorance of the traditions of any one country by an affectation of admiration for all countries."[11] This indolence, she assured her readers, was not Fiona Macleod's. But evidence that it existed in others is further provided by the animadversions in *Howards End* upon the leveling cosmopolitan spirit. Fear of such leveling was at the heart of Forster's assertion that Englishmen must return to being English, must look upon their land and love it, and not allow its distinctive character to be destroyed. Yet an examination of *Howards End* reveals Forster sharing another more essential mood of Sharp's cosmopolitanism, its transcendent nationalism. The cosmopolitanism Forster despised was represented for him by the same two forces for which Sharp had also found nothing but opprobrium: the spirit of urbanization and the spirit of imperialism. The "Imperial type," Forster wrote, "hopes to inherit the earth":

It breeds as quickly as the yeoman and as soundly; strong is the temptation to acclaim it as a super-yeoman who carries his country's virtue overseas. But the Imperialist is not what he thinks or seems. He is a destroyer. He prepares the way for cosmopolitanism, and though his ambitions be fulfilled, the earth he inherits will be grey.

And the city?

London was but a foretaste of this nomadic civilization which is altering human nature so profoundly, and throws upon personal relations a stress greater than they have ever borne before. Under cosmopolitanism, if it comes, we shall receive no help from the earth. Trees and meadows and mountains will only be a spectacle, and the binding force must be entrusted to Love alone. May Love be equal to the task.[12]

Forster's similarity with Sharp at these points suggests that in a deeper sense he was unjustified in calling these leveling forces "cosmopolitan." His real purpose in *Howards End* was not to propogate a narrow nativism, but to locate the "binding force" of which he spoke in a living community. His was a nationalism as transcendent as any of Yeats or Fiona Macleod. His England too was a melting pot; it absorbed, it did not exclude. It was an earth that even the exiled Schlegels, whose father had laid down the sword and sought refuge from an arrogant imperialism, could inherit.

Thus the miniature universe of *Howards End* has, like the panorama of western civilization in *A Passage to India*, a purpose in common with the big world beyond it. With a sense for the power of place to mold lives that had been exploited by the writers whom Sharp treated in *Literary Geography*, and by Sharp himself in *Silence Farm*, Forster went a step beyond them. He fabricated a community conceived not as a mold into which lives are behavioristically forced, but rather as a liberating spiritual force, one which challenges the best in man, commands, in a sense, the love out of him. Howards End is, as a true homeland ought to be, a positive agent, through which the spirit of the universe seeking to unite and not to divide might work its will. The distance between this and *A Passage to India* is not really great. In the later novel, Forster was only more courageously confronting the cosmopolitan challenge, in which "the binding force . . . must be entrusted to Love alone. May Love be equal to the task."

The unity the world seems to possess beneath its face of diversity has been arrived at by many different applications of the sense of symbolic place since William Sharp. Passage has been secured by means of Virginia Woolf's lighthouse—or better still, the quietly self-effacing house of Mrs. Ramsey, subtly reiterating its own image through Woolf's delicate novel. It has been achieved through the nature-mysticism of Katherine Mansfield, the Spain, the Italy, the Paris of Hemingway, or the Yoknapatawpha County of Faulkner.

All of these are indebted to the Victorian sense of place that gave to the romantic spirit new shape and concreteness. This process of translation found its quintessential expression in William Sharp. His work reveals, as though in summary of his era, that out of a sense of exile could emerge a dream of community, which, while borrowing partisan allegiances to place, did so only that it might go beyond them to contend the truth of the nonpartisanship of life.

APPENDIX

Sharp's Travels

This list of William Sharp's most significant travels and pauses during his lifetime is drawn largely from information scattered through Mrs. Sharp's *Memoir* and checked wherever possible against other external evidence of his movements. Mrs. Sharp's accuracy at all points is, of course, impossible to determine, though it is quite clear that she considered her husband's mobility an important matter for record. The fact that I have omitted several briefer summer excursions within England and Scotland and the possibility that she may have omitted some trips to Paris to cover the Salon exhibitions indicate that probably no gap of years can be construed as a standstill. Regardless of precision, it remains obvious from this itinerary that Sharp spent an incredibly large part of his lifetime in motion.

Sept. 12, 1855– Sept. 1876	Born, raised, and educated in Scotland (Paisley, Glasgow, and "the West").
Summer 1873	Joins troupe of wandering gypsies on "truant" excursion through western highlands.
Sept. 1876–June 1877	South Seas, Australia; travels through Australian bush country.
1877–1890	London established as home base, from which Sharp makes various other trips.
Feb.–June 1883	Italy, as art critic (Rome, Assisi, Florence, Venice).
April–June 1884	Paris, as art and literary critic.
[June 1884	Marriage to Elizabeth Sharp.]
August–Nov. 1889	Canada, New England, New York.
Summer 1890	Argyll, Scotland; beginning period of artistic retrenchment.
Fall 1890	Antwerp, Bonn, the Rhine Valley, and Stuttgart (to work out collaboration with Blanche Willis Howard on *A Fellowe and His Wife*).
Dec. 1890–Sept. 1891	Settles in Rome.
Sept. 1891	Stuttgart again.

Oct. 1891	Returns to London.
Jan.–March 1892	New York.
April–June 1892	Paris again (meets Verlaine, acquaints himself further with "decadents," "symbolistes").
Summer 1892– summer 1894	The Sharps make "home" of a cottage in Sussex.
Jan.–March 1893	Algeria and Tunisia.
July 1893	Scottish Highlands.
Summer 1894	Iona.
Fall 1894	Edinburgh (collaboration with Patrick Geddes and Edinburgh Celtic movement).
Feb. 1895	The Hebrides ("with Fiona").
Summer–fall 1895	Edinburgh; begins lecture series at University and collapses after first lecture; retires briefly to Isle of Bute.
Jan. 1896	France (Paris and Rémy de Provence to visit the Thomas Janviers).
May 1896	Venice.
Summer 1896	London, then Lake Country and Scotland.
Oct. 1896	New York.
Jan. 1897	Brief stop in London, then southern France again.
Summer 1897	Ireland (meetings with George Russell, Standish O'Grady, Edward Martin, Douglas Hyde, Lady Gregory).
May 1898	Holland.
Jan. 1899	Sharps settle briefly in Hampstead.
Summer 1899	Highlands, then Ireland again.
Fall 1900–fall 1901	Through France and Italy to Sicily for winter, then return to England with long pause in Florence.
Winter–spring 1902	Sicily again; stays near Taormina with Duke of Bronte (at Castello di Maniace).
Summer 1902	Lismore (Scotland).
Oct.–Dec. 1902	Castello di Maniace (Sicily).

Sharp's Travels

Jan. 1903	Athens and Greece.
Fall 1903	Wales.
Jan. 1904	Athens again.
Winter 1904	New York.
Feb. 1905	Rome.
April 1905	Scotland, especially Iona.
Oct. 1905	Switzerland, Italy (Venice and Florence), to Sicily again, where he plans and postpones a second trip to North Africa.
[Dec. 6, 1905	Dies at Castello di Maniace (Sicily).]

Selected Bibliography of Sharp's Works

All unpublished letters and manuscripts cited in the notes are from the Papers of William Sharp or the Papers of Patrick Geddes, both in the National Library of Scotland, Edinburgh. The list of Sharp's published works in volume II of Elizabeth Sharp's *Memoir* (2nd ed.; London: Heinemann, 1912), though omitting some titles and containing a few errors, is the most exhaustive bibliography available. The following bibliography contains Sharp's principal published works along with all others referred to in the text. Writings published under his pseudonym have been separated from those published under his own name for convenience of identification.

William Sharp

"American Literature," *Good Words*, XXX (June 1889), 56-71.

American Sonnets (ed.). Canterbury Series. London: Walter Scott, 1889.

"Cardinal Lavigerie's Work in North Africa," *Atlantic Monthly*, LXXIV (August 1894), 214-227.

"Celtic Literature" (with Ernest Rhys), *Library of the World's Best Literature, Ancient and Modern*, ed. Charles Dudley Warner (New York: The International Society, 1896-1897), VIII, 3403-3450.

"Chelsea Hospital and Its Inhabitants," *Good Words*, XXVI (November 1885), 705-711.

"The Child in Art," *Realm*, December 15, 1894, pp. 172-173.

The Children of To-morrow. London: Chatto and Windus, 1889.

"The City of Beautiful Towers," *Good Words*, XXVI (May 1885), 320-326.

Dante Gabriel Rossetti: A Record and a Study. London: Macmillan, 1882.

"The Dramas of Gabriele D'Annunzio," *Fortnightly Review*, LXXIV (September 1900), 391-409.

"Dust and Fog," *Good Words*, XXIV (October 1883), 721-723.

Earth's Voices: Transcripts from Nature; Sospitra and Other Poems. London: Elliott Stock, 1884.

Ecce Puella and Other Prose Imaginings. London: Elkin Matthews, 1896.

"Edward Burne-Jones," *Fortnightly Review*, LXX (August 1898), 289-306.

Fair Women in Painting and Poetry. Portfolio of Artistic Monographs, no. 7. London: Seeley, 1896.

A Fellowe and His Wife (with Blanche Willis Howard). New York: Houghton-Mifflin, 1892.

Flower o' the Vine. Introductory note by Thomas Janvier. New York: Webster, 1892.

For a Song's Sake and Other Stories (ed.), by Philip Bourke Marston. Canterbury Series. London: Walter Scott, 1887.

"Garden of the Sun: I-II" *Century*, LXXI (March 1906), 663-681, and LXXII (May 1906), 37-54.

"George Meredith's *Reading of Earth*," *Scottish Art Review*, I (February 1889), 263-265.

The Gipsy Christ and Other Tales. Carnation Series. Chicago: Stone and Kimball, 1895.

"Hersart de la Villemarqué: The Heroic and Legendary Literature of Brittany," *Library of the World's Best Literature, Ancient and Modern,* ed. Charles Dudley Warner (New York: The International Society, 1896-1897), XXXVIII, 15377-15391.

"The Hotel of the Beautiful Star," *Harper's,* CIII (October 1901), 673-679.

The Human Inheritance, The New Hope, Motherhood. London: Elliott Stock, 1882.

"Icelandic Literature," *Library of the World's Best Literature, Ancient and Modern,* ed. Charles Dudley Warner (New York: The International Society, 1896-1897), XX, 7865-7895.

"In the Days of My Youth," *Mainly About People,* November 14, 1900, pp. 484-485.

"The Isle of Arran," *Art Journal,* XLVII (July 1885), 205-208.

"Italian Poets of Today," *Quarterly Review,* CXCVI (July 1902), 239-268.

"La Jeune Belgique," *Nineteenth Century,* XXXIV (September 1893), 416-436.

"Land of Theocritus," *Harper's,* CVI (April 1903), 802-810.

The Life and Letters of Joseph Severn. London: Sampson, Lowe, and Marston, 1892.

Life of Browning. Great Writers Series. London: Walter Scott, 1890.

Life of Heinrich Heine. Great Writers Series. London: Walter Scott, 1888.

Life of Percy Bysshe Shelley. Great Writers Series. London: Walter Scott, 1887.

Literary Geography. London: Pall Mall Publications, 1904.

"Maeterlinck," *Academy,* March 19, 1892, p. 270.

"A Memory of Verona," *Good Words,* XXX (June 1889), 382-393.

"Monte Oliveto and the Frescoes of Sodona: I-II," *Art Journal,* XLVI (April-May 1884), 101-104, 133-136.

"Mr. George Meredith," *Good Words,* XL (July 1899), 477-482.

"Myths and Folklore of the Aryan Peoples" (with Ernest Rhys), *Library of the World's Best Literature, Ancient and Modern,* ed. Charles Dudley Warner (New York: The International Society, 1896-1897), XXVI, 10522-10542.

"A Note on Climate and Art," *Modern Thought,* III (June 1881), 153-155.

"A Note on the Aesthetic Development of America," *Scottish Art Review,* II (November 1889), 162-163.

"A Note on the Belgian Renascence," *Chap-Book,* IV (December 1895), 149-157.

Pagan Review, I (August [September] 1892).

The Poems of Eugene Lee-Hamilton (ed.). Canterbury Series. London: Walter Scott, 1903.

The Poems of Matthew Arnold (ed.). Canterbury Series. London; Walter Scott, 1896.

The Poems of Swinburne (ed.). Leipzig: Tauchnitz, 1901.

The Poetical Works of Walter Scott (ed.). Canterbury Series. London: Walter Scott, 1885.

The Progress of Art in the Nineteenth Century. London and Edinburgh: W. R. Chambers, 1902.

"Puvis de Chavannes," *Art Journal*, LX (December 1898), 377-378.

"Random Impressions from an Author's Note-Book," *Scottish Art Review*, I (January 1889), 237-240.

"Reminiscences of the Marble Quarries of Carrara," *Good Words*, XXXI (August 1890), 617-624.

Romantic Ballads and Poems of Phantasy. London: Walter Scott, 1888.

Selected Writings of William Sharp. 5 vols. London: Heinemann, 1912.

"The Sicilian Highlands," *Atlantic Monthly*, XCIII (April 1904), 471-478.

Silence Farm. London: Grant Richards, 1899.

"Sir Edward Burne-Jones," *Atlantic Monthly*, LXXXII (September 1898), 375-383.

"Some Personal Reminiscences of Walter Pater," *Atlantic Monthly*, XXIV (December 1894), 801-814.

"Some Reminiscences of Christina Rossetti," *Atlantic Monthly*, LXXV (June 1895), 736-749.

The Songs and Sonnets of Shakespeare (ed.). Canterbury Series. London: Walter Scott, 1885.

"The Sonnet in America," *National Review*, LXXIV (April 1889), 199-201.

The Sonnets of This Century (ed.). Canterbury Series. London: Walter Scott, 1886.

Sospiri di Roma. Rome: Società Laziale, 1891.

The Sport of Chance. 3 vols. London: Hurst and Blackett, 1888.

"Thomas Hardy and His Novels," *Forum*, XXVI (July 1892), 583-593.

Vistas. Green Tree Series. Chicago: Stone and Kimball, 1894.

"William Morris: The Man and His Work," *Atlantic Monthly*, LXXVIII (December 1896), 775-790.

Wives in Exile: A Comedy in Romance. London: Grant Richards, 1898.

Fiona Macleod

The Divine Adventure; Iona; By Sundown Shores. London: Chapman, 1900.

The Dominion of Dreams. London: Constable, 1899.

"A Field for Modern Verse," *Dome*, n.s. IV (March 1899), 207-210.

From the Hills of Dream, 2nd ed. rev. Edinburgh: Patrick Geddes, 1896.

From the Hills of Dream, Threnodies, Songs, and Later Poems. London: Heinemann, 1901.

Green Fire. New York: Harper's, 1896.

"The Irish Muse: I-II," *North American Review*, CLXXIX (November-

December 1904), 685-697, 900-912.

"The King's Ring," *Pall Mall Magazine*, XXXI (May-June 1904), 36-48, 222-243.

The Laughter of Peterkin. London: Constable, 1895.

The Mountain Lovers. Keynote Series. London: John Lane, 1895.

Pharais. Derbyshire: Frank Murray, 1894.

The Sin-Eater and Other Tales. Edinburgh: Patrick Geddes, 1895.

The Washer of the Ford. Edinburgh: Patrick Geddes, 1895.

The Winged Destiny: Studies in the Spiritual History of the Gael. London: Chapman and Hall, 1904.

The Works of Fiona Macleod. 7 vols. London: Heinemann, 1910-1912.

General Bibliography

Ausubel, Herman. *In Hard Times: Reformers among the late Victorians.* New York: Columbia University Press, 1960.

Babbitt, Irving. *Rousseau and Romanticism.* Boston and New York: Houghton Mifflin, 1919.

Baudelaire, Charles, *L'Art Romantique.* Paris: Garnier, 1931.

———— *Oeuvres complètes de Charles Baudelaire,* ed. Jacques Crepet. Paris: Conard, 1923.

Benedetti, Anna. *George Meredith, poeta; Fiona Macleod (William Sharp); studi letterari con l'aggiunta di alcune versioni dall'inglese.* Palermo: Trimarchi, 1913.

Bentley, Phyllis. *The English Regional Novel.* London: G. Allen and Unwin, 1941.

Branford, Victor. "Old Edinburgh and the Evergreen," *Bookman,* IX (December 1895), 88-90.

Buckle, Henry Thomas. *Essays.* New York: Appleton, 1864.

Burton, Richard. "Maeterlinck: Impressionist," *Atlantic Monthly,* LXXIV (October 1894), 673-680.

Caird, Mona. *The Morality of Marriage and Other Essays on the Status and Destiny of Women.* London: G. Redway, 1897.

Carpenter, Edward. *The Art of Creation.* London: G. Allen, 1904.

———— *Intermediary Types among Primitive Folk: A Study in Social Evolution,* 2nd ed. London: G. Allen and Unwin, 1919.

———— *Never Again! A Protest and a Warning Addressed to the Peoples of Europe.* London: G. Allen and Unwin, 1916.

Chew, Samuel C. "The Nineteenth Century and After," in *A Literary History of England,* ed. Albert C. Baugh (New York: Appleton-Century Crofts, 1948).

Clifford, William Kingdon. *Cosmic Emotion; also* [Virchow on] *the Teaching of Science.* Humboldt Library of Science Series. New York: Humboldt, 1888.

Conrad, Joseph. *Prefaces.* London: J. M. Dent, 1937.

Dickens, Charles. *Pictures from Italy.* London: Bradbury and Evans, 1846.

"Dual Personality in the Case of William Sharp," *Journal of the Society for Psychical Research,* X (April 1911), 57-63.

"The Effects of Civilization upon Women," *National Review,* IX (March 1887), 26-38.

Eliot, George. *Daniel Deronda.* 2 vols. New York: Doubleday, Page, 1901.

Ellis, Havelock. "The Changing Status of Women," *Westminster Review,* CXXVIII (October 1887), 818-828.

———— *The New Spirit.* London: Scott, n.d.

Ellmann, Richard. *The Identity of Yeats.* New York: Oxford University Press, 1954.

Fiechter, Sophia Charlotte. *von William Sharp zu Fiona Macleod.* Tubingen: Gulde, 1936.

Forster, E. M. *Howards End*. New York: Alfred A. Knopf, 1945.
———— *A Passage to India*. New York: Harcourt Brace, 1952.
Gaster, Theodore H. "England," in *Universal Jewish Encyclopedia* (New York: Universal Jewish Encyclopedia, Inc., 1941), IV, 110-130.
Geddes, Patrick, and J. Arthur Thompson. *The Evolution of Sex*. London: Walter Scott, 1890.
Gide, André. *Si le grain ne meurt*. Paris: Librairie Gallimard, 1928.
Goddard, Ethel. "*The Winged Destiny* and Fiona Macleod," *Fortnightly Review*, LXXVIII (December 1904), 1036-1044.
Greenacre, Phyllis, M.D. "Discussions and Comments on the Psychology of Creativity," *Journal of the American Academy of Child Psychiatry*, I (January 1962), 129-137.
———— "Experiences of Awe in Childhood," *The Psychoanalytic Study of the Child*, XI (1956), 9-30.
———— "The Relation of the Impostor to the Artist," *The Psychoanalytic Study of the Child*, XIII (1958), 521-528.
Handlin, Oscar, and John Burchard, eds. *The Historian and the City*. Cambridge, Mass.: M.I.T. Press and the Harvard University Press, 1963.
Hay, William Delisle. *The Doom of the Great City; being the narrative of a survivor written A.D. 1942*. London: Newman, 1880.
Hearn, Lafcadio. *The Writings of Lafcadio Hearn*. 9 vols. Boston: Houghton Mifflin, 1923.
Heine, Heinrich. *Werke und Briefe*. 8 vols. Berlin: Aufbau-Verlag, 1961.
Higginson, Thomas Wentworth. *The Writings of Thomas Wentworth Higginson*, vol. XIV: *Woman and the Alphabet*. Boston: Houghton Mifflin, 1900.
Hoare, Dorothy M. *The Works of Morris and Yeats in Relation to Early Saga Literature*. Cambridge, Eng.: At the University Press, 1937.
Janvier, Catherine A. "Fiona Macleod and Her Creator," *North American Review*, CLXXXIV (April 1907), 718-732.
King, Georgiana Goddard. "Fiona Macleod," *Modern Language Notes*, XXXIII (June 1918), 352-356.
Lawrence, D. H. *Studies in Classic American Literature*. New York: Viking Press, 1961.
Lefwich, Joseph. *Israel Zangwill*. New York: Thomas Yoseloff, 1957.
Le Gallienne, Richard. "The Mystery of Fiona Macleod," *Forum*, XLV (February 1911), 170-179.
Levi, Carlo. *Christ Stopped at Eboli*, trans. Frances Frenaye. New York: Farrar, Straus, 1947.
Lewis, Oscar. *Hearn and His Biographers: The Record of a Literary Controversy*. San Francisco: Westgate Press, 1930.
Lovett, Robert Morss, and Helen Sard Hughes. *The History of the Novel in England*. Boston: Houghton Mifflin, 1932.
Magnus, Katie. *Jewish Portraits*. London: Routledge, 1925.

Marcus, Steven. The Other Victorians: A Study of Sex and Pornography in Mid-Nineteenth-Century England. New York: Basic Books, 1966.
Mill, John Stuart. On Liberty; The Subjection of Women. New York: Holt, 1873.
More, Paul Elmer. The Drift of Romanticism. Shelburne Essays, Eighth Series. Boston: Houghton Mifflin, 1913.
Rea, Lilian. "Fiona Macleod," The Critic, XLVIII (May 1906), 460-463.
Read, Herbert. The Green Child. London: Grey Walls Press, 1945.
Reclus, Elie. Primitive Folk: A Study in Comparative Ethnology. Contemporary Science Series, ed. Havelock Ellis. London: Walter Scott, 1896.
Reichenkron, Günter, and Erich Haase, eds. Formen der Selbstdarstellung. Berlin: Duncker and Humboldt, 1956.
Restif de la Bretonne. Monsieur Nicolas, ed. Havelock Ellis. London: John Rodker, 1930.
Rhys, Ernest. Everyman Remembers. London: J. M. Dent, 1931.
———— "The New Mysticism," Fortnightly Review, LXXIII (June 1900), 1045-1056.
———— "Proteus," Century, LXXVI (August 1908), 508.
———— "William Sharp and Fiona Macleod," Century, LXXIV (May 1907), 111-117.
Rinder, Frank. "William Sharp—'Fiona Macleod': A Tribute," LVIII (February 1906), 44-45.
Rolt-Wheeler, Ethel. "William Sharp and Fiona Macleod," Fortnightly Review, CXII (November 1919), 780-790.
Rosenberg, John D. The Darkening Glass: A Portrait of Ruskin's Genius. New York and London: Columbia University Press, 1961.
Rousseau, Jean-Jacques. Emile, trans. Barbara Foxley. London: J. M. Dent, 1963.
Rudmose-Brown, Thomas B. "L'Idée celtique dans l'oeuvre de Fiona Macleod," Mercure de France, January 1906, pp. 161-169.
Schreiner, Olive. The Story of an African Farm. London: Chapman, Hall, 1892.
———— Woman and Labor. New York: Stokes, 1911.
Sharp, Elizabeth A., ed. Lyra Celtica. Introduction and notes by William Sharp. Edinburgh: John Grant, 1896.
———— William Sharp (Fiona Macleod): A Memoir. 1st ed. London: Heinemann, 1910. 2nd ed. 2 vols. London: Heinemann, 1912.
Symonds, John Addington. Essays Speculative and Suggestive. London: Smith Elder, 1907.
Temple, Ruth Z. The Critic's Alchemy: A Study of the Introduction of French Symbolism into England. New York: Twayne, 1953.
Texte, Joseph. Jean-Jacques Rousseau and the Cosmopolitan Spirit in Literature, trans. J. W. Matthews. New York: Stechert, 1929.
Tynan, Katherine. "William Sharp and Fiona Macleod," Fortnightly Review, LXXVI (March 1906), 570-579.

Unamuno, Miguel de. *Three Exemplary Novels*, trans. Angel Flores. New York: Grove Press, 1956.

Waugh, Arthur. "Fiona Macleod: A Forgotten Mystery," *Spectator*, August 14, 1936, p. 277.

Wells, H. G. *Experiment in Autobiography*. New York: Macmillan, 1934.

Woodward, E. L. *The Age of Reform, 1815-1870*. Oxford: Oxford University Press, Clarendon Press, 1938.

Yu, Beong-cheon. *An Ape of Gods: The Art and Thought of Lafcadio Hearn*. Detroit: Wayne University Press, 1964.

Zangwill, Israel. *The Melting Pot*. New York: Macmillan, 1910.

—— *Without Prejudice*. New York: Century, 1896.

Notes

Introduction

1. Richard Le Gallienne, "The Mystery of 'Fiona Macleod,'" *Forum*, XLV (February 1911), 170-179. An amusingly ironical clue to the effect the twentieth century had in turning these later Victorians upon one another is provided by Ernest Rhys's judgment of Le Gallienne: "There was something histrionic in his make-up." *Everyman Remembers* (London, 1931), p. 114.

2. Paul Elmer More, *The Drift of Romanticism*, Shelburne Essays, Eighth Series (Boston, 1913), pp. 119-143.

3. *Ibid.*, pp.125-128.

4. *Ibid.*, pp. 135-136.

5. Georgiana Goddard King, "Fiona Macleod," *Modern Language Notes*, XXXIII (June 1918), 352-356. For a reply to King's particular assertions regarding Fiona Macleod's sources, see note 45, Chap. 4.

6. Dorothy M. Hoare, *The Works of Morris and Yeats in Relation to Early Saga Literature* (Cambridge, Eng., 1937), pp. 101-102.

7. Samuel C. Chew, "The Nineteenth Century and After," in *A Literary History of England*, ed. Albert C. Baugh (New York, 1948), p. 1428.

8. Ernest Rhys "The New Mysticism," *Fortnightly Review*, LXXIII (June 1900), 1045-1056.

9. Ernest Rhys, *Everyman Remembers* (London, 1931), pp. 79-80.

10. Arthur Waugh, "Fiona Macleod: A Forgotten Mystery," *Spectator*, August 14, 1936, p. 277.

11. Thomas B. Rudmose-Brown, "L'Idée Celtique dans l'oeuvre de Fiona Macleod," *Mercure de France*, January 1906, pp. 161-169.

12. Elizabeth A. Sharp, *William Sharp (Fiona Macleod): A Memoir* (London, 1910). The Uniform Edition, published in 1912 to accompany *Selected Writings of William Sharp* and *The Works of Fiona Macleod*, asserted that division even more clearly than the first edition by separating the Memoir into two volumes, one for William Sharp (to 1894) and the other for Fiona Macleod (from 1894 to his death).

13. Sophia Charlotte Fiechter, *von William Sharp zu Fiona Macleod* (Tubingen, 1936), p. 74.

14. More, *Drift of Romanticism*, p. 126.

15. H. G. Wells, *Experiment in Autobiography* (New York, 1934), pp. 72-73. Quotations from *Experiment in Autobiography*, copyright 1934 by H. G. Wells, are reprinted by permission of Professor G. P. Wells and Collins-Knowlton-Wing, Inc.

16. Irving Babbitt, *Rousseau and Romanticism* (Boston, 1919), especially pp. 51-54.

1. The Changeling

1. Elizabeth A. Sharp, *William Sharp (Fiona Macleod)*: A *Memoir* (London, 1910). The second edition (London 1912), published in two volumes, will be used exclusively and will henceforth be referred to as *Memoir*, I, or *Memoir*, II, as the case may be. Quotations from the *Memoir* are reprinted by permission of William Heinemann, Ltd., and Dodd, Mead, and Co.

2. William Sharp, "In the Days of My Youth," *Mainly About People*, November 14, 1900, pp. 484-485. This article will be referred to hereafter as *MAP*.

3. *Memoir*, I, 4-5. Other less authoritative sources mistakenly give 1856 as Sharp's year of birth.

4. *Memoir*, I, 11.

5. *Ibid.*, p. 5.

6. *MAP*, p. 485.

7. *Memoir*, I, 5, and *MAP*, p. 485.

8. *Memoir*, I, 5.

9. *Ibid.*

10. *Memoir*, I, 5-6.

11. *Ibid.*, p. 9.

12. *MAP*, p. 485.

13. *Memoir*, I, 19, and *MAP*, p. 485.

14. *Mcmoir*, I, 21.

15. *MAP*, p. 485.

16. *Ibid.*

17. *Memoir*, I, 21.

18. *Ibid.*, pp. 9-10.

19. *Ibid.*, p. 6.

20. *Ibid.*, p. 7. See Fiona Macleod's "Barabal: A Memory," *The Dominion of Dreams* (London, 1899).

21. *Ibid.*, p. 18. See Fiona Macleod's "Seumas: A Memory," *The Winged Destiny* (London, 1904).

22. *Ibid.*, pp. 9-10.

23. *MAP*, p. 484.

24. *Ibid.*

25. *Memoir*, I, 6.

26. *Ibid.*

27. *Ibid.*, p. 15.

28. *MAP*, p. 485.

29. *Ibid.*

30. Fiona Macleod, "Prologue: The Laughter of Peterkin," *The Laughter of Peterkin* (London, 1895), pp. 5-20.

31. Fiona Macleod, "The Gaelic Heart," *The Winged Destiny*. Quoted in *Memoir*, I, 14; also in Thomas Rudmose-Brown, "L'Idée celtique dans

l'oeuvre de Fiona Macleod," *Mercure de France*, January 1906, p. 168, and Sophia Fiechter, *von William Sharp zu Fiona Macleod* (Tubingen, 1936), p. 25.

32. *Memoir*, I, 12-13. For a curious parallel to his supposedly factual experience, see the passage from Elie Reclus' contemporary anthropological study *Primitive Folk: A Study in Comparative Ethnology* (London, 1892), p. 73, evoking the visionary experiences of the priests of certain Indian tribes, quoted above, pp. 108-109.

33. *Ibid.*, p. 23.

34. *Ibid.*

35. William Sharp, "The Gipsy Christ," *The Gipsy Christ and Other Tales* (Chicago, 1895).

36. Compare especially Fiona Macleod, *Green Fire* (New York, 1896), and "Iona," *The Divine Adventure* (London, 1900).

37. Compare especially Fiona Macleod, "The Last Supper" and "The Anointed Man," *The Washer of the Ford* (Edinburgh, 1895), and the poem "The Moon-Child," *From the Hills of Dream* (Edinburgh, 1895).

38. Fiona Macleod, "The Annir-Choille" (sometimes reprinted as "Cathal of the Woods"), *The Washer of the Ford*. Herbert Read may have derived from Fiona Macleod the motif of the passage into "the green life" that appears in his novel *The Green Child* (London, 1945).

39. *Memoir*, I, 51.

40. Interview with Phyllis Greenacre, M.D., March 1964.

41. *Memoir*, I, 275.

2. Climate and Landscape

1. *Memoir*, I, 84.

2. *Dante Gabriel Rossetti: A Record and a Study* (London, 1882), p. 37.

3. *Memoir*, I, 57.

4. "A Note on Climate and Art," *Modern Thought*, III (June 1881), 153.

5. *Ibid.*, p. 154.

6. *Ibid.*, p. 155.

7. "Mr. George Meredith," *Good Words*, XL (July 1899), 481.

8. *The Songs and Sonnets of Shakespeare* (London, 1885); *The Sonnets of This Century* (London, 1886); *American Sonnets* (London, 1889).

9. *Memoir*, I, 187.

10. See *Memoir*, I, 33.

11. Charles Baudelaire, *L'Art Romantique* (Paris, 1931), p. 100 (trans. mine). For a suggestive, abundantly illustrated study of the use of landscape by nineteenth-century French writers, often to represent a highly fragmented and uncertain interior life, see Pierre Moreau, "De quelques paysages introspectifs," in *Formen der Selbstdarstellung*, ed. Günter Reichenkron and Erich Haase (Berlin, 1956), pp. 279-289.

12. *Earth's Voices: Transcripts from Nature: Sospitra and Other Poems* (London, 1884).

13. "The Human Inheritance," cycle I, part XII, *The Human Inheritance, The New Hope, Motherhood* (London, 1882), p. 23. Compare the remark of Charles de Guérin: "Pour l'homme interieur il n'est pas sous le ciel/ De forme qui ne cache un sens spirituel." See Moreau, "De quelques paysages," p. 283.

14. *Memoir*, I, 118.

15. "The Human Inheritance," cycle IV, part II, p. 72.

16. See *Memoir*, I, 47.

17. *Ibid.*, pp. 115-116.

18. *Ibid.*, p. 71.

19. "The flesh-and-blood man," Hearn wrote in "First Impressions," "is only the visible end of an invisible column of force reaching out of the infinite past into the momentary present—only the material Symbol of an immaterial host." This was the theoretical basis of his concept of "super-individuality," a likeness of which operated in Sharp's sense of his own special insight into the life of women. "Only by scientific psychology," Hearn continued, "can the mystery of certain formidable characters be even partly explained; but any explanation must rest upon the acceptance, in some form or other, of the immense evolutional fact of psychical inheritance. And psychical inheritance signifies the superindividual—preëxistence revived in compound personality." *The Writings of Lafcadio Hearn*, vol. IX: *Exotics and Retrospectives in Ghostly Japan* (Boston, 1923), pp. 143-144. (It may be pertinent to note that the original edition of *Exotics and Retrospectives* appeared in 1898, during Sharp's lifetime.) For Hearn's development of these ideas into the concepts of the oneness of humanity and "world literature," see Beong-cheon Yu, *An Ape of Gods: The Art and Thought of Lafcadio Hearn* (Detroit, 1964), pp. 152, 175-179.

20. William Kingdon Clifford, *Cosmic Emotion; also [Virchow on] the Teaching of Science* (London, 1888).

21. "The New Hope," *The Human Inheritance*, pp. 106-107.

22. Patrick Geddes and J. Arthur Thompson, *The Evolution of Sex* (London, 1890), p. 267.

23. *Ibid.*, p. 258.

24. "Transcripts from Nature," XVII, "Dawn Amid Scotch Firs," and XV, "A Green Wave," *The Human Inheritance*, pp. 142-143.

25. *Dante Gabriel Rossetti: A Record and a Study* (London, 1882), p. 335.

26. Glasgow University, Registration Roles and Catalogue, 1871-1873.

27. William Sharp, ed., *Poems of Swinburne* (Leipzig, 1901).

28. "Some Personal Reminiscences of Walter Pater," *Atlantic Monthly*, XXIV (December 1894), 804.

29. *Memoir*, I, 73-74.

). London

1. Arthur Waugh, "Fiona Macleod: A Forgotten Mystery," *Spectator*, August 14, 1936, p. 277.

2. Ernest Rhys, "William Sharp and Fiona Macleod," *Century*, LXXIV (May 1907), 111. Quoted in *Memoir*, I, 170.

3. Ernest Rhys, *Everyman Remembers* (London, 1931), pp. 76-77. Rhys liked to recall that it was he, and not Sharp, who was eventually forced to write the introduction for the De Quincey volume (over Sharp's name), when his "rosy" friend was taken ill with the first of his long, debilitating breakdowns. See *Everyman Remembers*, p. 77, and "William Sharp and Fiona Macleod," p. 112.

4. Richard Le Gallienne, "The Mystery of 'Fiona Macleod,'" *Forum*, XLV (February 1911), 174.

5. "Some Personal Reminiscences of Walter Pater," *Atlantic Monthly*, XXIV (December 1894), 812.

6. Perhaps there is evidence that Sharp never quite outgrew his childhood need to fantasize in his strong predisposition to tales of this kind of derring-do. He apparently tried to use his literary editorship of *The Young Folks' Paper*, for which he wrote adventure stories for children, as an outlet, so that he might better restrain himself in his other work. But the need to create almost theatrically romantic plots was always bursting out afresh. In 1904, he published, as Fiona Macleod's no less, a historical short story entitled "The King's Ring," which was based on events of bravado and intrigue in the American colonies during the Stuart era (*Pall Mall Magazine*, XXXI [May and June 1904], 36-48, 222-233). He planned with similar melodrama an unpublished tale (outlined in the nineties), to be called either "Nostalgia" or "The Ambitions of Zora," set in Constantinople and Paris during the Arabic revolts of the 1830's (Papers of William Sharp, National Library of Scotland, Edinburgh).

7. In a letter to a friend in 1888, Sharp wrote, "What has always impressed me deeply—how deeply I can scarcely say—is the blind despotism of fate . . . This blind, terrible, indifferent Fate, this tyrant Chance, slays or spares, mutilates or rewards, annihilates or passes by without heed, without thought, with absolute blankness of purpose, aim, or passion" (*Memoir*, I, 216).

8. Sharp's identification with Shelley, and the fact that he was working on his Shelley biography at this same time, may suggest that Fern Place had Field Place as a model.

9. Jean Jacques Rousseau, *Emile*, trans. Barbara Foxley (London, 1963), I, 26.

10. William Wordsworth, "Residence in London," *Prelude*, Book VII, lines 685 passim.

11. "Chelsea Hospital and Its Inhabitants," *Good Words*, XXVI (November 1885), 705.

12. Hyperesthesia seems to have been responsible for Ruskin's outcries against the city in his later years. See John D. Rosenberg, *The Darkening Glass: A Portrait of Ruskin's Genius* (New York, 1961), pp. 181-185.

13. "Madge o' the Pool: A Thames Etching," *The Gipsy Christ and Other Tales* (Chicago, 1895), p. 76.

14. *Ibid.*, p. 78.

15. "Chelsea Hospital," p. 705.

16. "A Memory of Verona," *Good Words*, XXX (June 1889), 383.

17. *Ibid.*, pp. 390-391.

18. Philip Bourke Marston, *For a Song's Sake and Other Stories* (London, 1887), ed. William Sharp. Introductory memoir, p. xl.

19. "Dust and Fog," *Good Words*, XXIV (October 1883), 721-723. This article is not included in the bibliography Elizabeth Sharp appended to volume II of her *Memoir*, but internal evidence suggests fairly conclusively that it is not the work of another William Sharp. Its topic is consistent with Sharp's early interest in science, and the range of cities used as examples is limited to those Sharp would have known best, Glasgow and London. The author's main point of departure is an essay by a Scottish scientist (John Aitken, Royal Society of Edinburgh). Also notable is that the article appeared in *Good Words*, a magazine with which Sharp was to have long and frequent association. Elizabeth Sharp's failure to mention "Dust and Fog" may be easily explained by its lack of literary interest.

20. *Ibid.*, p. 723.

21. *Ibid.*, p. 722.

22. William Delisle Hay, *The Doom of the Great City; being the narrative of a survivor written A.D. 1942* (London, 1880), p. 4. Hay appears to have been a wild utopian visionary who finally found his "place." A chronological list of his works is a biographical sketch in itself. After the sixty-years' perspective on "the Great City" came *Three Hundred Years Hence; or a voice from posterity* (London, 1881), then *Brighter Britain! or Settler and Maori in Northern New Zealand* (London, 1882). The *Fungus-Hunter's Guide and Field Memorandum Book* (London, 1887) was obviously intended to help converts survive their escape from civilization.

23. *Doom of the Great City*, p. 10.

24. *Ibid.*, p. 20.

25. *Ibid.*, pp. 21-22.

26. *The Children of To-morrow* (London, 1889), p. 21.

27. Letter to Patrick Geddes, 1896(?), Papers of Patrick Geddes, National Library of Scotland, Edinburgh.

28. In *The Gipsy Christ and Other Tales* (1895), which was largely a retrospective collection of short stories, some of which had previously appeared in magazines. Its publication was designed to occur simultaneously with that of Fiona Macleod's early writings, many of which appeared between 1894 and 1896, in order to provide circumstantial evidence that William Sharp was not the author of the Macleod work.

29. "Madge o the Pool," p. 102.
30. Ibid., pp. 75-77.
31. Ibid., p. 92.
32. Ibid., p. 93.
33. Ibid., p. 125.
34. The Sport of Chance (London, 1888), III, 44-45.
35. Ibid., II, 300-301.
36. Life of Heinrich Heine (London, 1888), p. 38.
37. Life of Browning (London, 1890), p. 11.
38. Ibid., pp. 11-12.
39. Ibid., p. 28.
40. Ibid.
41. Rhys, Everyman Remembers, Foreword, p. vii.
42. Ibid., p. 8.
43. Ibid., p. 9.
44. Carl E. Schorske, "The Idea of the City in European Thought," in The Historian and the City, ed. Oscar Handlin and John Burchard (Cambridge, Mass., 1963), p. 96.
45. Ibid., pp. 104-105.
46. See Oscar Handlin, "The City as a Field for Historical Study," in The Historian and the City, ed. Handlin and Burchard, p. 9.
47. Heine, p. 54.
48. Rhys, "William Sharp and Fiona Macleod," p. 112. Quoted in Memoir, I, 170-171.
49. Ernest Rhys, "Proteus," Century, LXXVI (August 1908), 583.
50. "The Isle of Arran," Art Journal, XLVII (July 1885), 205.
51. Though Wells's sense of place was very strong, he did not explicitly link it with the identity crises among his contemporary artists and writers; he considered the "artistic" persona a self-protective strategy among his associates, one which he says he himself consciously avoided. Experiment in Autobiography (New York, 1934), pp. 529-530.
52. Quoted in Oscar Lewis, Hearn and His Biographers: The Record of a Literary Controversy (San Francisco, 1930), pp. 6-7.

4. North and South

1. Memoir, I, 140.
2. "The Isle of Arran," Art Journal, XLVII (July 1885), 205.
3. Ibid.
4. Phyllis Bentley, The English Regional Novel (London, 1941), pp. 12-13.
5. Memoir, II, 104.
6. See Pierre Moreau, "De quelques paysages introspectifs," in Formen der Selbstdarstellung, ed. Günter Reichenkron and Erich Haase (Berlin, 1956), p. 280. Baudelaire may also have provided some reinforcement on

this score. Like Sharp, Baudelaire wrote a good deal of art criticism, and was inclined to make distinctions among forms of expression in painting and sculpture based on nationality, and particularly upon the northern-southern European dichotomy. See especially "Qu'est-ce que le romantisme?" in *Curiosités esthétiques, Oeuvres complètes de Charles Baudelaire* (Paris, 1923), I, 90-92.

7. William Sharp, ed., *Poetical Works of Walter Scott* (London, 1885), introductory notice, I, 15.

8. "Arran," p. 208.

9. *Memoir*, I, 117.

10. Ernest Rhys, *Everyman Remembers* (London, 1931), p. 79.

11. The *Scottish Art Review* lasted only through 1888 and 1889. It is an indication of the extent to which Sharp drew on the resources of a few well-placed friendships that the magazine was originally published by Elliott Stock, Ltd., the publisher of Sharp's first two volumes of verse, and was then taken over by Walter Scott, Ltd., the publisher of Sharp's third volume of verse, as well as the Canterbury Poets and Camelot Classics. In its Scoto-Celtic emphasis, the *Scottish Art Review* was an earlier—and in fact finer—*Evergreen* (the organ of the Edinburgh movement in the nineties). It was handsomely printed, and the contents—art, poetry, short stories, criticism—had a more sustained high quality than did its Edinburgh successor.

12. "Reminiscences of the Marble Quarries of Carrara," *Good Words*, XXXI (August 1890), 624.

13. "Random Impressions from an Author's Note-Book," *Scottish Art Review*, I (January 1889), 239.

14. *Ibid.*

15. "The City of Beautiful Towers," *Good Words*, XXVI (May 1885), 322.

16. "Random Impressions," p. 239.

17. *Memoir*, I, 133.

18. "Arran," p. 208.

19. *Memoir*, I, 138.

20. *Ibid.*, p. 147.

21. *Ibid.*, p. 128.

22. "Beautiful Towers," p. 324.

23. *Memoir*, I, 132.

24. *Ibid.*, p. 126.

25. "Random Impressions," p. 240.

26. *Memoir*, I, 140-141.

27. *Ibid.*, p. 141.

28. Fiona Macleod, "The Man on the Moor," *The Winged Destiny* (London, 1904), pp. 19-20.

29. "Random Impressions," p. 238.

30. *Ibid.*, p. 237.

31. *Memoir*, I, 139-140.

32. *Ibid.*, p. 133.

33. "Beautiful Towers," p. 326.

34. "Fröken Bergliot," *The Gipsy Christ and Other Tales* (Chicago, 1895), pp. 260-261.

35. *Ibid.*, p. 269.

36. *Ibid.*, p. 273.

37. *Memoir*, I, 310.

38. *Life of Browning* (London, 1890), p. 12.

39. *Ibid.*, p. 57.

40. In his biography of Heine (London, 1888, p. 26) Sharp describes the wandering poet's discovery of a statue of Venus, fallen in a deserted wood and covered with reedy grass. For Heine the sight is symbolic of the decadence of the ancient spirit of beauty: the goddess is allowed to lie unworshipped by a world tragically oblivious of the need that had created her. Precisely the same theme is contained in Sharp's poem "The Fallen Goddess" (*Sospiri di Roma*, Rome, 1891). Another parallel with Heine appears in Sharp's Fiona Macleod work. There the figure of "the Washer of the Ford" (*The Washer of the Ford*, Edinburgh, 1895), a woman who washes linen for shrouds in a running stream, is identical with a figure occurring in a poem in Heine's *Traumbilder* series, "Ein Traum, gar setsam schauerlich" (Heine, *Werke und Briefe* [Berlin, 1961], I, 15). Georgiana Goddard King's assertion that Fiona Macleod's source for the "Washer" was volume VIII of a contemporary collection of Spanish folklore, the *Biblioteca de las tradiciones españoles*, is therefore undoubtedly erroneous, since Sharp specifically alludes to the Heine image in his biography (pp. 32-33). King's parallel was meanly inspired as well as imperfect, requiring her to add that Sharp's substitution of shrouds for the handkerchief of the Spanish legend was, "of course, sheer literature." ("Fiona Macleod," *Modern Language Notes*, XXXIII [June 1918], 355.)

41. *Life of Heine* (London, 1888), p. 54.

42. *Ibid.*, p. 12.

43. *Ibid.*, p. 203. Heine, "Ein Fichtenbaum steht einsam," *Lyrisches Intermezzo*, 33, *Werke und Briefe*, I, 85.

44. *Ibid.*, p. 61.

45. *Ibid.*, pp. 186-187.

5. The Promised Land

1. See Poole's Index, I, "Jews," and especially the *Nineteenth Century*, the *Theological Review*, *Chambers Journal*, and the *London Quarterly*.

2. See Theodor H. Gaster, "England," *The Universal Jewish Encyclopedia* (New York, 1941), IV, 118.

3. Edward Dowden, "George Eliot: *Daniel Deronda* and *Middlemarch*," *Contemporary Review*, XXIX (February 1877), 365.

4. See Poole's Index, I and II, "Jews," and especially the *Nineteenth Century, Good Words, Fraser's, Eclectic,* and the *London Quarterly.*

5. Katie Magnus, *Jewish Portraits* (London, 1925), p. 159.

6. *Ibid.*

7. Dowden, "George Eliot," p. 366.

8. Hermann Adler, "Can Jews be Patriots?" *Nineteenth Century,* III (April 1878), 638. For the debate in general, see *Nineteenth Century,* 1877-1882.

9. *The Children of To-morrow* (London, 1889), p. 267.

10. Olive Schreiner, *Woman and Labor* (New York, 1911). See especially Chap. I.

11. *Children of To-morrow,* p. 13.

12. Preface to *Romantic Ballads and Poems of Phantasy* (London, 1888), p. iv.

13. *Children of To-morrow,* p. 41.

14. *Ibid.,* pp. 40-41.

15. *Ibid.,* p. 77.

16. *Ibid.,* p. 213.

17. *Ibid.,* p. 76.

18. *Ibid.,* p. 213.

19. *Ibid.,* p. 19.

20. Ibsen's *Rosmersholm* (1886) bears enough resemblance to Sharp's novel to suggest that Sharp was perhaps influenced by Ibsen's concept of sexual and social daring. Both tales are constructed around a marital triangle, in which the enlightenment and conversion of the husband functions as the key action, and, though Rebecca and Sanpriel are substantially different, they are both women of talent and personal power, and the crucial agents of the hero's change. Unlike Rosmer and Rebecca, of course, Dane and Sanpriel do not choose to die together, but there is a similarity in their choice of an outlaw life in preference to submission to any of the pressures of convention, and, just as in Ibsen, an enormously fatalistic element in their deaths. Like Rosmer's and Rebecca's, too, their relationship is ultimately defined by a complex combination of personal guilt and retribution with social defiance.

21. *Life of Browning* (London, 1890), p. 16.

22. *Ibid.*

23. "The Sonnet in America," *National Review,* VIII (April 1889), 192-193.

24. *Memoir,* I, 240.

25. *The Harvard Monthly* devoted its Christmas issue for 1903 to Fiona Macleod and the Celtic movement.

26. Catherine A. Janvier, "Fiona Macleod and Her Creator," *North American Review,* CLXXXIV (April 1907), 719.

27. *Memoir,* I, 246.

28. *Flower o' the Vine* (New York, 1892), introductory note by Thomas Janvier, p. viii.

29. *Ibid.*, p. ix.

30. *Memoir*, I, 247.

31. "A Note on the Aesthetic Development of America," *Scottish Art Review*, 11 (November 1889), 162.

32. *Ibid.*, pp. 162-163.

33. *Ibid.*, p. 163.

34. Israel Zangwill, *Without Prejudice* (New York, 1896), p. 291.

35. Israel Zangwill, *The Melting Pot* (New York, 1910), p. 199.

36. "American Literature," *National Review*, XVII (March 1891), 71.

37. Introduction to an unfinished *Life of Rossetti*, planned to make up for the weaknesses of his earlier *Dante Gabriel Rossetti: A Record and a Study* (1882); quoted in *Memoir*, I, 112.

6. Italy Again

1. *Memoir*, II, 9.

2. *Ibid.*, I, 310.

3. *Ibid.*, pp. 291-299.

4. *Ibid.*, p. 293. Considering Charles Dickens's significant place-consciousness, it is interesting to compare his reactions to the Roman Campagna with Sharp's, especially since they touch at some curious points. Dickens in *Pictures from Italy* (London, 1846, pp. 162-163) described the Campagna as

> an undulating flat . . . where few people can live; and where, for miles and miles, there is nothing to relieve the terrible monotony and gloom. Of all kinds of country that could lie outside the gates of Rome, this is the aptest and fittest burial-ground for the Dead City. So sad, so quiet, so sullen; so secret in its covering up of great masses of ruin, and hiding them; so like the wasteplaces into which the men possessed with devils used to go and howl, and rend themselves, in the old days of Jerusalem.

When Sharp paused some forty years after Dickens to contemplate a Campagna shepherd and compose a poem to celebrate him ("The Shepherd," *Sospiri di Roma* [Rome, 1891]), he simply emotionally inverted Dickens's picture of "a villainous-looking shepherd: with matted hair all over his face, and himself wrapped to the chin in a frowzy brown mantle, tending his sheep" (p. 473).

5. Richard Burton, "Maeterlinck: Impressionist," *Atlantic Monthly*, LXXIV (October 1894), 675.

6. *Sospiri*, pp. 52-53.

7. *Memoir*, I, 295.

8. *Sospiri*, pp. 74-76.

9. See *Memoir*, I, 298.

10. *Sospiri*, pp. 49-50.

11. See especially *Memoir*, II, 5. Sharp himself may have confused Rhys —perhaps intentionally. See Ernest Rhys, *Everyman Remembers* (London, 1931), p. 79.

12. *Memoir*, I, 284.

13. Fiona Macleod, *Where the Forest Murmurs, The Works of Fiona Macleod* (London, 1912), VI, 173. The essay in which this phrase appeared, called "The Tribe of the Plover," was first published in *Country Life*, April 15, 1905.

14. *Pagan Review*, I (August [September] 1892), 4. The editor's preface is quoted in its entirety in *Memoir*, I, 323-328.

15. With typical whimsy, Sharp mentioned his own name once, on the back cover of the review, in an advertisement for a "forthcoming" volume of "Living Scottish Poets."

16. Interesting to note, Sharp originally planned the publication of *Vistas* (1894) under the name of Siwaärmill (*Memoir*, I, 306).

17. *Pagan Review*, p. 43.

18. *Life of Browning* (London, 1890), p. 87.

19. *Ibid.*, p. 37.

20. *Ibid.*, p. 45.

21. *Ibid.*, p. 36.

22. *Ibid.*, p. 133.

23. *Memoir*, I, 305.

24. *Ibid.*, II, 45.

25. "Fragments from the Lost Journals of Piero di Cosimo," *Ecce Puella and Other Prose Imaginings* (London, 1896), p. 50.

26. *Ibid.*, pp. 50, 59.

27. *Ibid.*, p. 62.

28. *Dante Gabriel Rossetti: A Record and a Study* (London, 1882), pp. 285-301.

29. "Monte Oliveto and the Frescoes of Sodona," *Art Journal*, XLVI (April 1884), 104.

30. *Rossetti*, p. 137. The prologues to "The Weird of Michael Scott" and "Sospitra" in *Romantic Ballads and Poems of Phantasy* (London, 1888) contained references to this legend.

31. Philip Bourke Marston, *For a Song's Sake and Other Stories* (London, 1887), ed. William Sharp. Introductory memoir, p. xli.

32. *Ibid.*, pp. xxvi-xxvii.

33. *Life of Shelley* (London, 1887), p. 14.

34. "George Meredith's *Reading of Earth*," *Scottish Art Review*, I (February 1889), 264.

35. *Memoir*, I, 307.

36. *Ibid.*, pp. 302-303.

37. *Ibid.*, II, 68.

38. *Memoir*, I, 23. See p. 21.

39. Elie Reclus, *Primitive Folk: Studies in Comparative Ethnology*, Contemporary Science Series, ed. Havelock Ellis (London, 1892), p. 73.

40. "Maeterlinck," *Academy*, March 19, 1892, p. 270.

41. "Some Personal Reminiscences of Walter Pater," *Atlantic Monthly*, LXXIV (December 1894), 813.

42. "Sir Edward Burne-Jones," *Atlantic Monthly*, LXXXII (September 1898), 376. An impulse for such analysis, especially self-analysis, in terms of a dual racial strain was obviously one of the by-products of the current ethnological fad. Two instances among French writers who grew up in the nineteenth century may be cited offhand—Ernest Renan (who was himself largely responsible for the popularization of race theories in his day) analyzed the tensions in his own personality in terms of his Celtic-Gascon origins; and André Gide, studying his ancestry for keys to self-understanding, was so concerned with the significance of dual racial strains that he pored over entries in current biographical dictionaries to discover the racial genealogies on both sides of the families of notable men and women (*Si le grain ne meurt* [Paris, 1928], p. 22).

43. "William Morris: The Man and His Work," *Atlantic Monthly*, LXXVIII (December 1896), 781.

44. *The Progress of Art in the Nineteenth Century* (London, 1902), pp. 223-224.

45. *Ibid.*, p. 155.

46. *Memoir*, I, 275.

47. *Ibid.*, p. 82.

48. Lilian Rea, "Fiona Macleod," *The Critic*, XLVIII (May 1906), p. 460.

49. *Ibid.*

50. See Reclus, *Primitive Folk*, pp. 70-75. Edward Carpenter developed Reclus' data into a broad system of hypotheses about the cultural importance of homosexuality in *Intermediary Types among Primitive Folk: A Study in Social Evolution* (London, 1919).

51. *Rossetti*, p. 35.

52. "Desolation," *The Human Inheritance, The New Hope, Motherhood* (London, 1882), p. 163.

53. "Dover Beach," ll. 29-30, 33. The apparent inconsistency is Arnold's; the italics are mine.

54. *Memoir*, II, 308.

7. Woman

1. John Stuart Mill, *On Liberty and The Subjection of Women* (New York, 1873), p. 244.

2. See Thomas Wentworth Higginson, *The Writings of Thomas Wentworth Higginson*, vol. XIV: *Woman and the Alphabet* (Boston, 1900). In the opening essay of this volume Higginson confirms the modern reader's

reaction to nineteenth-century woman-consciousness: "It has been seriously asserted, that during the last half-century more books have been written by women and about women than during all the previous uncounted ages. It may be true . . . As to the increased multitude of general treatises on the female sex, however,—its education, life, health, diseases, charms, dress, deeds, sphere, rights, wrongs, work, wages, encroachments, and idiosyncracies generally,—there can be no doubt whatever; and the poorest of these books recognizes a condition of public sentiment of which no other age ever dreamed" ("Ought Women to Learn the Alphabet," pp. 5-6). Higginson concludes that the century has, in relation to women, undergone a "new Reformation."

3.   Olive Schreiner, *Woman and Labor* (New York, 1911), pp. 60-64. Chaps. I and II are principally devoted to the concept of "female parasitism," its history and effects.

4.   Henry Thomas Buckle, "The Influence of Women on the Progress of Knowledge," *Essays* (New York, 1864).

5.   Steven Marcus, in *The Other Victorians* (New York, 1966), notes that William Acton, in writing his authoritative medical treatise *The Functions and Disorders of the Reproductive Organs, in Childhood, Youth, Adult Age, and Advanced Life, Considered in their Physiological, Social, and Moral Relations* (1857), barely mentions women at all, and "seems perfectly unconscious of the fact that he has anything to account for in this connection" (p. 13).

6.   *Ibid.*, pp. 196-197.

7.   S. E. Gay, *Modern Thought*, December 15, 1879; Frances E. Hoggan, M.D. (Manchester, 1884); J. H. Garfit (Boston, 1886); William Reeves (London, 1888); Henry C. Wright (London, 1888). Victorian physiologists were remarkably versatile: Garfit, it is claimed on the title page of his essay, was also the author of *A Short Account of the Giraffe.*

8.   Havelock Ellis, "The Changing Status of Women," *Westminster Review*, CXXVIII (October 1887), 16. He was quoting from Whitman's *Democratic Vistas.*

9.   Patrick Geddes and J. Arthur Thompson, *The Evolution of Sex* (London, 1890), pp. 270-271.

10.   "A Woman," "The Effects of Civilization upon Women," *National Review*, IX (March 1887), 26-38. Sharp's essay was "Rossetti in Prose and Verse," pp. 111-124.

11.   *Memoir*, I, 39.

12.   *Ibid.*, II, 7.

13.   "William Morris: The Man and His Work," *Atlantic Monthly*, LXXVIII (December 1896), 780.

14.   Mona Caird, *The Morality of Marriage and Other Essays on the Status and Destiny of Women* (London, 1897). Elizabeth Sharp discusses Mona Caird's writings on marriage in *Memoir*, I, 226.

15 "Madge o' the Pool: A Thames Etching," *The Gipsy Chilst and Other Tales* (Chicago, 1895), p. 102.

16. He held this post from 1886 to 1889.

17. "To Esther Mona," *The Laughter of Peterkin* (London, 1895).

18. Fiona Macleod, "The Unborn Child," *From the Hills of Dream* (Edinburgh, 1895), p. 32.

19. *Memoir*, I, 198. Sharp's career was nearly one long season of illness. Speaking in public was apparently a great strain for him, and he tried to avoid it by limiting his attempts to talks before small groups. It was for this reason that he did not take a chair of poetry at the University of London, though encouraged by the fervent recommendations of many associates, and also refused an opportunity to deliver a lecture at Harvard in 1892. On the one occasion when he ignored advice and delivered the first of a projected series of lectures at the University of Edinburgh in 1895, he suffered a total collapse. This was followed by intermittent relapses for years afterward. One anguished letter to Geddes in 1896 is a litany of pleas for commiseration. He begged Geddes to send him a secretary while his wife was in Paris covering art exhibitions: "*I must not be alone*" (Papers of Patrick Geddes, National Library of Scotland, Edinburgh; letter undated, but apparently from January or February 1896). In 1898 he suffered another total nervous collapse from which he recuperated only partially. From then on until his death in 1905 he required resuscitating trips to the Mediterranean at least once a year.

20. *Memoir*, I, 303.

21. Richard Le Gallienne, "The Mystery of 'Fiona Macloed'," *Forum*, XLV (February 1911), 173, and *Memoir*, II, 5.

22. *Memoir*, II, 5.

23. *Ibid.*, I, 277.

24. *Ibid.*, II, 5.

25. "A Winter Evening," "Prologue," and "Epilogue: Il Bosco Sacro," *Sospiri di Roma* (Rome, 1891), pp. 67, 1, 122.

26. Such references occur in a letter from Sharp to Geddes dated April 29, 1895, and in another, undated, but probably from late 1895; a prospectus for the *Evergreen* (then not yet the *Evergreen*, but "The Celtic World") shows Sharp anxious to keep the Celtic sources broad, and have them include "Irish, Scottish, Welsh, Manx, Cornish, and Breton writers" (Geddes Papers).

27. Edith Wingate Rinder, ed., *Poems and Lyrics of Nature* (London, 1897).

28. *Memoir*, II, 5-6.

29. *Ibid.*, p. 39.

30. Ernest Rhys, *Everyman Remembers* (London, 1931), p. 80.

31. Sharp seems to have used the name "Esclarmoundo" for Mrs. Rinder after *Pharais*, to convey the idealization of his passion. *Green Fire*

239

carried the dedication "to Esclarmoundo," followed by a passage from Ovid suggestive of Sharp's own attitude: "Nec sine te nec tecum vivere possum." "The Silence of Amor," a group of prose-poems (first appearing in *From the Hills of Dream* and reprinted in *The Works of Fiona Macleod* [London, 1910], vol. VI), was similarly dedicated—"To Esclarmoundo: There is one word never spoken in these estrays of passion and longing."

32. Frank Rinder, "William Sharp—'Fiona Macleod': A Tribute," *Art Journal*, LVIII (February 1906), 44-45.

33. *Memoir*, I, 316-317.

34. *Ibid.*, pp. 320-321.

35. *Ibid.*, II, 123-124. The letter is dated March 29, 1898.

36. *Ibid.*, p. 124.

37. "Mr. George Meredith," *Good Words*, XL (July 1899), 481.

38. *Memoir*, II, 124-125.

39. *Ibid.*, p. 123.

40. Sarah G. Bowerman, "Blanche Willis Howard," *Dictionary of American Biography* (New York, 1943). Sympathy with feminism seems to have been von Teuffel's most outstanding trait of character. He is, wrote Sharp, "one of the few Germans who seem to regard women as equals" (*Memoir*, I, 273).

41. A curious sidelight on Sharp's feminism—perhaps Victorian feminism—is provided by the husband's analysis of his wife's desire for freedom: he says it came from seeing her mother's spirit totally suppressed by her father's masterful, dominating will (*A Fellowe and His Wife* [Boston, 1892], pp. 51-52).

42. *Memoir*, II, 78. Richard Le Gallienne's wife died in childbirth in 1895.

43. "Fragments from the Lost Journals of Piero di Cosimo," *Ecce Puella* (London, 1896), p. 73.

44. "The Birth of a Soul," *Vistas* (Chicago, 1894), p. 50.

45. *Memoir*, II, 92.

46. Shelley and "Epipsychidion" are, in fact, invoked by the "wife" in *Fellowe and Wife*, pp. 26-27.

47. *Memoir*, I, 83.

48. Ibsen was a penetrating student of the psychopathology of feminism, and he provides another suggestive parallel to Sharp's situation in *Rosmersholm* (1886), where Rosmer, Rebecca West, and Beata form a mutually dependent and reciprocally self-sacrificing triangle. Perhaps such curious relationships were not then as far-fetched, in life or literature, as they may seem now.

49. Papers of William Sharp, National Library of Scotland, Edinburgh. His notes for the volume of short stories are particularly copious; he planned to dedicate it to George Meredith, "great captain in the army of students of life."

50. *Ibid.*, MS essay on "Maeterlinck's *Pelléas et Mélisande*."

51. "The Hotel of the Beautiful Star," *Harper's*, CIII (October 1901), 673.
52. *Ibid.*, p. 679.
53. See "Dual Personality in the Case of William Sharp," *Journal of the Society for Psychical Research*, X (April 1911), 57-63, in which the possibility of technical duality is rejected. "The view that [Sharp and Macleod] were two personalities seems to turn on [Sharp's and Mrs. Sharp's] clear and unwavering impression that so it was—an impression apparently never divorced from their belief in their underlying unity" (p. 57). The following arguments against "classic" duality are given: (1) no clear or marked superiority, either moral or intellectual, (2) no pathological element, and (3) no breach of memory. The Fiona Macleod pose does not provide a classic case of imposture, either, as that is defined by Phyllis Greenacre, M.D.—"far surpassing in interest and apparent ability the impostor's ordinary 'other self'" ("The Relation of the Impostor to the Artist," *The Psychoanalytic Study of the Child*, XIII [1958], 521).
54. *Memoir*, II, 208.
55. *Fellowe and Wife*, p. 34. The Comedy of Woman was planned as an ambitious project of exploration: each story was conceived as a study of some prevailing female passion—e.g., "woman consciously making pleasure her one aim," "woman who gladly forfeits all for passion," "woman in love with herself," "religious mania," "the passionate, basic craving for maternity," etc.(Sharp Papers).
56. "Ecce Puella," *Ecce Puella*, p. 24.
57. *Ibid.*, p. 19.
58. *Ibid.*, p. 27.
59. An indication of the kind of reaction he avoided is provided by George Meredith's letter thanking Sharp for *not* dedicating to him his *Fair Women in Painting and Poetry* (Portfolio of Artistic Monographs, no. 7 [1894]; a bit of critical fluff). "Thousands of curdling Saxons," wrote Meredith, "are surly almost to the snarl at the talk about 'woman.' Next to the Anarchist, we are hated" (*Memoir*, II, 35).
60. *Pharais* (Derbyshire, 1894); *The Mountain Lovers* (London, 1895). Both novels were reprinted as vol. I of *Works*.
61. *Green Fire* (New York, 1896), p. 279.
62. "Some Reminiscences of Christina Rossetti," *Atlantic Monthly*, LXXV (June 1895), 745.
63. See especially "Iona," *The Divine Adventure; Iona; By Sundown Shores* (London, 1900). One spiritualistic commentator on Fiona Macleod posed the view that Sharp's pseudonymous personality was the result of his being "possessed" by the spirit of St. Bridget (Edith Rolt Wheeler, "Fiona Macleod," *Fortnightly Review*, CVI [November 1919], 780-790).
64. Beong-cheon Yu, *An Ape of Gods: The Art and Thought of Lafcadio Hearn* (Detroit, 1964), pp. 208-210.
65. Some of Miguel de Unamuno's stories supply hints of a further

development in the twentieth-century symbolic use of women. His characterizations of women in terms of raw sexual or maternal impulse bring some of Fiona Macleod's Celtic heroines up to date and suggest that Sharp was prefiguring the anti-intellectual bent of many experimental treatments of women in modern literature. See *Three Exemplary Novels*, trans. Angel Flores (New York, 1956).

66. *Works*, VII, 82-86. The poem first appeared in the second edition of *From the Hills of Dream*.

67. "The Distant Country," *Dominion of Dreams* (London, 1899), pp. 210-213.

68. *Silence Farm* (London, 1899), pp. 188-193.

69. *Ibid.*, p. 218.

70. Obviously not in his line either was the comic treatment of woman's desire for freedom, attempted in *Wives in Exile* (London, 1898).

71. Sharp made an intensive study of Hardy's work to 1892, and one would expect that he followed Hardy closely thereafter. See "Thomas Hardy and His Novels," *Forum*, XXVI (July 1892), 583-593.

8. The New Cosmopolitanism

1. *Memoir*, I, 309.
2. *Ibid.*, p. 287.
3. "Maeterlinck," *Academy*, March 19, 1892, p. 270.
4. *Ibid.*
5. Richard Burton, "Maeterlinck: Impressionist," *Atlantic Monthly*, LXXIV (October 1894), 676. Another veiled personal controversy may have found expression in this article; without mentioning Sharp as a Maeterlinck supporter, Burton attacks him, together with Whitman and Henley, as among the "dubious experimenters" in *vers libre* (p. 675).
6. "La Jeune Belgique," *Nineteenth Century*, XXXIV (September 1893), 417-418.
7. *Ibid.*, p. 418.
8. Patrick Geddes expressed the same view when he said that the object of the Edinburgh movement was "to arrest the tremendous centralizing power of the metropolis of London" (quoted in *Memoir*, II, 49).
9. "A Note on the Belgian Renascence," *Chap-Book*, IV (December 1895), 151.
10. *Ibid.*, p. 154.
11. *Ibid.*, p. 156.
12. Quoted in *Memoir*, II, 50.
13. Israel Zangwill, *Without Prejudice* (New York, 1896), p. 291.
14. Victor Branford, "Old Edinburgh and the *Evergreen*," *Bookman*, IX (December 1895), 89. Sharp himself was emissary to Paris for the formation of the Franco-Scottish Society; letters of Sharp to Geddes through

1895 refer to such arrangements (Papers of Patrick Geddes, National Library of Scotland, Edinburgh).

15. Compare Sophia Fiechter, von William Sharp zu Fiona Macleod (Tubingen, 1936), p. 69; also Ernest Rhys, Everyman Remembers (London, 1931), p. 80.

16. Memoir, II, 60.

17. Sharp to Geddes, April 29, 1895, Geddes Papers.

18. "The Dramas of Gabriele D'Annunzio," Fortnightly Review, LXXIV (September 1900), 391-409.

19. "Italian Poets of Today," Quarterly Review, CXCVI (July 1902), 239-268.

20. William Kingdon Clifford, Cosmic Emotion; also [Virchow on] the Teaching of Science (London, 1888), pp. 11-13. Rhys, in Everyman Remembers, cites Clifford's work as causing a great deal of excitement and playing a major part in setting the intellectual tone of London in the late eighties; see Prologue, p. ii.

21. Ibid., p. 15.

22. Beong-cheon Yu, An Ape of Gods: The Art and Thought of Lafcadio Hearn (Detroit, 1964), pp. 175-177. Yu's references in this connection are to Hearn's essays "A Language Question" and "The Prose of Small Things."

23. Edward Carpenter, The Art of Creation (London, 1904), p. 34. Carpenter was a friend of Rhys, and one of the originals of the "Vita Nuova" Fellowship in the late eighties (Rhys, Everyman Rebembers, p. 2). His universalist philosophy took on the distinctly political cast of anti-nationalism during the First World War, when he wrote his outraged reaction to the war, Never Again! (London, 1916).

24. Herman Ausubel, In Hard Times: Reformers among the Late Victorians (New York, 1960), p. 32.

25. See especially Ruth Z. Temple, The Critics' Alchemy (New York, 1963), Chapters I-III, and Christophe Campos, The View of France: Arnold to Bloomsbury (London, 1965), pp. 30-48.

26. Joseph Texte, Jean-Jacques Rousseau and the Cosmopolitan Spirit in Literature, trans. J. W. Matthews (New York, 1929), Introduction, p. xxi. The text used here is a reprint of the original translation published in London in 1899.

27. Ibid., p. xvi.

28. Life of Heine (London, 1888), p. 93.

29. Havelock Ellis, The New Spirit (New York, n.d.), pp. 22, 25. The Introduction is dated 1892.

30. Charles Dudley Warner, ed., Library of the World's Best Literature, Ancient and Modern (New York, 1896-97). Sharp's contributions to this encyclopedic work were "Celtic Literature" (with Ernest Rhys), VIII, 3403-3450; "Icelandic Literature," XX, 7865-7895; "Myths and Folklore of the Aryan Peoples" (with Ernest Rhys), XXVI, 10522-10542; and "Hersart de

la Villemarqué: The Heroic and Legendary Literature of Brittany," XXXVIII, 15377-15391.

31. Cosmopolitans did not, of course, stop with the west. Indian and oriental cultures were also enjoying popularity. Even Sharp had intentions of invading Lafcadio Hearn's domain with an article on "Lyric Japan" (*Memoir*, I, 350).

32. *Texte, Rousseau*, pp. 79-80.

33. Foreword to *The House of Usna* (Portland, Me., 1903). This essay is reprinted in *The Works of Fiona Macleod* (London, 1912), VII, 291-307, and in revised form was published as the title essay in *The Winged Destiny* (London, 1904), pp. 367-390.

34. "Land of Theocritus," *Harper's*, CVI (April 1903), 802-804. This essay was only one of a series of projected "Greek Backgrounds" (*Memoir*, II, 246). Sharp visited Greece in the winter of 1903.

35. *Memoir*, II, 209.

36. *Texte, Rousseau*, p. 366.

37. Letter from Fiona Macleod to Katherine Tynan, March 24, 1897; quoted in Tynan, "William Sharp and Fiona Macleod," *Fortnightly Review*, LXXVI (March 1906), 578. Chambers' and other contemporary biographical dictionaries contained special entries for Fiona Macleod, invented by Sharp to maintain the illusion of her separate existence.

38. Sharp's concept of racial "reorganization" is a reminder that the fundamentally cosmopolitan principle underlying the Catholic Church bore renewed and influential significance. Even so positivist a thinker as H. G. Wells found it worthy of comment: "It dawned upon me," he wrote in *Experiment in Autobiography* (New York, 1934) of his mental life at about the turn of the century, "that there had been a Catholic Reformation as drastic as and perhaps profounder than the Protestant Reformation, and that the mentality of clerical Rome, instead of being an unchanged system *in saecula saeculorum* had been stirred to its foundations at that time and was still struggling—like everything else alive—in the grip of adaptive necessity. In spite of my anti-Christian bias I found something congenial in the far flung cosmopolitanism of the Catholic proposition. Notwithstanding its synthesis of decaying ancient theologies and its strong taint of other-worldliness, the Catholic Church continues to be, in its own half-hearted fashion, an Open Conspiracy to reorganize the whole life of man . . . Catholicism is something greater in scope and spirit than any nationalist protestantism . . . It is a question too fine for me to discuss whether I am an outright atheist or an extreme heretic on the furthest verge of Christendom . . . But certainly I branch from the Catholic stem" (pp. 486-487).

39. "Cardinal Lavigerie's Work in North Africa," *Atlantic Monthly*, LXXIV (August 1894), 226.

40. "Iona," *The Divine Adventure; Iona; By Sundown Shores* (London, 1900), p. 167.

41 "The Wayfarer," Winged Destiny. The story first appeared in Cosmopolis in 1898.

42. "The Gael and His Heritage," Winged Destiny, p. 235. The essay first appeared in the Nineteenth Century in 1900.

43. The Dominion of Dreams (London, 1899). This series of tales was continued from The Sin-Eater and Other Tales (Edinburgh, 1895).

44. Winged Destiny. See also "Lost," Dominion of Dreams.

45. "Cuilidh Moire" and "Man on the Moor," Winged Destiny. "Cuilidh Moire" first appeared in the Contemporary Review in 1902.

46. "To E.W.R.," Pharais (Derbyshire, 1894), p. ix.

47. Lyra Celtica (Edinburgh, 1896), Introduction, p. li.

48. Ibid., p. 427.

49. "Iona," pp. 245-246.

50. "Celtic," Winged Destiny, p. 200. The essay first appeared in the Contemporary Review in 1900.

51. "Prelude," Winged Destiny, p. 169. The essay first appeared as the Foreword to a reprint of the essay "Celtic" in book form (Portland, Me., 1901).

52. Ibid., p. 177.

53. "The Irish Muse: I," North American Review, CLXXIX (November 1904), 689. Part II of this essay appeared the following month (pp. 900-912).

54. "Prelude," p. 178.

55. "Iona," p. 119.

56. Ethel Goddard, "The Winged Destiny and Fiona Macleod," Fortnightly Review, LXXVIII (December 1904), 1038. Fiona Macleod had spoken glowingly of Miss Goddard's Dreams for Ireland in the very volume she was reviewing (Winged Destiny, p. 270).

57. Ibid., pp. 1037, 1044; quoting from Winged Destiny, pp. 193, 198.

58. Wind and Wave (Leipzig, 1902).

59. "To E.W.R.," Pharais, p. vii.

60. "Iona," p. 167.

61. "Celtic," p. 189.

9. The Geography of the Mind

1. Joseph Texte, Jean-Jacques Rousseau and the Cosmopolitan Spirit in Literature, trans. J. W. Matthews (New York, 1929), pp. 79-80.

2. Ibid., Introduction, pp. xviii-xix.

3. Ibid., p. 336.

4. Ibid., p. 369.

5. The Progress of Art in the Nineteenth Century (London, 1902), Introduction, p. v.

6. Ibid.

7. Ibid., p. 3.

8. *Ibid.*, p. 32.
9. *Ibid.*, p. 46.
10. *Texte, Rousseau*, p. 293.
11. *Progress of Art*, pp. 79-81.
12. *Ibid.*, p. 81.
13. *Ibid.*, p. 89.
14. Edward Carpenter, *The Art of Creation* (London, 1904), p. 33.
15. *Ibid.*, pp. 56-57.
16. *Literary Geography* (London, 1904), pp. 7-8.
17. *Ibid.*, pp. 93-95.
18. *Ibid.*, pp. 109-112.
19. *Ibid.*, pp. 132-133.
20. *Ibid.*, p. 136. Consistent with Sharp's now fully-flowered sense of place were the projected "Greek Backgrounds" (*Memoir*, II, 246).
21. Compare Phyllis Bentley, *The English Regional Novel* (London, 1941), in which the author defines the "true" regional novel in just such narrow, almost Marxian terms (pp. 21-23).
22. *Silence Farm* (London, 1899), pp. 138-139.
23. "La Jeune Belgique," *Nineteenth Century*, XXXIV (September 1893), 434.
24. *Green Fire* (New York, 1896), pp. 282-283.
25. *The Sin-Eater and Other Tales* (Edinburgh, 1895).
26. Foreword to *The Silence of Amor* and *Where the Forest Murmurs*, *The Works of Fiona Macleod* (London, 1910), VI, 7. *The Silence of Amor* first appeared as part of the second edition of *From the Hills of Dream* (Edinburgh, 1896).
27. *The Silence of Amor, The Works of Fiona Macleod* (London, 1910), VI, 15, 22, 27, 30.
28. "The Lynn of Dreams," *The Winged Destiny* (London, 1904), p. 152. The story first appeared in the *Contemporary Review* in 1902.
29. See *Memoir*, II, 333, where Mrs. Sharp documents this phase, which she says was followed by an attempt on Sharp's part to bring his two "personalities" into harmony.
30. "Celtic," *Winged Destiny*, p. 197.
31. "The Tribe of the Plover," *Works*, VI, 173. All of the essays incorporated into *Where the Forest Murmurs* first appeared in *Country Life* during 1904 and 1905.
32. *Ibid.*, p. 411.
33. Prologue to *The Washer of the Ford* (Edinburgh, 1895), p. 4.
34. *The Divine Adventure; Iona; By Sundown Shores* (London, 1900), p. 414.
35. *Ibid.*, p. 430.
36. *From the Hills of Dreams: Threnodies, Songs, and Later Poems* (London, 1901).

37. "The Shadowy Waters," Winged Destiny, pp. 325-326, 337. The essay first appeared as "The Later Work of Mr. Yeats" in the North American Review in 1902.

38. Ibid., pp. 332-333.

39. Sharp did not resist the pressures to have Fiona Macleod's closet dramas played, and The House of Usna was performed by the Stage Society at the Globe in 1900, under his own direction. After Sharp's death, The Immortal Hour was turned into an opera by Rutland Boughton, with apparent success. Mrs. Sharp then dedicated the latter play's posthumous reprinting to E.W.R.

40. Sharp spoke in his Foreword to The House of Usna ("Fatality in the Tragic Drama") of D'Annunzio's La Città Morta as "that most perturbing of all modern dramas" (Works, VII, 300). See also "The Dramas of Gabriele D'Annunzio," Fortnightly Review, LXXIV (September 1900).

41. Dorothy M. Hoare, The Work of Morris and Yeats in Relation to Early Saga Literature (Cambridge, Eng., 1937), p. 102.

42. Carlo Levi, Christ Stopped at Eboli, trans. Frances Frenaye (New York, 1947), pp. 183-184.

43. "The Winged Destiny" (revised version of Foreword to The House of Usna), Winged Destiny, p. 367.

44. Foreword to The House of Usna, Works, VII, 292.

45. Ibid., p. 299.

46. Ibid., p. 304.

47. Ibid., pp. 294-295.

48. Carpenter, Art of Creation, p. 22.

49. Foreword to The House of Usna, Works, VII, 303.

50. Ibid., p. 305.

51. Ibid., p. 306.

52. "A Field for Modern Verse," Dome, n.s. IV (March 1899), 207.

53. Ibid., p. 209.

54. Ethel Rolt Wheeler, "William Sharp and Fiona Macleod," Fortnightly Review, CXII (November 1919), 786.

55. Quoted in Memoir, II, 335, from lecture given to the Aberdeen Center of the Franco-Scottish Society in 1907.

56. "Edward Burne-Jones," Fortnightly Review, LXX (August 1898), 291-292.

57. Ibid., p. 294.

58. Ibid., pp. 298, 300.

59. Ibid., p. 297.

60. Ibid., p. 305.

61. "Puvis de Chavannes," Art Journal, LX (December 1898), 377.

62. "Land of Theocritus," Harper's, CVI (April 1903), 802-804. This same theme appears, with varying degrees of development, in all Sharp's essays on Sicily.

63. "Garden of the Sun: I," *Century,* LXXI (March 1906), 681.
64. "The Sicilian Highlands, *Atlantic Monthly,* XCIII (April 1904), 474.
65. "Garden of the Sun: II," *Century,* LXXII (May 1906), 50.
66. *Ibid.,* p. 53.
67. *Ibid.,* p. 54.
68. *Memoir,* II, 326.

Conclusion

1. See Phyllis Greenacre, M.D., "Discussion and Comments on the Psychology of Creativity," *Journal of the American Academy of Child Psychiatry,* I (January 1962), 129-137, and "Experiences of Awe in Childhood," *The Psychoanalytic Study of the Child,* XI (1956), 9-30.

2. H. G. Wells's judgments on his own schoolboy sense of England's glorious superiority sustain this generalization, particularly his comment that he was then (in the late seventies) at a stage of puerility "at which the brains of great multitudes of English people halted for good . . . Adolf Hitler," he continued, from the enlightened vantage point of 1933, "is no more than one of my thirteen year old reveries come real. A whole generation of Germans has failed to grow up." *Experiment in Autobiography* (London, 1934), pp. 70, 74.

3. Many of the city-dwellers of the seventies and eighties were first-generation urbanites: the population of urban areas in England tripled between 1821 and 1871, and Irish- and Scottish-born immigrants to England doubled within the same period. See E. L. Woodward, *The Age of Reform, 1850-1870* (Oxford, 1938), pp. 579-580. The Great Depression only served to heighten a sense of dislocation among the poor by causing severe unemployment and underemployment. "To the respectable public, workers remained semi-savages—brutal, dirty, ignorant, lazy, untrustworthy." Herman Ausubel, *In Hard Times* (New York, 1960), pp. 35-37. Under the circumstances, the poor could have felt only slightly less foreign than foreigners. Some literary men surely thought so: Henry James devoted his novel *The Princess Casamassima* and Joseph Conrad *The Secret Agent* to the anarchistic impulses of these déclassés. And E. M. Forster's *Howards End* succinctly identified the outcast sense of the poor in the naming of his character Leonard Bast—undoubtedly typical Forster shorthand for "bastard."

4. *Daniel Deronda* (New York, 1901), I, 19.

5. "The Poet of Ballyshannon" (1888), quoted in Richard Ellmann, *The Identity of Yeats* (New York, 1954), pp. 14-15.

6. It is no wonder Conrad could say in a private moment, "I am an alien." The same secure English character made aliens of men who did not have Conrad's reasons for feeling foreign. Shaw was allegedly described by some of his contemporaries as an alien, H. G. Wells as having "an alien mentality," with the result that even Wells is said to have spoken of himself

as Jewish, and as possessing "no God, no King, no nationality." See Joseph Lefwich, Israel Zangwill (New York, 1957), pp. 139-147.

7. Prefaces (London, 1937), pp. 50-52; Preface to The Nigger of the Narcissus (1897).

8. Ibid., p. 154; Preface to Within the Tides (1920).

9. Studies in Classic American Literature (New York, 1964), pp. 3, 5-6. In the respects suggested here, but also in many other respects, the likenesses between Sharp and Lawrence are striking. Both in his consciousness of multiple personality in himself and in his quasi-metaphysical treatment of the dual sexual principle, especially the "Woman-Idea," Lawrence seems to have reembodied Sharp. Their equally restless wandering, their obsession with place, their concern with reconstituting the sexual relationship through a literary strategy of primitivism and the use of folk symbology—these are all remarkably strong points of contact. The Etruscans, the Sicilians, and Italy in general profoundly stirred them both, and the free-verse Sospiri that resulted from Sharp's Italian experience bears suggestive resemblances to Lawrence's Birds, Beasts, and Flowers. Perhaps there is evidence that all these crossed lines were not merely coincidental in the fact that Heinemann was in the process of printing all the Sharp-Macleod writings, as well as Mrs. Sharp's Memoir, at precisely the time they were publishing Lawrence's first novel. And the title of that novel, The White Peacock, apparently suggested by someone at Heinemann, is also, curiously, the title of one of the best and most frequently anthologized poems of Sharp's Sospiri.

10. A Passage to India (New York, 1952), p. 282.

11. "The Winged Destiny and Fiona Macleod," Fortnightly Review, LXXVII (December 1904), 1037.

12. Howards End (New York, 1945), pp. 370-371, 298.

Index

Index

Index

Schreiner, Olive. on women and evolutionary process, 37; concept of "female parasitism," 84, 117; her feminism, 121-122, 141
Science: and art, 32, 86, 90; and poetry, 37-38, 39
Scotland: Sharp's youthful ties with, 28; use of, as background in Sharp's early poetry, 33-34; in Sharp's travels, 211-212
Scott, Sir Walter, 13, 67
Scott, William Bell, 29
Scottish Art Review, 68, 93, 95, 105, 232
Seer, the, 113, 182, 190-191
Serao, Matilda, 152
Shadow of Arvor, The, 126
"Shadowy Waters, The," 186, 187
Sharp, David Galbraeth (Sharp's father), 18-22 *passim*, 27
Sharp, Elizabeth (Sharp's wife): on Sharp–Fiona Macleod division, 6; her interpretations of Sharp's childhood and family relations, 19-20, 21-23; in Sharp's early poetry, 35; marital relationship with Sharp, 124, 134-135; on Edith Rinder and Fiona Macleod inspiration, 126-130; her contribution to Edinburgh Celtic movement, 152
Sharp, Katherine Brook (Sharp's mother), 18-22 *passim*
Sharp, Mary (Sharp's sister), 19
Sharp, William: relations with family, 1, 18-26; psychological motives behind creation of Fiona Macleod, 2, 7, 24, 26-27, 97, 126-130, 134-139; internal sexual tension of, 2, 26-27, 135; restlessness of, 2, 14-15, 20-22, 48, 62-63, 75-77, 96-97, 128, 194, 198-200, 211; problem of identity, 13, 44, 62-63, 71-73, 75-77, 103-107, 115, 198-199; autobiographical writings, 18, 35-36, 41; excursion with gypsies, 20, 21-22, 24, 108; childhood fantasies, 21; psychic experience, 23, 191; early literary career, 45-48; effects of illness, 115, 124, 239; sympathy with women, 116, 143-145; travel, 211-213; unresolved biographical problems, 3, 16; misinterpretations of, 3-6
philosophic and literary influences on his development: response to contemporary movements in

early career, 8, 30-32, 34-35, 37, 38, 39-40, 43-44; Scotland in early work, 15; anti-English sentiment, 15, 61, 93-95, 146, 155, 159-161, 199; romanticism, 15, 177, 196-197; Pre-Raphaelites, 30, 45, 86; scientific interest, 32, 52-53, 71; interest in sonnet, 32, 91; Celtic associations, 44, 67, 95, 146-147; reaction to London, 45-48, 59; effects of travel to Italy, 45, 65-66, 68-80 *passim*, 96-99, 101-102, 162-163, 192-195; cosmopolitanism, 77-80, 90-95, 97, 146-172, 203; Heine and Judaism, 79-82; America, 91-95, 202; Celtic movement, 126, 152-153; Belgian literary movement, 126, 147, 179-180
literary themes and preoccupations: opposition to nationalism, 12, 159, 168-172, 199, 203-204, 208; duality, 24-25, 41, 87, 107-115, 127, 131, 134, 173-174, 191-192, 241; messianic view of woman, 25; childbirth, 27, 56-57, 123, 132-133; feminism, 35, 116, 121, 141; religion, 38, 72-75, 164-167; the child, 40, 123; nature and landscape, 41-42, 177-179; the city, 47, 48-65, 70, 85, 199; the artist, 76-77; Judaism, 82-84, 87-91, 95; marriage and sexual union, 84, 114, 128-130; concepts of drama, 103-104, 147, 152, 161-162, 204-205; symbolism, 177-190, 202-203
special aspects of career: variety of literary methods and activities, 2, 45; spiritualism and the occult, 24, 136, 191; art criticism, 45, 96, 174-176; use of pseudonym, 103, 135, 136, 138; transvestism, 135; weaknesses of his literary art, 145, 203; need for community, 172; cosmic consciousness, 176-177. *See also* Macleod, Fiona
Shaw, George Bernard, 248
Shelley, Percy Bysshe: as influence on Sharp, 8, 33; Sharp's identification with, 27, 229; Sharp's biography of, 77-78; duality in, 107; love and

Index

261